T0305130

Business Strategy and National Culture

NEW HORIZONS IN INTERNATIONAL BUSINESS

Series Editor: Peter J. Buckley
Centre for International Business,
University of Leeds (CIBUL), UK

The New Horizons in International Business series has established itself as the world's leading forum for the presentation of new ideas in international business research. It offers pre-eminent contributions in the areas of multinational enterprise – including foreign direct investment, business strategy and corporate alliances, global competitive strategies, and entrepreneurship. In short, this series constitutes essential reading for academics, business strategists and policy makers alike.

Titles in the series include:

A Yen for Real Estate
Japanese Real Estate Investment Abroad – From Boom to Bust
Roger Simon Farrell

Corporate Governance and Globalization
Long Range Planning Issues
Edited by Stephen S. Cohen and Gavin Boyd

The European Union and Globalisation
Towards Global Democratic Governance
Brigid Gavin

Globalization and the Small Open Economy
Edited by Daniel Van Den Bulcke and Alain Verbeke

Entrepreneurship and the Internationalisation of Asian Firms
An Institutional Perspective
Henry Wai-chung Yeung

The World Trade Organization in the New Global Economy
Trade and Investment Issues in the Millennium Round
Edited by Alan M. Rugman and Gavin Boyd

Japanese Subsidiaries in the New Global Economy
Edited by Paul W. Beamish, Andrew Delios and Shige Makino

Globalizing Europe
Deepening Integration, Alliance Capitalism and Structural Statecraft
Edited by Thomas L. Brewer, Paul A. Brenton and Gavin Boyd

China and its Regions
Economic Growth and Reform in Chinese Provinces
Edited by Mary-Françoise Renard

Emerging Issues in International Business Research
Edited by Masaaki Kotabe and Preet S. Aulakh

Network Knowledge in International Business
Edited by Sarianna M. Lundan

Learning in the Internationalisation Process of Firms
Edited by Anders Blomstermo and D. Deo Sharma

Business Strategy and National Culture

US and Asia Pacific Microcomputer Multinationals in Europe

Denise Tsang

Lecturer in the Department of Management, School of Business University of Reading, UK

NEW HORIZONS IN INTERNATIONAL BUSINESS

Edward Elgar
Cheltenham, UK • Northampton, MA, USA

© Denise Tsang 2002

Published by
Edward Elgar Publishing Limited
Glensanda House
Montpellier Parade
Cheltenham
Glos GL50 1UA
UK

Edward Elgar Publishing, Inc.
136 West Street
Suite 202
Northampton
Massachusetts 01060
USA

A catalogue record for this book
is available from the British Library

Library of Congress Cataloguing in Publication Data

Tsang, Denise, 1965-
    Business strategy and national culture : US and Asia Pacific microcomputer
  multinationals in Europe / Denise Tsang.
            p. cm. -- (New horizons in international business series)
    Includes bibliographical references and index.
    1. Computer industry--United States. 2. Computer industry--Pacific Area. 3.
  International business enterprises--Europe. I. Title. II. New horizons in
  international business

    HD9696.2.U62 T773 2002
    338.8'871004'094--dc21
                                                                                            2002022061

ISBN 1 84064 480 X

Printed and bound in Great Britain by Biddles Ltd, *www.biddles.co.uk*

Dedicated to Jim Clarke

Contents

List of Figures

List of Tables

Preface

Although much has been written about the bounded rational business strategists and their cognitive limitations, the cultural influence on business strategy has been largely neglected. This book examines one of the most puzzling issues concerning business strategy — the inter-firm variations of strategic patterns within a fast-paced and highly competitive industry. This book is concerned with the effect of core cultural values on the backward linkage strategy of US and Asia Pacific microcomputer multinational firms in Europe. Studies on managerial values as early as the 1960s by William Guth and Renato Tagiuri revealed that personal values of managers were important determinants of strategy. As the business strategies of US and Asia Pacific microcomputer firms are formulated by headquarters managers whose personal values are subordinated by different sets of cultural values, it is imperative to examine the core values associated with the cultures from which these managers originate in order to gain a comprehensive view of their strategies.

This book focuses on the backward linkage strategy of fourteen multinational microcomputer firms, namely, the US firms IBM, Hewlett-Packard, Compaq, Dell, Gateway, Sun and Silicon Graphics, the Japanese firms Fujitsu, NEC and Toshiba, the Taiwanese firms Acer, Mitac and Twinhead as well as the Korean firm Samsung. In various parts of this book, the term Asia Pacific firms will be used interchangeably to refer to the aforementioned Japanese, Taiwanese and Korean firms headquartered in the Asia Pacific region. The fourteen multinational firms not only shared over 60 per cent of the individual personal computer, workstation and server segments of the European microcomputer market, they also established a manufacturing presence in Europe by 1999 to assemble their own brand of microcomputers. IBM for instance set up its assembly lines in its Greenock plant in Scotland in 1982 while Dell expanded its capacity by the opening of a new plant in Limerick in 1999.

I will present a cultural theory that explicates the core values of individualism, continuous improvement and flexibility on backward linkage strategy. Core cultural values are pervasive and are reflected in business values across nations; they filter down through managerial values, which consciously and unconsciously determine their concepts concerning backward linkage strategies (the ownership structure concerning component inputs). Core cultural values also shape social perceptions and underlie firms' accumulation of diverse sets of capabilities, which in turn influence their pattern of integration into components. In their early attempts to describe individuals across culture, Alex Inkeles and Daniel Levinson identified some values that were universally important across nations. These core values embodied relation to authority, concept of self and conflict handling; they were substantiated by later studies that presented similar classifications of values. Despite the possession of a universal set of core values, some cultures are characterised by additional core values. As the thrust of this book is concerned with the backward linkage strategy of US and Asia Pacific firms, the focus will be, therefore, on a specific set of relevant core cultural values rather than a universal set of values within the USA, Japan, Korea and Taiwan.

The material in this book is based on directly and indirectly collected data: indirectly collected data include content analysis of firm and industry materials for the 1980s and the 1990s. In addition, unstructured face-to-face interviews with representatives from ten of the aforementioned microcomputer firms conducted primarily between 1996–97 were the source of direct data collection. The topic areas of the interviews incorporated their direct investment strategy as well as backward linkage strategy. The interviews were usually one and a half hours in length, and some were followed by guided facility tours. Additional interviews were also conducted with six microcomputer peripheral and component firms operating in Europe. These interviews were invaluable to this book, and I sincerely appreciated the time provided by various interviewees such as Vice President, General Manager, Controller, Plant Manager, Marketing Manager, Commodity Manager... that have taken part in the interviews despite their extremely busy schedules.

Although the bulk of this book was written over the past two years, I began work that covered the subject matter in 1996 when I was working on a PhD thesis concerning foreign direct investment strategy in the European microcomputer industry. I am deeply grateful to the Economics Department in the University of Reading for financing the research. In addition, I am indebted to my supervisors Professor Mark Casson and Professor Geoffrey Jones for their critical and inspirational comments both on the thesis itself and on general issues concerning knowledge acquisitions. Finally, I would also like to extend my gratitude to the Bristol Business School for the provision of database support and research facility.

1. The Strategy of Microcomputing

In its September 1999 issue titled *'Young and Rich'*, Fortune looked at the wealthiest Americans under the age of forty whom the magazine described in its front cover as 'amassing fortunes faster than any generation in history'. The leading candidates of this hyper rich lists were entrepreneurial founders of Dell and Gateway, microcomputer multinational firms with net income of US$1,460 million and US$427 million in 1999. As a matter of fact, profitability has not only been associated with the microcomputer industry, but also with some of the upstream and downstream industries. Most notably, the leading microcomputer software firm Microsoft generated a net income that totalled at US$9,421 million in 2000.[1]

The unrelentless pursuit of profitability in the microcomputer industry and its adjacent industry are synonymous with the economic model of firms. As Friedman (1953 p. 22) pointed out that 'unless the behaviour of businessmen in some way or other approximated behaviour consistent with the maximisation of returns, it seems unlikely that they would remain in business for long'. Knight (1941 p. 252) also perceived the importance of economising and suggested that 'men in general, and within limits, wish to behave economically, to make their activities and their organisation efficient rather than wasteful'.

It is the contention of this book to examine the business strategy utilised by US and Asia Pacific firms in the European microcomputer industry; in particular, it examines microcomputer firms that have undertaken market-seeking manufacturing investment. Table 1.1 shows the list of manufacturing investment in the industry in 2000, which are all located in, or with close proximity to, the major markets the UK, Germany and France. This table shows that six microcomputer firms are located in either Scotland[2] or Ireland, which highlights the fact that more than a third of the systems sold in Europe are assembled in the two regions. The remaining firms, with the exception of Silicon Graphics (SGI) and Acer's major manufacturing facility, are all located within the major markets.

The purpose of this chapter is to clarify the underlying concepts and the competing perspectives on backward linkage strategy that have been propounded by various theorists. I will, however, begin with a review of the microcomputer industry in Europe. This will be followed by two consecutive sections that elaborate the concepts in conjunction with business strategy and component technology; I will then discuss the backward linkage strategies utilised by US and Asia Pacific firms and the theoretical perspectives arguing for disintegrated linkage strategy or integrated linkage strategy. The final section will provide a summary of the cultural perspective adopted in this book.

Table 1.1: US and Asia Pacific Microcomputer Firms, 2000

	Europe Manufacturing Location
US Firms	
Compaq	Erskine, Scotland, the UK
Dell	Limerick, Ireland
Gateway	Dublin, Ireland
Hewlett-Packard	Grenoble, France
IBM	Greenock, Scotland, the UK
Sun	Linlithgow, Scotland, the UK
Silicon Graphics	Cortalliod, Switzerland
Japanese Firms	
Fujitsu	Augsburg, Germany
NEC	Scotland, the UK and Angers, France
Toshiba	Regensberg, Germany
Korean Firm	
Samsung	Teeside, the UK
Taiwanese Firms	
Acer	Den Bosch, the Netherlands and Ahrensburg, Germany.
Mita	Telford, the UK
Twinhead	Basingstoke, the UK

Note: Gateway closed its Irish operation in December 2001. Compaq and HP had agreed to merge their operations in March 2002; nevertheless, they were counted as two separate firms in this book.[3]
Source: Various Directories.

THE MICROCOMPUTER IN EUROPE

Table 1.2 reviews the European microcomputer industry in the broader context of the computer and telecommunication industry. It shows that the total revenue derived from the computer and telecommunications in the UK, Germany and France was more than twenty times higher than that of Ireland, which is the smallest market on the list. Despite its limited market size, Ireland is a leading microcomputer manufacturing base. It is the chosen location for a number of facilities which include among others, Intel's two microprocessor fabrication plants, Gateway's computer assembly facility and European call centre, Dell's three manufacturing plants, SCI[4]'s printed circuit boards assembly operation[5], Hewlett-Packard's (HP) inkjet printer cartridge supply bases as well as IBM's personal computer telephone customer support centre for Europe and the US.

Table 1.2: Computer and Telecommunication Market in Europe

	Sales Revenue in 2000 (billion of euros)
Austria	12.0
Belgium/Luxembourg	14.7
Denmark	10.6
Finland	7.9
France	85.3
Germany	115.1
Greece	7.3
Ireland	4.8
Italy	61.4
Netherlands	26.3
Norway	8.5
Portugal	7.4
Spain	38.3
Sweden	18.3
Switzerland	19.5
UK	100.2

Note: A billion is a thousand million.
Source: European Information Technology Observatory as quoted in Wall Street Journal Europe 22 March 2001 p. 29.

Microcomputers incorporate personal computers, workstations and servers. Personal computers, which can be traced to Apple Computers' garage operations in 1976, represent the largest segment of the industry. In comparison, workstations and servers account for less than one-tenth of the total volume of personal computers. Workstations were invented in 1980 by the US firm Apollo Computer. The original concept was to build systems with enhanced computing power and data storage in comparison to personal computers; in addition, they were designed for network integration. During the 1980s, workstations were used simply for the purpose of running the computer-assisted design program called AutoCAD program. Servers[6], on the other hand, provide services to personal computers or workstations on the same network. Examples of servers are print servers, file servers or internet servers. Servers are designed with redundant parts in order to be fault tolerant; for instance, the system will be able to continue its function even when a microprocessor fails. Table 1.3 shows that the aggregated European market shares of eight industry participants in personal computer accounted for approximately 65 per cent of market shares in early 1999.

Table 1.3: European Personal Computer Unit Market Shares, 1999

	Market Shares
Compaq	17.5%
Fujitsu-Siemens	12.6%
Dell	9.3%
IBM	9.0%
Hewlett-Packard	5.9%
Packard Bell NEC	4.7%
Toshiba	4.0%
Acer	2.7%

Source: Context as quoted in Wall Street Journal 17 June 1999 p. A21.

Personal computers, workstations and servers used to differ substantially in their price and technical capabilities; the price and specification of the low end workstations and servers, however, have been converging with the high end personal computers since the mid-1990s. For example, microcomputer firms used microprocessors from the MIPs, Alpha, PowerPC or PA-RISC families in workstations or servers previously; however, the Intel microprocessors have now become widely accepted alternatives. The similarities of personal computer, workstation and server in key specifications such as microprocessors, memories and hard disk drives are demonstrated by Dell's system illustrated in the following Table 1.4.

The European microcomputer industry consists of own brand marketers[7] such as Hitachi, Sony, Apple and Quantex, own brand manufacturers and marketers such as IBM, Compaq and Dell, contract manufacturers[8] such as SCI Systems, Solectron and First International Computer as well as firms that engage in both activities such as Acer, Samsung and Twinhead; because of this the term 'microcomputer firms' as adopted in this book will be confined to firms that have undertaken some degree of own brand manufacturing in Europe. The percentage of own brand manufacturing among US firms such as Dell and Gateway is 100 per cent whereas for Taiwanese firms such as Acer and Twinhead is about 40 to 60 per cent.[9]

Table 1.4: System Specifications of Microcomputers at Dell

	Dell Dimension L800 Desktop PC	Precision 220 Workstation	Dell PowerEdge 300 Server
Processor	Intel Pentium III 800 Mhz 256 KB Cache	Intel Pentium III 866Mhz 256 KB Cache	Dual Intel Pentium III 800 Mhz 256 KB Cache
Memory	64 MB SDRAM	65 MB RDRAM	64 MB SDRAM
Storage	10 GB Hard Disk Drive	10 GB Hard Disk Drive CD R/W Iomega Zip Drive	10 GB Hard Disk Drive plus optional tape backup
Video	Intel Integrated 810 Video Controller	32 MB nVidia GeForce II GTS Graphics Card	2MB Integrated Video Memory
Audio	Creative Labs SoundBlaster 64Voice PCI Sound Card	Integrated AAC '97 Sound	
Communi-cation	56K V90 Modem	Integrated 3Com 3C920 Fast Etherlink XL 10/100 PCI	Intel Pro 100+ Server Adaptor 3 Com 3C980C 10/100 PCI Adapter 56 K v90 Modem

Source: Dell UK (2000).

BUSINESS STRATEGY AND MICROCOMPUTER FIRMS

The business strategy of microcomputer firms deserves detailed investigation as the industry has witnessed the rise and decline of a number of legendary firms since its inception. In addition, the microcomputer industry is a leading manufacturing industry with worldwide sales of approximately 140 million units in 2000. Though the growth rate of the personal computer segment, which accounted for more than 80 per cent of the total volume in the microcomputer industry has slowed down in recent years, the market research consultancy International Data Corporation has maintained its optimism on personal computers and stated that 'the profound influence of the PC and the growth (era) is over. But it's still a big market. The PC business is still a sizeable, established business'.[10] As a matter of fact, executives of IBM's personal computer unit[11] stated in the early 2001 that personal computers still held strong sales potential for the firm and would help to boost its computer service business.

Business strategy is concerned with the manner in which a firm competes, and is particularly significant in the highly competitive microcomputer industry. Dunning (1993) defined business strategy as a deliberate choice taken by managers to organise the resources and capabilities within their control to achieve corporate objectives over a specified time period. Within this context, business strategy can be interpreted as the configuration of internal structure, culture and systems of firms in order to achieve competitiveness in the industry. Firm structure refers to the division, grouping and co-ordination of tasks whereas its culture relates to the common perception held by its members. The systems of the firm, on the other hand, incorporate the various inter-related aspects of management such as supply chain, human resources, accounting, information and international investment.

Various microcomputer firms have publicly discussed their business strategies. For instance, Dell depicts its business strategy in terms of a model where it emphasises serving its customers directly via telephone sales or person-to-person sales teams and then builds the products according to customers' orders. This means that Dell does not carry any inventory of fully assembled microcomputers and hence avoids any potential loss in conjunction with the depreciation of components[12].

Acer has used fast food as a metaphor for its business strategy. Acer's strategy encompasses its European operation and receives the relatively light-weight components with changing technology such as motherboards from the Far East by air; it then receives bulky components with a relatively long life-cycle such as display monitors and cases by sea. In addition, it procures high value items such as microprocessors, memories and hard disk drives in Europe. These two examples demonstrate that the concept of business strategy has been defined in terms of microcomputer firms' supply chain system, specifically the linkage of component supply and distribution.[13] These two linkages are referred to as backward linkage strategy and forward linkage strategy respectively.

The backward linkage strategy relates to the ownership strategy concerning the organisation of hardware components for microcomputer assembly whereas the forward linkage strategy is associated with the ownership strategy in conjunction with the marketing of fully assembled microcomputers. These strategies are important in the current stage of the industry life-cycle in the European microcomputer industry as they impinge upon profitability.

Figure 1.1: Structure of Linkage Strategy

Backward Linkage
(Procurement of microcomputer components)

Microcomputer Assembly

Forward Linkage
(Distribution of microcomputers)

Source: Author.

Commenting on its future operating results in 2000, Sun referred to the importance of backward linkage along its supply chain: 'If we were unable to timely develop, manufacture, and introduce new products in sufficient quantity to meet customer demand at acceptable costs, or if we were unable to correctly anticipate customer demand for our new and existing products, our business and operating results could be materially adversely affected'.[14] Sun therefore pointed out that microcomputer firms' backward linkage strategy should allow for the supply of components at the appropriate quantity and cost.

The profit implication of backward linkage strategy has been acknowledged by various writers (Curry and Kenney 1999; Chapman et al. 1997....) Chapman et al. (1997) wrote that 'after pricing, reducing purchasing costs is the most powerful way to improve shareholder returns'. They estimated that external procurement of goods and services accounted for about 85 per cent of the total expenditure in the computer and electronics sector; hence, a 10 per cent reduction in procurement spending would increase shareholder returns by 22 per cent. The cost structure of microcomputer products at Dell in 1999 as shown in Table 1.5 reflected Chapman et al.'s estimation, in which external procurement of components accounted for some 80 per cent of total expenditure. External procurement was based on the estimation of one per cent direct labour costs during the assembly process.[15]

Table 1.5 : Dell's Cost Structure, 1999

Total Expenditure	*US$22,434 million*	*(100%)*
Costs of Production	US$20,047 million	
Material costs	US$19,847 million	*(88%)*
Direct Labour	US$253 million	*(1%)*
Indirect Labour	US$2,387 million	*(11%)*

Source: Dell 2000 Annual Report.

COMPONENTS AND BACKWARD LINKAGE STRATEGY

The backward linkage strategy can be classified into integrated linkage strategy and disintegrated linkage strategy. Disintegrated linkage strategy relates to firms entering into contractual relationships with specialist component suppliers, rather than organising component productive activities internally. Integrated linkage strategy, on the other hand, describes firms organising some productive activities internally and substituting market transactions with hierarchical transactions among subsidiaries.

As the breadth of technologies in microcomputer components varies widely, no microcomputer firm is self-sufficient in all types of component. Examples of technical variance in components can be seen in the rather low skill for design activity required for desktop tower cases and the extremely high skill embedded in operating system software. In the area of manufacturing, technological complexity in relation to the assembly process of display monitors and keyboards is low whereas that for semiconductor assembly is among one of the most sophisticated manufacturing processes in the world. A working definition of integrated backward linkage strategy that will be used throughout this book is therefore integration in some but not necessarily all of the microcomputer hardware components. Microcomputer firms pursuing integrated linkage, nevertheless, may integrate into one of the three main component areas, which are quite different in terms of the demand for labour skill, the initial capital requirement, the minimum efficient scale in production, the transportability of the end products and the profit margins obtained by producers. Table 1.6 compares their distinctive features.

Table 1.6 : Classification of Microcomputer Components

Attributes	Concept-intensive components (software, microprocessor)	Capital-intensive components (DRAM, hard disk drive)	Labour-intensive components (keyboards, display monitors)
Labour skill intensity	High	Medium	Low
Minimum efficient scale	Low	High	Medium
Initial capital investment	Low	High	Medium
Product cycle	Short	Short	Long
Transportability	High	Medium	Vary
Profitability	High	Medium	Low

Source: Author.

The demand for skilled labour is highest in the design of concept-intensive components. For instance, it took IBM, Motorola and Apple designers in the Somerset Joint Design Centre, Texas nearly two years to complete the Power PC Architecture, which is implemented in the Power PC601, 603, 604 and 620 microprocessors. The representatives from the three firms were experienced designers and the project was also co-ordinated by a 16-member committee as well as a 14-member implementation team.[16] In addition, the supply of skilled labour for concept-intensive components is rather limited in nature. Bill Gates remarked that the individual ability to engage in the skillful design of software is difficult to attain. He stated that he could screen the best programmers among new graduate recruits in three or four years, and that he could not think of any initially mediocre programmer at Microsoft who later become a world-class programmer. He also asserted that: 'There is no way of getting around [the fact] that in terms of IQ, you've got to be very elitist in picking the people who deserve to write software; 95 per cent of the people shouldn't write complex software'.[17] Concept-intensive components, on the other hand, require very little initial capital investment. For example, the most important capital equipment for a new software venture is microcomputers and the relevant software design tools.

The critical feature of capital-intensive components such as dynamic random access memory (DRAM), hard disk drives and liquid crystal display panels is that they contain the highest level of initial capital investment and minimum efficient scale within the production process. For instance, the minimum efficient scale for the assembly stage of 64 megabytes DRAM as estimated from Taiwan's Walton Advanced Electronics was 6.6 million per month in 2000.[18] The initial capital investment for the latest technology in DRAM is also substantial. It has increased from about US$4 million in 1971 to more than US$2,000 million in 1998; it has further been estimated that a new facility will cost more than US$10,000 million by 2015.[19] For instance, the initial capital requirement for DRAM for Hyundai's abandoned project of 256 megabytes DRAM semiconductor plant in Scotland amounted to about US$5,000 million in 1998.[20] The largest cost components of the initial capital investment in semiconductors are the clean-room and the fabrication equipment, the latter accounts for approximately 85 per cent of the initial cost. Table 1.7 shows the consistently high levels of annual capital equipment spending by Samsung's semiconductor business between 1990–98. The highest level of spending was US$2,853 million in 1995 whereas the lowest level of spending was US$715 million in 1998. The average spending during this period was US$1,553 million.

Table 1.7: Capital Equipment Spending by Samsung

								(US$ million)
1990	1991	1992	1993	1994	1995	1996	1997	1998
849	736	743	872	2,489	2,853	2,593	2,129	715

Source: Leham Brothers (1999).

Finally, labour-intensive components such as display monitors and keyboards have the longest product life cycle. For example, the specification of a high quality display monitor is relatively up-to-date for five years as compared to two years for a specific generation of microprocessor. Another essential characteristic of labour-intensive components is that their transportability varies. Table 1.8 highlights the variation of transportation costs within labour-intensive components. Bulky items such as display monitors that can weigh more than 20 kilograms are far less transportable than mice or keyboards, in the sense that it is economically unjustifiable to transport them by air when there is disruption in sea freight services or a sudden surge of demand in microcomputer systems.

Table 1.8: Transportability in Labour-intensive Components

	Standard Labour-intensive Components e.g. mice, keyboards	Bulky Labour-intensive Components e.g. display monitors
Air Freight as a percentage of Cost of Goods Sold	5.4%	20.9%
Sea Freight as a percentage of Cost of Goods Sold	1.2%	1.0%

Source: Levy (1997).

Finally, the profitability of the three types of microcomputer components as indicated by operating profit margins differs, with concept-intensive components ranked the highest and the labour-intensive components ranked the lowest. Examples can be cited from concept-intensive software producer Microsoft's operating profit margins of 50 per cent in 2000 and labour-intensive component manufacturer Acer's one per cent.[21] The profitability of labour-intensive manufacturers, in this respect, relies on a substantial sales volume that generates streams of income. The profitability of capital-intensive components, on the other hand, can vary widely. Most of them are dependent on specific business cycles in their industries; for instance, memory chip manufacturers have experienced cyclical profits and losses as a result of the fluctuation of memory prices.

INTEGRATED AND DISINTEGRATED LINKAGE

Table 1.9 illustrates a unique pattern of backward linkage strategy among US and Asia Pacific firms in the European microcomputer industry in 2000. It can be seen that youthful US firms SGI, Sun, Dell and Gateway, which were established by entrepreneurial individuals without substantial industry experience during the 1980s, engaged in the disintegrated linkage strategy. The value of their externally procured hardware components as a percentage of total procurement was 100 per cent. As a contrast, the remaining firms pursued integrated linkage strategy.

Table 1.9: Backward Linkage Strategy in Europe

	Disintegrated Linkage	Integrated Linkage
US Firms	SGI, Sun, Dell, Gateway	IBM, HP, Compaq
Japanese Firms		NEC, Fujitsu, Toshiba
Korean Firm		Samsung
Taiwanese Firms		Acer, Mitac, Twinhead

Source: Various.

The distinction between the youthful US firms and the established US firms such as IBM and Hewlett-Packard deserve considerable attention. Established firms are those run by management with mainframe and minicomputer industry experience while youthful firms are those established by amateurs in the 1980s. Even though Compaq was founded by Rod Canion, Jim Harris and Bill Murto in 1982, it is classified as an established firm on the grounds that the three founders were ex-technical managers of the established firm Texas Instruments (TI). Table 1.10 demonstrates the amateurish background of youthful US firms' founders.

An industry reporter, for example, described Gateway's founder as 'to picture Ted Waitt, just imagine Woody Harrelson, who plays the bartender on the TV show "Cheers". Except instead of exuding, goofy Midwestern naïveté, Waitt seems nourished by... well, what is he on, anyway?'[22]

Table 1.10: Founders of Youthful US Microcomputer Firms

	Year of Establish-ment	Founders	Background of Founders
SGI	1982	James Clark	Professor of Computer Science, Stanford University
Sun	1982	Scott McNealy, Vinod Khosla, William Joy, Andreas Bechtolsheim	MBA and Engineering graduates from Stanford
Dell	1983	Michael Dell	University Student
Gateway	1985	Ted Waitts	Computer Store Salesman

Source: Various.

Indeed, Tom Peters wrote that the founders of youthful US firms were more interested in the elegance of their ideas and experiments than the financial rewards of setting up new ventures.[23] Dempsey, in particular, referred to Sun as embodying 'all the clichés of the West Coast IT entrepreneurs' and 'the antithesis of the blue chip hardware manufacturer'.[24] Similarly, Morris et al. (2000) described the design of Dell's headquarters as 'anti-corporation'. They wrote:

> Looming out of the flat landscape are its white Bauhaus buildings, one pretty much like the next, as far as the eye can see. Nothing too tall. Nothing too fancy. Definitely sterile; each building named with a number. 'Modern prison', one observer described it. Dell seems to be thumbing its nose at all those self-important old-economy companies that built monuments to themselves.

Another example can be cited in the 'serious fun' atmosphere of SGI. Jager and Oritz's (1997) depicted the firm's self conception as '... conferences rooms are christened after movies in which SGI technology was used. The company sponsors bungee-jumping events and lip-sync competitions, and has even held wakes for divisions that have been merged into others'. Cringely (1996) contrasted the youthful US firms with the established US firms. According to him, the former were founded by 'groups of boys who banded together to give themselves power... They weren't rebels; they resented their parents and society very little' (ibid. p. 14). The latter, on the other hand, were described by Cringely as: 'smoke stacks, skyscrapers, half-acre mahogany desks, corporate jets, grey hair, the building of things in enormous factories by crowds of faceless, time-card punching workers' (ibid. p. 16).

Existing Literature on Backward Linkage Strategy

I will first provide a brief review of the literature in relation to backward linkage strategy. The rationale for backward linkage strategy can be approached from economics, sociology, history and organisation. The economic justification has been focused predominantly on transaction cost and market imperfection. The former argues that firms will minimise the sum of transaction costs and production costs when determining backward linkage strategy. Within the behaviour assumption of bounded rationality and opportunism, Williamson (1985) showed that asset specificity was a major cause of transaction cost that would lead to the use of integrated linkage strategy. Asset specificity refers to assets that are dedicated to the disintegrated linkage strategy and cannot be re-deployed without incurring additional costs when the backward linkage terminates; the nature of these transaction specific assets might generate opportunistic behaviour among suppliers in terms of holding up[25] and as a result increase the costs of the disintegrated linkage. When both buyers and suppliers anticipate the problem of hold up, the contract negotiation for the disintegrated linkage tends to be more lengthy as contracting parties attempt to safeguard their interests against being held up later on. As firms operating within a single industry will encounter similar issues concerning asset specificity, the co-existence of integrated linkage strategy and disintegrated linkage strategy within the European microcomputer industry does not support the application of the theory.

The market imperfection theory points to the information asymmetry regarding the quality of components between buyer and seller as an explanation for backward linkage strategy. It has been suggested that the desire to acquire information concerning component quality is a motivating factor among firms that pursue integrated linkage strategy. Casson (1987 p. 133) wrote that 'quality control is most effective when administered through close supervision of the production process, since this avoids inferior quality items being produced in the first place'. Person-to-person interviews with microcomputer firms, however, suggests that there was adequate information to evaluate component suppliers across the industry.[26] For example, one of the microcomputer firms mentioned in a personal interview in 1997 that its knowledge concerning the quality standards of monitor suppliers was based on systematic data collection from customers concerning malfunction or other quality issues. Another interview with a Procurement Manager of another microcomputer firm at the same time suggested that the firm's purchasing officer in Taiwan had some 30 years of experience in the field, and possessed the necessary contacts and knowledge of indigenous manufacturers. Similarly, its purchasing officer in Japan facilitated the firm's procurement of memory integrated circuits. As even the youthful participants have accumulated approximately a decade of experience in the microcomputer industry by the end of the 1990s, they would have acquired in that time considerable information concerning the suppliers. The conception of market imperfection therefore cannot satisfactorily explain the divergence of backward linkage strategy in the European microcomputer industry.

A further development within the economic perspective is on the notion of firm capability. Langlois (1992) argued that the choices of backward linkage strategy were determined by the relative strength of capabilities internal to the firm and those available through contracts with other firms. He specifically raised the time dimension in his discussion, and suggested that transaction costs affected backward linkage strategy in the short run. He wrote that '… a firm may wish to internalise a stage of production even when the market possesses the requisite capabilities to at least the same degree as does the firm itself. If the firm does internalise, it must be because there are other costs to using the market' (ibid. p. 114). Langlois wrote that IBM's entry into the personal computer market with disintegrated linkage strategy was because 'the market possessed a high level of capabilities' and 'IBM's own capabilities were severely lacking' (ibid. p. 119). Indeed, IBM UK's Sir Edwin Nixon pointed out that, as a late entrant in personal computer, IBM could not afford to undertake the normal developmental process for personal computers (which at the time took three-and-a half years), it therefore needed to change its backward linkage strategy.[27]

The social embeddedness perspective suggests that the various sub-units within a society are the most important units for understanding backward linkage strategy. Saxenian (1994) suggested that backward linkage was associated with the social structure of the local business environment where firms originated. She wrote that the widespread practice of disintegrated backward linkage in Silicon Valley arose from the co-operative culture among the engineers and executives who knew each other through informal socialising as students or as participants in local affairs. Hence, external procurement was preferred and suppliers were treated as 'partners in a joint process of designing, developing, and manufacturing innovative systems' (ibid. p. 145). On the other hand, the adoption of integrated backward linkage strategy on the East Coast reflected the formal interpersonal relationships among executives and engineers. This explanation can be compared with Whitley's (1990) emphasis on the impact of social institutions on backward linkage. However, the idea of social embeddedness has not considered the transference of backward linkage practice when firms undertake investment abroad. It does not incorporate the fact that when US and Asia Pacific firms invested in Europe, their backward linkage strategies were independent of the local social network. Hence, the location bound nature of this perspective does not accommodate the dynamism of backward linkage strategy within the microcomputer industry.

Parallel with the above perspective drawn from the wider impact of social environment is the isomorphic process that forces rivals to pursue similar backward linkage strategies within an industry. In a seminal paper DiMaggio and Powell (1983) suggested that the pressure to become more similar to the other firms accounted for the spread of bureaucracy during the 20th century. They suggested that one of the reasons managers' imitated the structures of other firms was to demonstrate their awareness of the best prevailing practice, which also served the purpose of reducing uncertainty in a rapidly changing industry. They stated that firms competed for resources, customers, legitimacy as well as social fitness. Accordingly, the diverse pattern of backward linkage in the European microcomputer industry can be seen as a continuous process of participants' miming the dominant strategy in attempts to adapt to the uncertain industry environment. Though providing a plausible explanation towards the evolutionary pattern of backward linkage strategy, the diverged pattern at the beginning of the industry and after two decades of development suggests that this perspective does not extrapolate the different extent of uncertainty among firms that encountered the same industry dynamics.

Finally, the historical perspective of backward linkage strategy is related to the politics of past decisions. Hannan and Freeman (1977) suggested that the inertia pressure within firms was due to established standards of procedure, past investments and power distribution. When diversifying into the microcomputer business, some personal computer firms have inherited an established business portfolio including component areas such as storage, semiconductors and display monitors; these firms tend to pursue integrated linkage strategy as inherited businesses are powerful groups for maintaining the status quo. Saunders (1994 p. 128) adopted this deterministic view on backward linkage strategy and wrote: 'Most businesses, of course, usually find themselves with an initial position which has been inherited from the past. Their position in the supply chain is already established ... and mapped out'.

However, it has been suggested that firms can learn and unlearn strategies over time (Grant 1998). Indeed, the evolution of IBM's backward linkage strategy did demonstrate aspect of learning and unlearning. IBM pursued disintegrated linkage strategy when it first introduced the IBM PC.[28] It then gradually reverted to its traditional practice of integrated linkage during the 1980s and is currently a leading producer in hard disk drives and liquid crystal displays. As the European microcomputer industry has evolved for two decades, it can be argued that industry participants have had sufficient time to discard the constraint imposed by their inheritance and configure efficient backward linkage strategies.

Cultural Orientation of Backward Linkage

While the aforementioned perspectives provide persuasive theoretical grounds towards the determinants of backward linkage strategy, considerable variation on backward linkage remains across US and Asia Pacific firms which the various perspectives do not satisfactorily explain (as shown in Table 1.8). This book aims to fill the gap in the existing literature concerning backward linkage strategy, and illuminate the impact of national culture on firms' strategy within the isomorphic process perspective and the capability perspective. It argues that the norm of integrated linkage in the computer industry has been advocated by established US firms and replicated indiscriminately by Asia Pacific firms during the 1980s. It also provides a rationale for youthful US firms' pioneering of the disintegrated backward linkage in terms of managers' non-conformity to the industry recipe. In addition, it explains the distinctive pattern of integration in conjunction with the three microcomputer component areas among US and Asia Pacific firms (i.e. US microcomputer firms specialising in concept-intensive components, Japanese and Korean firms in capital-intensive components as well as Korean and Taiwanese firms in labour-intensive components).

National culture examines the concept of culture within the boundaries of modern political states such as the US, Japan, Korea and Taiwan.

However, it should be noted that culture first appeared in the English language in the late 19th century. Tylor (1871 p. 1) wrote: 'Culture... taken in its wide ethnographic sense, is that complex whole which includes knowledge, beliefs, arts, morals, custom, law and any capabilities and habits acquired by man as a member of society'. Contrary to this wholistic definition, Rohner (1984) suggested that culture is an organised system of meanings which members of that culture attributed to the persons and objects comprising the culture; Rohner's definition viewed culture as socially constructed and a product of human interaction. Following this more precise conceptualisation, Casson (1996) defined culture as collective subjectivity while Hofstede's (1980 p. 21) definition elaborated it in terms of 'the collective programming of the mind which distinguishes the members of one group or category of people from another'.

Due to the diverse meanings that could be attributed to the concept of culture, a discussion of cultural implication on backward linkage strategy should concentrate upon a specific area of the complex concept. As Trompenaars (1993 p. 3) pointed out '... the essence of culture is not what is visible on the surface. It is the shared ways groups of people understand and interpret the world'. Indeed, Kroeber and Kluckhohn (1952 p. 35) stated that 'the essential core of culture consists of traditional (i.e. historically derived and selected) ideas and especially their attached values'. It is therefore appropriate to abstract a cultural theory on backward linkage strategy that differentiates culture in terms of core values. Core values are the dominant values in a culture; they consistently reflect 'the broad tendency to prefer certain states of affairs over others' (Hofstede op. cit. p. 19).

National culture is a critical cognitive factor that influences the business strategy among microcomputer firms. Firstly, the divergent backward linkage strategy among US and Asia Pacific firms in Europe reflects the different core values among their top management, who are predominantly nationals of the nations in which their headquarters are located.[29] Secondly, the pattern of integration reflected culturally derived firm capabilities. The cultural implications in business strategy have been suggested by Schneider (1989 p. 149) who stated that 'assessments of the environment and the organisation are not necessarily objective but are a function of perceptions'. She stated that national culture shaped our perceptions regarding the environments and the nature of relationships within firms, and hence affected issues related to the business strategy formulation (e.g. scanning the environment, preferences for types and sources of information, methods of interpretation and validation and criteria for establishing priorities). Indeed, a growing body of literature has shed light on the influence of cultural values upon business strategy. Some of these studies will be reviewed in the final section of chapter three.

CONCLUSION

US and Asia Pacific firms have pursued rather different backward linkage strategies in tackling the competitive environment of the European microcomputer industry. Leading firms that utilised the disintegrated strategy included Dell and Sun while those which practised integrated strategy included IBM and Fujitsu. The material presented here raises an interesting question, i.e. why does the diversity of backward linkage strategy persist within the extremely competitive industry and in the current European setting. Continuing with the existing economic, behavioural and cultural literature, this book pursues a complementary line in the formulation of a cultural theory to explain the persistence of divergent backward linkage strategy among US, Japanese, Korean and Taiwanese firms which are driven by the same industrial dynamics. I will describe the historical conjectures affecting the European microcomputer industry in the following chapter before proceeding to lay the theoretical groundwork that elaborates on the influence of national cultural values on backward linkage strategy within the confines of business logic.

NOTES

[1] The net incomes of Dell, Gateway and Microsoft are quoted from their annual reports.

[2] However, microcomputer firms such as Compaq has cut 700 jobs in Scotland in 2001.

[3] 'Light at end of the tunnel for Gateway employees', *The Irish Times*, 21 December 2001. 'Compaq shareholders overwhelmingly approve Hewlett-Packard', *Compaq Press Release*, 20 March 2002; it was announced that the HP-Compaq integration team involved more than 1,200 employees as in 26 March 2002 (*CNET New.com site,* 26 March 2002).

[4] SCI, which was founded as Space Craft Inc. in 1961, changed its name to SCI Systems Inc.

[5] SCI Systems Inc. merged with Sanmina Corporation in December 2001. The new firm Sanmina-SCI Corporation has over 100 manufacturing facilities

throughout the world. See *SCI Press Release* 'Stockholders approves merger of Sanmina and SCI' 6 December 2001.

[6] Servers were originally classified as minicomputers.

[7] Own-brand marketers manufacture their systems outside Europe; in other words, they have only undertaken marketing investment in Europe. For example, the own brand marketer Sony keeps its higher value-added notebook computer production in Japan where it can scrutinise closely the quality; however, it has undertaken manufacturing investment in conjunction with television sets and display monitors in the UK.

[8] Contract manufacturers are firms that provide manufacturing services to other firms such as building microcomputers according to clients' specifications.

[9] See 'Fast food approach hits the spot at Acer', *Electronic Buyers' News*, 11 May 1998 p. 42.

[10] The International Data Corporation (IDC) is a market research firm that based in Framingham, Massachusetts. The data is reported in 'Influences of PC era over but still a big market', *the Financial Times* 24 September 1999 p. 20.

[11] This comment was quoted from William M Bulkeley 'IBM successfully turns around its personal computer unit', *The Financial Times*, 20 February 2001. Also, IBM's 2001 Annual Report shows that its computer services accounted for 40 per cent of the firms' sales revenue in 2000 while its personal computers contributed to about 20 per cent towards its sales revenues.

[12] Components refer to items such as resistors, screws, capacitors and memories as well as subassemblies such as hard disk drives and printed circuit boards.

[13] The supply chain comprises six connected series of links; these links represent the aspect of management in product design, component supply, product assembly, marketing, distribution and service.

[14] See Sun 2000 Annual Report.

[15] Recent industry estimation of direct labour cost is about 1 per cent (*Wall Street Journal Europe* 9 June 1997 p. 5) as compared to 5 per cent in the early 1990s.

[16] Diefendorff, K., R. Oehler and R. Hochsprung (1994), 'Evolution of the PowerPC Architecture', *IEEE Micro*, April pp. 47–9.

[17] Stross (1998) p. 35.

[18] Walton was established in 1998. Its investors are Taiwan's Walsin and Winbond as well as Japan's Mitsui. The microcomputer firm Toshiba also has 19.9 per cent equity stakes of the firm.

[19] Cost of DRAM facility was estimated by VLSI Research as quoted in Tom Foremski 'Costs are soaring to record levels', *The Financial Times*, 5 April 2000, IT Survey p. 6.

[20] The projected amount was reported by Matthew Reed and Douglas Lavin 'Picture Brightens for European Chip Firms', *Wall Street Journal Europe*, 21 January 1998 p. 5.

[21] See 2001 Annual Reports of the two firms.

[22] Joshua Hyatt, 'Betting the farm', *Inc.*, December 1991, p.38.

---

[23] Cheryll Aimee Barron, 'Silicon Valley Phoenixes', *Fortune*, 23 November 1987 p. 109

[24] *The Financial Times,* IT Survey 26 May 1993 p. II

[25] This means threatening to terminate the relationship after the other party has undertaken asset specific investment.

[26] This information concerning the reputation of suppliers included industry awards as well as firms' historic data on incoming parts quality.

[27] Simon Caulkin, 'Nixon's IBM', *Management Today,* January 1985 p. 60.

[28] IBM's strategy was hinged on its determination to enter the market within the time constraint in 1981.

[29] Personal interviews with microcomputer firms suggested that headquarters managers have considerable influence over European subsidiaries. They are not only managing directors of the subsidiaries at the European level, they also maintain close contacts with top managers in Europe with constant telephone contact.

2. US and Asia Pacific Multinationals and European Microcomputers

The geographical boundary of the European microcomputer industry adopted in this book is Western Europe[1], which is one of the most important markets in terms of total sales revenue. It shared over 20 per cent of the global personal computer market in 2000. Though no longer a fast growing segment of information technology, the microcomputer and the supercomputer hardware segments still enjoy moderate growth in Europe. Table 2.1 shows the recent market growth rate of microcomputers, mainframes and supercomputers, and provides a comparison of their growth rate with other information technology sub-segments. It can be seen that their expected growth rate in Europe in 2001 is 7.5 per cent and is much higher than office equipment such as photocopiers.

Table 2.1: European Information Technology Market, 1998–2001

	Computer Hardware	Office Equipment	Network Equipment	Communication Equipment
1999	7.8%	1.0%	14.4%	38.4%
2000	9.0%	1.5%	14.2%	25.6%
2001*	7.5%	1.5%	14.3%	17.4%

Note: * Estimation.
Source: European Information Technology Observatory as quoted in Wall Street Journal Europe 22 March 2001 p. 29.

As microcomputer multinational firms mainly undertake assembly activities in Europe, the total amount of Europe's microcomputer production severely lagged behind total sales revenue. Despite its large market, Europe is rather insignificant in terms of microcomputer productive activities. Nevertheless, microcomputer firms' European operations are highly competitive in global terms. An interview with the Scottish operation of a multinational firm in 1997 revealed that the subsidiary had scored the highest in a number of internal efficiency indices among the multinational's global manufacturing sites. The measurement of internal efficiency included items such as customer satisfaction, productivity, inventory, human resources and external quality. Table 2.2 shows that the USA, Japan, Taiwan, Singapore and China are the most important manufacturing locations for personal computers by total value of production in 1999.[2] Though their home markets are very small, Taiwan and Singapore play critical roles in personal computer assembly as well as in the manufacturer of certain microcomputer components.

Table 2.2: Key Personal Computer Manufacturing Locations, 1999

	Total Output
USA	US$95,160 million
Japan	US$44,050 million
Taiwan	US$21,020 million
Singapore	US$18,470 million
China	US$18,450 million

Source: Market Intelligence Centre, Taiwan as quoted in Wall Street Journal 11 December 1999 p. A23.

This chapter provides the background to an understanding of the context of US and Asia Pacific firms' direct manufacturing investment in the European microcomputer industry, spanning two decades. The first period of investment was undertaken exclusively by US firms while the second period witnessed the entrance of their Asia Pacific counterparts. Though Asia Pacific firms utilised indirect exports to serve the European market in the early 1980s, they did not embark on manufacturing investment until the late 1980s. The general trend of the microcomputer industry will be discussed in the next section, followed by a review of the growth of the European microcomputer industry. The evolution of the industry, as a matter of fact, is intertwined with the development of indigenous firms and foreign firms. I will therefore first discuss the growth of the indigenous firms and then the entry of US and Asia Pacific firms in Europe.

THE NEW INDUSTRY OF COMPUTING

The microcomputer industry was conceived in the mid-1970s by US firms such as MITS and Apple which marketed pre-assembled computer circuit boards (or computer kits) for enthusiasts who wanted to build their own systems.[3] The implication of these computer kits was first illustrated by Steve Dompier who wrote the software for MITS Altair to play popular tunes.[4]

Apple II was launched in 1977. It was a complete microcomputer system with keyboard, memory, cassette tape ports, BASIC and a display screen. Its attractive beige plastic cases incorporated the firm's half-eaten apple logo designed by the public relations consulting firm Regis McKenna. In retrospect, the Apple II symbolised the dawn of an era where computers have become consumer products in addition to their previous industrial product status. Though there were competing products such as Tandy's TRD-80 and Commodore's Vic20, Apple II was the most successful with over 100,000 units sold by the end of 1980. US firms have not only pioneered the microcomputer industry, but also driven the industry's growth. Table 2.3 shows the largest microcomputer firms worldwide in 2000. It can be seen that US firms have maintained entrenched market positions, which were at least 40 per cent in all three segments of microcomputers.

Table 2.3: Leading Microcomputer Firms Worldwide, 2000

(million units)

Personal Computers		Workstations		Servers	
Compaq	13%	Dell	23%	IBM	27%
Dell	11%	Sun	21%	Sun	16%
HP	8%	HP	16%	Compaq	16%
IBM	7%	IBM	14%	HP	14%
Fujitsu Siemens	5%	Compaq	13%	Dell	6%
Others	56%		13%		21%
Global shipment	132 million		1.7 million		4.4 million

Source: Various.

The microcomputer industry can be considered as a natural extension of the mainframe and minicomputer era, where the technological trajectory over time is towards smaller and more powerful systems. Theoretically, this historical continuity would favour firms that have already established daunting positions in the markets. However, as suggested in the previous chapter, the current generation of industry leaders such as Compaq, Dell and Sun have indeed since the early 1980s built their businesses from scratch. Though they have grown rapidly in the last decade, they are smaller than the established firms in the industry.

Figure 2.1 shows the size of microcomputer firms in terms of their consolidated sales revenues in 2000; it should be noted that the sales revenue of the Samsung Group refers to that of 1999. Figure 2.1 demonstrates that the sales revenue of Samsung was approaching US$94,000 million[5]; the lighter portion represents its US$28,580 million of information communication technology product revenue, which is derived from Samsung Electronics, Samsung SDI and Samsung Electro-Mechanics and Samsung-Corning. Samsung Electronics is the largest among them and has attained a sales revenue of US$27,220 in 2000. The darker portion of the bar represent Samsung's revenues from machinery and heavy industry, financial, chemicals and from a number of miscellaneous businesses.

Figure 2.1 also shows that IBM's sales revenues, which derived solely from information technology, were about US$90,000; this, therefore, illustrates the enormous size of IBM in the industry. The figure also shows that Japanese firms, as a group, exhibit very similar level of sales revenue at about US$50,000 million. Hewlett-Packard and Compaq's consolidated sales revenues were US$48,782 and US$42,383 million respectively, and were similar to those of the Japanese firms Fujitsu, NEC and Toshiba. Nevertheless, with the completion of the proposed merger between Hewlett-Packard and Compaq in 2002, the sales revenues of the new firm will be very close to those of IBM. As Michael Capellas, Compaq's CEO stated that: '... this merger is about market leadership'.[6] In addition, the remaining youthful US and Taiwanese firms' sales revenues ranged from about US$300 million to US$16,000 million.

In summary, this figure exhibits the differences of firm size across nations; for instance, established US firms, Japanese firms and Korean firms are typically larger than their Taiwanese counterparts. In fact, the largest microcomputer firms in Taiwan such as Acer and Mitac are relatively small when compared to larger firms in the industry. Moreover, this figure reiterates the differences in terms of firm size among established US firms and youthful US firms.

Figure 2.1: Sales Revenue of Microcomputer Firms, 2000

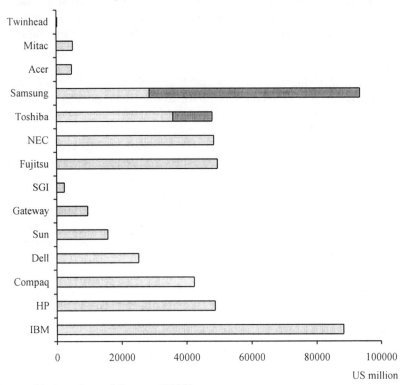

Source: Various Annual Reports (2000).

Microcomputer As a Research Focus

The microcomputer industry has presented its observers with a fascinating history associated with the rise and decline of captivating US firms in the contemporary industrial landscape. An interesting example includes the decline of Osborne Computer and Digital Equipment Corporation.

Demise of US innovators

Osborne was found by Adam Osborne, a former technology columnist in 1981 who launched the portable Osborne I in that year. The Osborne I was an instant success despite the industry's scepticism. Osborne's rate of production approached 25,000 units a month in early 1982, which was similar to that of the industry leader Apple at the time.[7] Nevertheless, Osborne's announcement of the Osborne II in 1984, the next generation of system with superior features and performance, led to plummeting sales for the Osborne I as users delayed their purchasing decisions. Unfortunately, the late introduction of the Osborne II coupled with the decline in sales of the Osborne I resulted in the dramatic bankruptcy of the four year old firm.

The story behind Digital, the inventor of the minicomputer and the second largest firm in the computer industry at its peak was its failed attempts to enter the personal computer market. Digital introduced its Professional 300 series and Rainbow 100 series in the early 1980s as an attempt to secure a position in the personal computer market. Digital advertised the Rainbow at the time as follows: 'The gap, believe us, is wide... Digital was the first company to mass produce minicomputers, and the PDP-11 is, in fact, the world's most popular minicomputer today... And the Digital difference becomes even wider when you consider Digital's unique service back-up'.[8] The Rainbow ran Microsoft's DOS operating system, yet it was not compatible with the IBM PC and therefore did not achieve much success. The sophisticated Professional series, which was sold with little profitability, on the other hand, gained a reputation of not being able to format its own floppy disks.[9] Digital attempted to tackle the personal computer industry again in 1992 with a IBM compatible model amid a shrinking minicomputer market. It allocated a few assembly lines in its Ayr plant in Scotland to production and recruited experienced managers from Hewlett-Packard to oversee its UK marketing operation, which was one of its most important European markets. Though Digital achieved some success in the UK, its overall market penetration in Europe was relatively low. Digital merged with Compaq in 1997.

Dynamics in Product Development

The attractiveness of the microcomputer industry also lies in its dynamic evolutionary pattern in terms of product configuration and processing capability. Seven significant stages of microcomputer product development can be identified. The first stage was the introduction of the Apple II, which commercialised the product concept of the personal computer. The next product evolution was brought about by Apollo Computer in 1980 who designed microcomputers containing superior computing power and data storage. This microcomputer was named a workstation and was designed for network integration. Then Osborne Computer's portable Osborne I marked the third stage of microcomputer development in 1981. Although the Osborne I weighed about 30 pounds and 'bore an incongruous resemblance to a World War II field radio'[10], it was extremely popular at the time. Its founder stated that its systems served as an indictment of the microcomputer industry's failure to innovate. Portable microcomputers continue to evolve and currently the weight of a portable computer is about three pounds.

Accompanying the concept of portability in design, the microcomputer industry witnessed the ascendancy of the IBM personal computer standard that operated on Microsoft's Disk Operating System in 1981. The configuration of the IBM PC cannot be regarded as a technological breakthrough as it incorporates the Intel 8088 microprocessor, 16 kilobytes of memory (expandable to 256 kilobytes), one or two Tandon floppy disk drives, Zenith's power supply and an optional colour monitor and printer. Nevertheless, IBM sold 136,000 units of the IBM PC in 18 months and led the market to accept a new definition of the personal computer, one which is synonymous with the IBM PC. IBM stated in its archives: 'although it enters an already-crowded field, the IBM PC becomes an overnight sensation'.

IBM exploited its technological and marketing heritage, and positioned its personal computer (which was the same colour as the mainframes and started at £2,800[11]) as a high quality, premium priced product that was perfectly compatible with businesses operating in the mainframe and minicomputer environment. Thus, for mainframe and minicomputer users, the IBM PC was a logical choice for their corporate computing needs. The IBM PC captured approximately 70 per cent of the Fortune 1000 accounts during its first four years and its worldwide market share peaked at nearly 30 per cent between 1984 and 1985.[12]

The 5th period of product development that followed witnessed systems based on Windows operating system (i.e. IBM PCs and their compatible systems) taking the place of the Apple operating systems. The idea of an IBM-compatible personal computers originated from Compaq (which stands for compatibility and quality). Compaq was established (shortly after IBM PCs were introduced) with financial support from venture capitalists who believed in Compaq's plan of marketing IBM-compatible systems. Other US firms that followed Compaq into the new IBM-compatible personal computer market included Dell, Packard Bell, Gateway and Zenith Data System. The spread of the IBM compatible systems led to from the late 1980s a decline in prices. A technology reporter in 1992 that: 'what's in a name? Not much, it seems, when it comes to a personal computers'; another analyst also stated that 'when there are too many suppliers and too much undifferentiated product, a shakeout inevitably occurs.'[13] There was indeed a consolidation in the industry, with established brand names gaining market shares in all major markets.

The sixth product evolution that began in 1984 was Apple's Macintosh, which Apple's Steve Jobs named it an 'insanely great' computer. The user friendly Macintosh transformed the display screen into an electronic desktop and allowed the user to interact with the system by moving and pointing to positions on the screen via a mouse. Despite a slow start, the Macintosh had received increasing acceptance by 1986. Indeed, its popularity enabled Apple to share an average of 9 per cent of the worldwide personal computer market between the years 1986–91. Macintosh's product feature, however, was found in the IBM PC and compatible systems when Microsoft launched Windows 3.1 in 1992.

The next watershed in microcomputer production was the launch of the network computers by Oracle and Sun in 1996; the network computers are systems with minimum hardware components which rely on software in a central network. Since the mid-1990s, there is also a development towards the assimilation of microcomputers with areas of consumer electronics and telecommunications. For example, the convergence of consumer electronics and microcomputer technology is exhibited in products such as the PC-TV, PC-phone or net camera. Video conferencing, on the other hand, represents the application of computer and telecommunication technology in distant person-to-person interaction. Moreover, the set-top box, that enables households to connect to cable or satellite television, is equipped with functions of personal computers such as web browsing. It can be seen from this brief review of product evolution that the microcomputer industry has intertwined with the development of technology among US firms, and corresponds with the theme of US firms' critical position in the market discussed earlier.

INDIGENOUS MICROCOMPUTER FIRMS IN EUROPE

The total value of data processing shipments of IBM, Digital and Hewlett-Packard in Europe amounted to the total value of shipments from the European firms Bull, Siemens, Olivetti and ICL in 1983;

moreover, IBM's market shares were two and a half times greater than those of the four European firms.[14] This illustrates the dominance of US firms in Europe as early as 1983. Though US firms have been and are important in the European microcomputer industry, other indigenous firms that have exerted influence on the industry at various times included Amstrad, Evesham, Apricot, Acorn, Viglen, Tiny, Elonex and Time in the UK, Nixdorf Computer, Escom, Vobis and Max Data of Germany, Philips and Tulip in the Netherlands, Stern Computing and Cibox in France.

European Engagement in the Microcomputer

In fact, ICL, Siemens-Nixdorf, Bull, Philips and Olivetti[15] were regarded by their respective governments as national champions prior to the 1990s. The concept of national champions was linked to government policies in the form of procurement and subsidies. IBM UK's Managing Director Sir Edwin Nixon recalled that: 'one of the major problems of IBM UK in the 1970s was the government procurement policy in favour of ICL. I went 10 years without a single new account in central government'.[16] As for subsidies, ICL was rescued twice by the UK government before it was finally sold to STC for £411 million in 1985. Similarly, Bull lost FF2,925 million between 1981 and 1984 and about FF22,000 million between 1990 and 1994, and was depicted as 'almost a parody of industrial policy gone awry. The annual taxpayer subsidy just to cover Bull's losses exceeds the entire American Venture capital infusion into new computer start-ups' (Ferguson et al. 1993 p. 233). The rationale for supporting the European champions was commented on sympathetically by IBM's chairman Thomas Watson, Junior:[17]

> It is easy to see why an Englishman or a Frenchman or a German would not want absolute foreign control of an industry crucial to his security and survival or even to his country's economic future; why he would not want all its shots called by men of another country thousands of miles away, whatever the advantages of American management and technology can bring him and his fellow countrymen.

The European champions entered the microcomputer industry in response to the success of Apple and IBM. They had grown organically as well as by acquisition throughout the 1980s and the early 1990s. For example, Olivetti acquired 49.3 per cent of the Cambridge-based firm Acorn[18] in the UK for £10.4 million in 1985 while Bull bought the US firm Zenith Data Systems in 1989 and engaged in minority equity stakes in another US firm Packard Bell in the year 1993. Siemens' computer division merged with the private firm Nixdorf Computer in 1990; Siemens-Nixdorf Informationsssyteme AG (SNI) further acquired minority shares in the troubled Vobis and Escom in 1996. The president of SNI explained that 'the primary motivation for this strategic move was to create opportunities for joint bulk buying and to benefit from resulting economies of scale in the purchasing sector'.[19]

Market shares of European Champions

The European champions did achieve some international significance. Siemens-Nixdorf[20], Olivetti, Bull, ICL and Philips were among the top 50 firms worldwide in 1991 as shown in Table 2.4. In addition, Olivetti was by far the most successful European firm with a revenue at least 1.7 times higher than other European firms.

Table 2.4: Personal Computer Revenue of European Firms in 1991

Olivetti	US$1,578.20 million
Groupe Bull	US$889.50 million
Siemens-Nixdorf	US$596.75 million
Philips	US$307.60 million
Amstrad	US$271.60 million
Tulip	US$215.50 million

Global Benchmark		
No. 1 firm:	IBM	US$8,505.00 million
No. 50 firm:	Northgate	US$167.14 million

Source: Datamation 1 December 1992 p. 37.

Olivetti had 5.5 per cent of the Ecu22,213 million worth of the European personal computer market in 1991; its market position was behind US firm IBM's 18.8 per cent, Compaq's 9.3 per cent and Apple's 8 per cent.[21] It cannot be denied that Olivetti (under the leadership of Carlo de Benedetti in the 1980s) had migrated rather successfully from its office equipment business (i.e. typewriters) to personal computers as contrasted with other national champions' attempts to make the necessary transition from mainframe computers to microcomputers. Indeed, Olivetti designed a M20 personal computer in its research centre in California in the early 1980s and then mass produced them in its Ivrea plant in Italy.[22]

A Decade of Retreat

Most European champions encountered financial difficulties in the late 1980s as competition in the microcomputer industry intensified; their losses reached insurmountable levels over time and resulted in a series of withdrawals from the industry. Even Olivetti who managed to prosper in the 1980s suffered the same fate as its other European counterparts. It was reported in the mid-1990s that 'Olivetti's PC unit accounts for 20 per cent of the whole group's revenue, but its operating losses and restructuring needs had caused most of the group's combined 3,852 trillion lire in losses since 1991'.[23] Olivetti eventually disposed its personal computer business in March 1997 for a sum of around US$150 million.[24]

Other European champions have also been acquired or have divested themselves of their microcomputer business interests. Indeed, 80 per cent of ICL was sold to the Japanese firm Fujitsu in 1990 (Fujitsu obtained the remaining 20 per cent by 1998). ICL was transformed over time into a service oriented firm. Its personal computer section merged with Fujitsu in July 1996. The new firm Fujitsu ICL Computer Ltd[25] based its manufacturing in the former East German firm Aquarious Robotron Systems which Fujitsu had acquired in 1995. ICL's remaining manufacturing were re-oriented with a contract manufacturing service focus. On the whole, ICL maintains a strong focus on the emerging segment of computer software and service. It was described by an industry observer as follows: 'ICL has undergone a radical transformation from a problem-ridden mainframe computer maker into an expanding computer software and services company with no manufacturing operations'.[26]

Siemens-Nixdorf retreated from the microcomputer business in 1999 through a joint venture partnership with Fujitsu (i.e. the former Fujitsu ICL). One analyst commented that 'the deal may allow Siemens to exit the computer business in a face-saving way since it would effectively contract out the assembly to Fujitsu'.[27] Prior to its joint venture with Fujitsu, Siemens-Nixdorf had engaged in negotiations with Acer for the disposal of its computer operation. However, Acer abandoned the plan as a result of a disagreement over price and payment terms.[28] Immediately following the announcement of the failure of the negotiations with Acer, Siemens-Nixdorf's manager stated that the firm's search for a new partner would continue since it could not operate its personal computer assembly on its own in the face of heavy competition from abroad.[29]

Bull transferred its loss-making Zenith Data System to Packard Bell in February 1996.[30] As a result, Bull increased its equity stakes in Packard Bell to 19.9 per cent. Its manager at the time stated that if Packard Bell were to become profitable, Bull might increase its equity stakes so as to include its financial results in the firm's consolidated account.[31] However, Bull reduced its commitment and sold nine Packard Bell shares in 1997.

To a great extent, the evolution of the European champions has been intertwined with US firms and their strategies. Olivetti developed its early personal computers in its Silicon Valley subsidiary and its eventual sale was led by the US financier Edward Gottesman. Bull have expanded their personal computer businesses with the acquisition of equity stakes in US firms Zenith Data Systems and Packard Bell. Finally, the transformation of ICL, under the majority ownership of Fujitsu, has followed IBM's well-trodden path of focusing on services and software.

More Nimble European Competitors

European microcomputer firms such as the UK's Apricot, Acorn, Amstrad, Tiny, Time and Viglen and Germany's MaxData as well as France's Cibox have specialised in niche segments within their national markets and have managed to establish a market presence at various points in the industry's development. For example, Alan Sugar's Amstrad targeted the low-end mass consumer market in the 1980s while his later firm Viglen[32] focused on the educational segment in the 1990s. Amstrad was in fact one of the fastest growing medium-sized British firms between 1980–90, with 1,841 per cent growth in profits and 4,087 per cent growth in sales revenue.[33]

MaxData grew steadily following its formation in 1987 and has built up a reputation for speedy delivery where customers could receive their systems within 3 to 4 days. Cibox, on the other hand, skilfully used the hypermarket channels such as Auchan and Carrefour to mass distribute its personal computer systems and grew rapidly in the late 1990s. It is interesting to note that these niche marketers have grown considerably during different stages of the microcomputer industry's development despite the overall dominating position of US firms. Unlike the former national firms, some of the small European firms such as Tiny and MaxData have even undertaken direct investment in the USA in 2000. Tiny operates a number of retail outlets similar to those in the UK while

MaxData utilises internet sales to approach its customers. Their assumptions are that indigenous firms that survive in the highly competitive European market will be able to grow in the USA. So time will tell if the investment of these firms proves to be successful.

Table 2.5: Market Shares in Major European Markets in late 1999

Germany		UK		France	
Siemens	17%	Tiny	6%	Cibox	4%
Maxdata	6%	Time	6%	Unika	5%
Fujitsu	13%	Fujitsu	4%	Siemens	4%
Compaq	11%	Toshiba	5%	Toshiba	4%
IBM	5%	Packard Bell	16%	Packard Bell	13%
Dell	4%	Dell	17%	Dell	12%
HP	4%	Compaq	16%	Compaq	16%
		IBM	5%	IBM	12%
		HP	5%	HP	10%

Source: Fortune (Asia) 6 March 2000 p. 45.

US AND ASIA PACIFIC MICROCOMPUTER INVESTMENT

As microcomputer firms' direct investment in Europe coincided with US and Asia Pacific's historical outflow of manufacturing investment into Europe, which itself is a manifestation of the global trend of international production in the post Second World War period, I will provide a broad discussion of US, Japanese, Taiwanese and Korean investment activities in Europe prior to the discussion of their national firms' microcomputer investments.

Figure 2.2 compares the recent foreign direct investment stock of the USA, Japan, Taiwan and Korea in Europe in 1995. Direct investment relates to either manufacturing investment or marketing investment in Europe, and differs from portfolio investment. The stock of foreign direct investment relates to the total accumulated value of assets at a given time. Figure 2.2 shows that the USA had an entrenched position in Europe, with a total value of US$394,000 million worth of investment. Though their investment stock in the 1950s and 1960s was hardly noticeable, Japanese firms had expanded rapidly overseas and had attained a total value of investment of US$58,696 million. Taiwan's and Korea's level of investment in Europe was US$5,899 million and US$10,223 million respectively, which are relatively insignificant amounts.[34]

Figure 2.2 Foreign Direct Investment Stock in Europe, 1995

US$ million

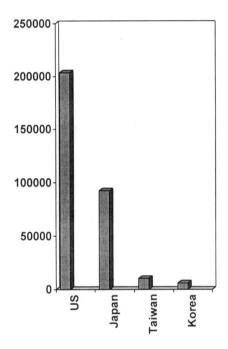

Source: UNCTC 1992 p. 244 and p. 494, UN 1997 p. 20, Van Hoesel 1998 and Business Week 7 October 1996 p .25.

American Foreign Direct Investment

America is one of the early pioneers in contemporary manufacturing investment with the first US foreign investment being in the Panama Railroad Company in 1849. The Singer Sewing Machine Company, on the other hand, was a pioneer US firm that opened its factory in

Glasgow, Scotland in 1867. By 1914, America shared 14 per cent of the worldwide stock in foreign investment (Jones 1996 p. 30). With the ascendancy of mass production, US firms such as Ford, General Motors and Coca-Cola undertook more investment abroad. Their activities were reflected in the increase of the percentage shares of US investment within the total world direct investment, which were 28 per cent by 1938 (ibid. p. 42). The structural change of the US economy that favoured the service sector, however, soon altered US manufacturing firms' positions in total US foreign direct investment.

Figure 2.3 reveals that the most important sectors among US investment in both 1988 and 1990 were finance and insurance. The electrical equipment sector had less than US$20,000 million worth of investment (i.e. less than 5 per cent of the total investment). Figure 2.4 shows the increase of investment stock by US firms between 1980 and 1988 in Europe. It can be seen that one-third of the investment was directed to the UK, while approximately one-tenth was towards France, Germany and the Netherlands. Another recent development of US investment in Europe is the doubling since 1990 of investment. US firms invested approximately US$150,000 million into Europe in 1996; consequently, the total stock of US investment in Europe in 1990 was about three times greater than that in Asia Pacific, while in 1996 it was nearly four times.[35]

US microcomputer firms' investment can be interpreted in the light of the nation's total investment. Firstly, like the early US investors such as Singer, US microcomputer firms Apple and IBM were leaders in microcomputer investment in Europe. They demonstrated their commitment in Europe by establishing manufacturing operations at the early stage of the industry's development; most notably, Apple set up its manufacturing plant in Ireland in 1980 while IBM established its manufacturing division in Scotland in 1982. Secondly, US microcomputer firms such as IBM, Compaq, Dell, HP and Sun have shown resilience and the ability to sustain foreign investment, which goes against the irreversible trend of decline in the US manufacturing sector. They maintain their positions by innovative marketing as well as leveraging capabilities of low cost producers. For instance, Dell and Sun have introduced innovative products and marketing channels whereas Dell has pioneered the trend of utilising contract manufacturing in the industry. By the early 1990s, US firms had obtained experiences in organising networks of original equipment manufacturing firms in Taiwan, Korea as well as in major microcomputer markets. I will discuss their leveraging of Taiwan and Korea's manufacturing capabilities in a later chapter.

Figure 2.3: Industry Distribution of US Investment, 1980–90

US$ million

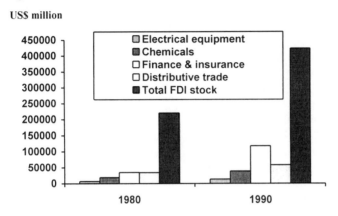

Source: UNCTC 1992 p. 492.

Figure 2.4: US Investment by Area, 1980–90

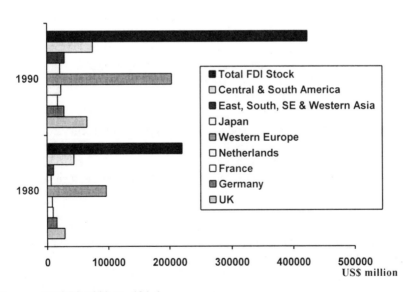

Source: UNCTC 1992 pp. 494-6.

Japanese Foreign Direct Investment

The foreign direct investment of Japanese firms can be traced back to the late 19th century when Japan, following the Meiji Restoration in 1868, embarked on the path of economic modernisation. During the 1900s, Japanese textile firms began to acquire cotton mills in China. It was estimated that 83 per cent of the US$260.5 million Japanese foreign investment in 1914 was directed to China (Yasumuro 1984 p. 84). By the 1930s, Japanese investment had reached a large size relative to that of the Japanese economy, although not in relation to the size of foreign investment in the world as a whole (Jones 1996 p. 42). Despite the loss of its accumulated foreign investment stock after the country's defeat in the Second World War, Japanese firms embarked on foreign investment again in the 1960s with the rapid post-war economic recovery. This was encouraged by the removal of various governmental restrictions on outward foreign direct investment e.g. in the late 1960s and the early 1970s.

Figure 2.5 illustrates Japanese investment by geographical areas in 1990. It can be seen that Japanese investment was concentrated in the US and, to a lesser extent, South East Asian nations such as Indonesia, Malaysia, the Philippines, Singapore, Taiwan and Hong Kong. As for Europe, the UK is the most preferred location while the Netherlands, France and Germany are also key locations. Figure 2.6 shows that investment in finance and insurance, real estate, communications and electrical equipment accounted for 21 per cent, 15 per cent, 10 per cent and 7 per cent of the total investment respectively in 1990.

Two observations can be made about Japanese investment in general. Firstly, Japan's foreign investment has continued to recover at a steady pace since the end of the Second World War; it is indeed remarkable that Japan is currently one of the leading investors after the US. Secondly, Japanese firms show a tendency to locate their investment in the UK, which is a pattern exhibited by the US investors as discussed above. The geographical concentration of Japanese firms in the UK has been explained typically in terms of the language factor and the usual pattern of clustering among Japanese communities and firms. Munday (1990 p. 40) studied Japanese investment in Wales and wrote: 'the success of Wales as a location for Japanese manufacturers, is concerned with the aspect of the welcome mat provided for the respective firms. The Japanese are newcomers to foreign manufacturing activity in the West... Signs of any host unfriendliness, or any other frictions within the host nation against the Japanese company, may alter the course of an investment decision...'. Nevertheless, it may also be a conscious replication of US firms' business strategies on the part of the Japanese investors.

Figure 2.5: Japanese Investment by Geographical Area, 1990

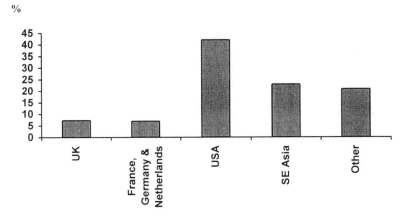

Source: UNCTC 1992 pp. 289–90.

Figure 2.6: Japanese Investment by Sector, 1990

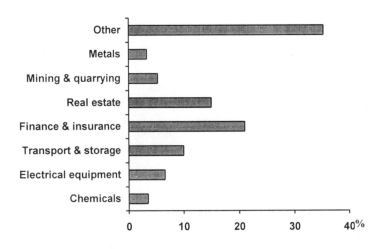

Source: UNCTC 1992 pp.242–3.

Taiwanese Foreign Direct Investment

With the onset of the economic miracle in the 1960s, some Taiwanese firms replaced their initial export strategies with direct manufacturing investment. Taiwanese firms began to invest abroad on a large scale in the 1980s. Since 1984 they have played increasingly important roles as investors. In that year, their foreign investments approved by the Taiwanese government's Investment Commission amounted to US$40 million. The amount of Taiwanese investment increased more than five times between 1980 and 1988. The geographical distribution of Taiwanese firms' investment in 1988 can be seen in Figure 2.7. The USA was the predominant recipient of Taiwanese investment; the next important recipients were the Philippines and Indonesia. The distribution of Taiwanese firms' investment by the industrial sector is illustrated in Figure 2.8. It can be seen that over 70 per cent of the investment has been predominantly in the secondary sector between 1979 and 1988. As for a more detailed analysis at the industry level, Figure 2.9 shows that the industries with the highest share of investment in 1988 were chemicals and electrical equipment.

Figure 2.7: Taiwan's Investment by Geographical Area, 1988

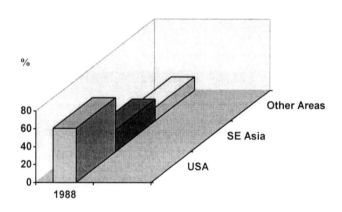

Source: UNCTC 1992 p. 305.

A more recent development is Taiwanese investment in China, which has surged since the mid-1990s. Despite the complexity of Taiwan's foreign direct investment procedure, Taiwanese microcomputer firms managed to set up facilities in China to capture its labour cost competitiveness, which were/are essential for these firms to compete. Major US and Japanese microcomputer firms such as Dell, Compaq, IBM and Toshiba have in fact all established manufacturing facilities in China. Hence, Taiwanese microcomputer firms' migration to China is critical (despite its political incorrectness from the Taiwanese government's point of view) for accessing resources for the labour-intensive assembly process of microcomputer and component manufacturing.[36] China has attracted investment from microcomputer component manufacturers in the southern provinces in recent years, which allows microcomputer firms to undertake local procurement in most components. Besides, China is also an enormous market for the industry. The importance of the Chinese market is supported by Dell's operation in Xiamen, which became profitable shortly after its establishment. Despite its lucrative market and labour cost competitiveness, business operations in China always demand considerable management skills.[37]

Figure 2.8: Taiwanese Investment by Industrial Sector, 1979–88

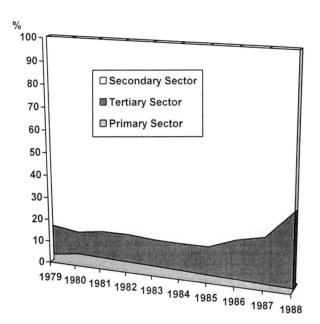

Source: UNCTC 1992 p. 302.

Figure 2.9: Taiwanese Investment by Industry, 1986

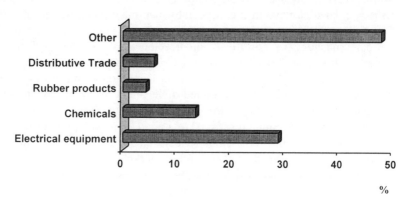

%

Source: UNCTC 1992 p. 303

Korean Foreign Direct Investment

At the end of the 1950s, South Korea was one of the world's poorest nations. Nevertheless, with an export-led growth since the 1960s, it has become one of the most prosperous economies in the Asia Pacific region. The Korean government intervened heavily in the operation of the economy; for example, it used to provide long-term low interest loans to the family-owned conglomerates, the *chaebols*. Korean firms' overseas investment activities became prominent in 1986, when the government liberalised the regulations concerning foreign investment in order to mitigate the inflationary impact of trade surpluses and to accommodate the demand for more freedom in capital movement. The amount of recent Korean investment is illustrated in Figure 2.10. The total value of direct investment in 1989 was US$1,444 million, whilst that in 1992 reached US$4,507 million. Korean firms' quickened their expansion and invested abroad US$230 million in 1994, US$307 million in 1995 and US$413 million in 1996. Its total stock of foreign investment, as a consequence, increased to US$5,583 million in 1996.[38]

The geographical distribution of Korean firms' investment in 1988 is illustrated in Figure 2.11. One of the characteristics of the distribution of the investment is that South East Asia represented over 20 per cent of the total investment. The investment in USA and Canada amounted to 43 per cent of the investment in 1988 whereas Europe was 3.7 per cent. By 1993, Korean investment in the EU had risen to US$534 million, of which 32 per cent was in Germany, 30 per cent was in the UK and 20 per cent was in France (Nam and Slater 1991 p. 40).

Figure 2.10: Korea's Foreign Investment, 1970–92

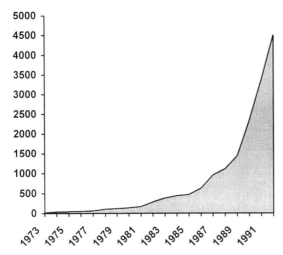

Source: Jin 1994 p. 186.

Figure 2.11: Korean Investment by Geographical Area, 1988

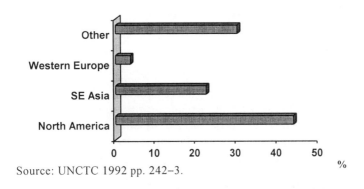

Source: UNCTC 1992 pp. 242–3.

The sectional distribution of Korean firms' investment in 1992 is shown in Figure 2.12; approximately half of the total investment was in manufacturing. This reflected the Korean economy's successful transition from reliance on primary production activities to secondary activities derived from a successful industrial base. However, the economic crisis in Korea in late 1997 has led to a retrenchment policy among Korean firms such as Hyundai who abandoned its semiconductor plant project in the UK in 1988.

Figure 2.12: Korean Investment by Industry, 1992

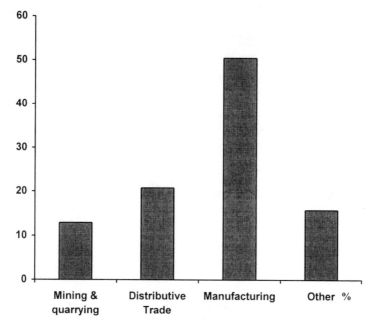

Source: UNCTC 1992 p. 240; Jin 1994 p. 191.

The investment by the Korean microcomputer firm Samsung correlates in the late 1990s with the expansion of Korean investment. The reason Europe is under-represented as a destination for investment is that Korean firms targeted low-cost localities for labour-intensive manufacturing related processes. In addition, they prefer to tackle the more homogenous market in the USA. When entering the European microcomputer industry, Samsung chose acquisition (of the US firm AST) as the market entry mode. At the time, Samsung considered it could build on the firm's existing brand recognition in the USA and Europe. However, AST continued to lose market shares, incurred heavy losses and was eventually disposed of by Samsung. Nevertheless, an extraordinary feature of recent Korean investment is the speed of its expansion; this is particularly impressive given the enormous size of Korean firms and the usual time required for decision making process to go through different levels and units of large firms. To a certain extent, one can interpret this in terms of the flexibility of these very large firms that incorporate rapid decision making processes.

Direct Manufacturing Investment in European Microcomputer Firms

The previous section has provided the historic context of US and Asia Pacific microcomputer firms' investment. I will now describe their manufacturing investment since the industry's inception. The first wave of microcomputer manufacturing investment in Europe was led by the US firms Apple, IBM, Hewlett-Packard, Compaq, SGI, Sun and Tandy's setting up of facilities prior to the late 1980s. The location of Apple's manufacturing plant was Ireland while that for SGI was, and still is, Switzerland. The remaining firms, on the other hand, chose the Silicon Glen in Scotland.

These early investments were succeeded by those initiated by youthful US firms AST, Packard Bell, Dell, Gateway and Tandem as well as Asia Pacific firms from the late 1980s onwards. Asia Pacific firms included Fujitsu, NEC, Toshiba, Mitsubishi, Toshiba, Acer, Twinhead, Mitac and Samsung. The manufacturing investment of these late entrants (with the exception of Dell, Gateway, Mitac and Twinhead) took the form of acquisition.

Acer acquired the Dutch firm Kangaroo Computer in 1989. Mitsubishi and Fujitsu purchased the British firms Apricot[39] and ICL's operation in 1990. AST bought Tandy's plant in Scotland in 1993 while Packard Bell acquired two of Bull's plants in Angers also in 1993. In addition, NEC obtained 40 per cent equity stakes in Packard Bell in 1996. Samsung's investment, as mentioned earlier, was associated with the acquisition of AST. Among those firms who established their own facilities, Dell and Gateway located in Ireland in 1991 and 1993 with the help of the Industrial Development Authority (IDA). Gateway established its European manufacturing and marketing facility in the Clonshaugh Industrial Estate in Dublin in 1993. Its Senior Vice President Robert Spears stated that Gateway received Irish government incentives under EU guidelines for training and cost reimbursement. He added that the ten per cent corporate tax was an incentive that 'you don't come across every day'.[40] Mitac's facility in Telford was also associated with local grants from the Telford Development Corporation. Mitac agreed to undertake a £3.5 million investment in buildings, plant and machinery in January 1993 that would generate 120 jobs. Upon the completion of its plant within three years, Mitac would receive a grant of £400,000.[41]

Nevertheless, the position of microcomputer firms' manufacturing investment is rather dynamic. Apple sold its plant in Cork, Ireland to Singapore's NatSteel Electronics in 1999. NatSteel Electronics was in turn acquired by the US contract electronics manufacturer Solectron in 2000.[42] Mitsubishi withdrew from the European market in 1999.[43] Acer expanded into Germany in 1994 and relocated to the current plant in the Netherlands in 1996. However, it closed its plant in Germany in 1999. Mitac also announced its intention to expand its Telford facility in 2000. Compaq expanded its manufacturing capacity by acquiring US firms Tandem in 1997 and Digital in 1998 and, as a result, inherited their manufacturing facilities in Scotland. Sun, which opened a US$132 million showcase manufacturing facility in Scotland in 1990, planned to expand the facility further with an additional £26 million investment in 2000. In addition, Samsung diverted its AST investment in January 1999[44] and focused its assembly operation in the Wynyard Park, Teeside. This facility is a purpose built electronics manufacturing complex with a sales revenue of £204 million in 1999, where approximately one-third of its sales were to the UK market.[45]   Dell purchased the AST plant in Limerick from Samsung in 1997 and also opened an additional plant in Limerick in 1999. Finally, NEC increased its commitment in Packard Bell to 53 per cent in 1998; this investment in Packard Bell signified NEC's majority ownership of the former US firm. The other shareholders of the firm are Beny Alagem and his partners (who founded Packard Bell in 1986), they maintain 36 per cent ownership. Bull maintains 11 per cent shares of Packard Bell NEC.[46]

To a great extent, the continuous changes in manufacturing investment reflects the competitive environment of the European microcomputer industry and provides an interesting setting from which to explore the backward linkage strategy of US and Asia Pacific microcomputer firms. It clearly sets out the premise that economic rationalism (i.e. profit maximisation) is the underlying principle of successful backward linkage strategy. Furthermore, it also highlights the importance of US firms as an underlying theme in the development of the European microcomputer industry, which parallels their impact on the product and market evolution of the microcomputer.

CONCLUSION

The historical development of the microcomputer industry was presented in the context of the foreign direct investment of the USA, Japan, Korea and Taiwan into Europe. This chapter pinpointed some established US firms' manufacturing experience in Europe can be traced back to the pre-Second World War period. It also described the weakness of indigenous firms, and their acquisitions by Asia Pacific firms. This chapter has further discussed the product and market dynamics of the microcomputer industry that contributed to the surge of manufacturing investment within Europe in past decades, and furnishes us with information concerning the distinct contributions of US firms that shape the industry. Closely related to the spread of US manufacturing investment is the influence of US managerial practice, a topic which has been acknowledged in the past decades. Dunning (1958) found significant American influence on their British subsidiaries. He reported that the overall policy and thinking of the British subsidiaries were dominated by the parents. The Managing Directors of these subsidiaries were either Americans, controlled by the US headquarters or had assimilated American managerial values. He quoted a British Managing Director's acquisition of business values: 'my constant contact with, and visits to, our US parent company makes me more receptive to new ideas than would otherwise have been the case' (ibid. p. 251). In his book *'The American Challenge'*, Servan-Schreiber (1968) also observed the superior technology and marketing possessed by US firms during the 1950s and 1960s, and suggested that their leadership and innovativeness should be the model for European firms. The conception of a unique US model, to a great extent, can also be applied to the backward linkage strategy in the microcomputer industry; in a sense that earlier best practice of integrated linkage strategy is associated with the established US firms such as IBM while succeeding practice is linked with Dell's disintegrated linkage strategy. I will explore this idea further in chapter six and chapter seven.

NOTES

[1]   Western Europe includes Austria, Belgium, Luxembourg, Denmark, Finland, France, Germany, Greece, Ireland, Italy, the Netherlands, Norway, Portugal, Spain, Sweden, Switzerland and the UK.

[2]   However, Taiwan's Market Intelligence Centre predicted that China would replace Taiwan's position in the near future as a result of the influx of Taiwanese firms' investment in China (See 'China is likely to supplant Taiwan

as No. 3 manufacturer of PC hardware', *Wall Street Journal,* 11 December 1999).

[3] Apple's pre-assembled computer circuit board Apple I retailed at the price of US$666.66.

[4] The historical event that took place on 16 April 1975 in California was described as 'the Altair's first recital'.

[5] Samsung Group's sales revenue in 2000 should be at comparable level. For instance, its larger group subsidiaries Samsung Electronics and Samsung Trading had reported US$38,491 million and US$35,939 million sales revenue in 2000 respectively.

[6] 'Compaq shareholders overwhelmingly approve Hewlett-Packard', *Compaq Press Release,* 20 March 2002.

[7] Bro Uttal, 'A computer Gadfly's Triumph', *Fortune,* 8 March 1982 p. 74.

[8] Advertised in *Management Today,* July 1983 p. 31.

[9] One could, however, purchase formatted floppy disks from Digital.

[10] Uttal (op. cit.).

[11] See Microcomputer Land's advertisement for IBM PC in *Management Today* July 1982 p. 36.

[12] Cusumano and Yoffie (1998); Levy (1997) and Apple Computer 1992.

[13] Louis Kehoe, 'Price is the name of the game', *The Financial Times,* 16 June 1992 p. 17.

[14] *Data Management* June 1985 p. ix.

[15] ICL, Siemens Nixdorf, Bull and Olivetti were regarded as the Big Four.

[16] Simon Caulkin, 'Nixon's IBM', *Management Today,* January 1985 p.60.

[17] Philip Sielcman 'Now it's the European versus IBM', *Fortune,* 15 August 1969 p. 90.

[18] Acorn's founder Christopher Curry and Herman Hauser reduced their shares of the firm at 37 per cent.

[19] *The Financial Times,* Survey 3 April 1996 p. IV.

[20] Siemens' computer division and Nixdorf Computer were independent concerns prior to 1990. The inventive Nixdorf Computer was a leading mainframe and minicomputer firm in Germany; however, it encountered severe financial problems in the late 1980s.

[21] Estimation by Dataquest Europe, a unit of Gartner Group which headquartered in San Jose, California.

[22] Robert Bail 'The durable turnaround at Olivetti', *Fortune,* 21 February 1983 p. 114.

[23] Maureen Kline 'Olivetti undergoes its latest revamping', *Wall Street Journal Europe,* 2 May 1996.

[24] 'Olivetti seals deal with Gottesman on PC division', *Wall Street Journal Europe,* 3 March 1997 p. 3.

[25] Fujitsu dropped ICL from the title in 1999.

[26] Paul Taylor 'Fujitsu buy clears way for ICL flotation', *The Financial Times,* 1 October 1998.

[27] This view is among analysts such as Ingo Queiser at Bankhaus Metzler, Frankfurt and Yoshiharu Izhmi at Warburg Dillion Read in Tokyo, see *The Financial Times,* 18 June 1999 p.33.

[28] 'Key Developments in Germany', *Crossborder Monitor,* 7 October 1998.

[29] Dow Jones Newswires 'Siemens Unit Seeks PC Partner' as quoted in *Wall Street Journal Europe,* 29 September 1998.

[30] Douglas Lavin, 'Bull logs its first profit in six years', *Wall Street Journal Europe,* 21 February 1996.

[31] Ibid.

[32] Viglen Technology was founded in the UK in 1975, however, it was acquired by Amstrad in 1984. Two years later, Amstrad also purchased Sinclair, the early industry entrant that was associated with the rudimentary ZX81.

[33] Amstrad was one of the fastest growing British firms according to a study in the Henley Management College. See *Management Today,* February 1996 p. 63.

[34] The total amount of outward foreign direct investment for the USA, Japan, Taiwan and Korea as in 1995 was US$705,570 million, US$305,545 million, US$24,344 million and US$11,079 million respectively. See UNCTC (1996 pp. 245–7).

[35] US Commerce Department as quoted in 'US investment in Europe', *Business Week,* 7 October 1996 p. 25.

[36] The Taiwanese government has permitted investments in some selected areas such as motherboards and monitors but legally prohibited the direct investment of more technological intensive areas such as the manufacturing of notebook computers. Nevertheless, Taiwanese firms have created shell corporations in other nations and channelled their investment into China (See Michael Kanellos and Jack Kuo, 'Notebook manufacturers shift to China to lower costs', *CBET News.com site,* 28 December 2000).

[37] It was reported that some 20 years after China's Open Door Policy, industrial workers still consider reading the Chinese Communist Party's newspaper and attending party meeting as their work roles. See 'Dell crack China', *Fortune,* 21 June 1999.

[38] Bank of Korea as reported by Charles S. Lee, 'Tomorrow the world', *Far East Economic Review,* 1 May 1997 p. 44.

[39] Apricot was originally a computer distributor named ACT which was established in Birmingham in 1966. ACT forward integrated into manufacturing by acquiring Victor Technologies in 1984 and obtained its plant in Glenthrones, Scotland.

[40] *Corporate Location,* July–August 1996 p. 14.

[41] Michel Wu, *Taiwan's Outward Direct Investment with special reference to the Computer/Information Industry in Europe,* 1996 MSc Dissertation, University of Reading, UK.

[42] Natsteel's business suffered as the demand for Apple's iMac (its largest customer and accounted for about 50 per cent of its sales revenues) fell. See Michael Shari, 'Why Singapore is unloading an icon', *Business Week,* 20 November 2000 p. 58.

[43] Mitsubishi was one of the Japanese firms that entered Europe via direct marketing in Europe since the early 1980s; others included Fujitsu, Toshiba, NEC, Hitachi and Sanyo.

[44] *Business Week,* Special Report, 'Overhauling Samsung', 10 January 2000 p. 75.

[45] Samsung's Wynard Park project had drawn six Korean suppliers to the UK, which produced casings, wiring, coils, cables... For example, Woo One invested in a £2.5 million factory in Hartlepool, the North East to produce computer casings. Poong Jeon, Fine Electromechanics and Sung Kwang established electronic component manufacturing plants in South Yorkshire that were estimated to be about £2.2 million. (See T*he Financial Times*, 24 April 1996). Samsung's sales revenue were from FAME database (2000).

[46] David P Hamilton 'NEC to boost Packard Bell investment', *Wall Street Journal Europe,* 3 August 1998 p. 7.

3. Microcomputer Strategic Paradigm

I pointed out in chapter one that US and Asia Pacific microcomputer multinational firms' backward linkage strategies can be divided into integrated strategy and disintegrated strategy, which differ in the ratio of the value of external procurement to the total value of hardware components. Table 3.1 illustrates the differing ratios of two micro-computer firms in Europe in 1990. The total costs of procurement as a percentage of sales for Firm A was about 40 per cent whereas for Firm B it was 50 per cent. Firm A utilises a disintegrated backward linkage strategy where its ratio of external procurement to total procurement was 100 per cent; Firm B, on the other hand, pursued an integrated strategy and attained a ratio of 36 per cent. The ratio therefore points to the fact that 64 per cent of Firm B's procurement was manufactured at its headquarters or by other subsidiaries.

Table 3.1: Component Procurement in Microcomputer Firms, 1990

	Firm A Disintegrated Linkage	Firm B Integrated Linkage
	US$ m	US$ m
Total Value of Procurement	439.5	589.3
Internal Procurement	0.0	378.0
External Procurement	439.5	211.3
Ratio of external procurement to total value of procurement	*100%*	*36%*

Source: Historic Firm Data.

The breakdown of Firm B's procurement spending is shown in Table 3.2. Firm B undertook internal procurement of US$378 million worth of main circuit boards from the Far East and the US, which constituted over 60 per cent of Firm B's total value of procurement in 1990. The high percentage of main circuit boards in terms of total procurement is due to the fact that they contained more expensive semiconductor components such as micro-processors and memories. Firm B procured US$211.3 million components externally, which comprised important items such as US$76 million worth of hard disk drives and US$73 million worth of display monitors. The table shows that hard disk drives and display monitors were 24 per cent of Firm B's total value of procurement. Finally, Firm B also undertook purchases in Europe on items such as keyboards and modems.

The present chapter has three main purposes. Firstly, the concept of integrated linkage strategy and disintegrated linkage strategy will be elaborated with examples; in doing so, I will touch on the nature of supplier relationships among US and Asia Pacific microcomputer firms. Secondly, the two opposing modes of backward linkage strategy will be interpreted in terms of the business strategy paradigm of market orientation and resource orientation. Finally, the theoretical background of a cultural theory, that expands the dichotomous paradigm of market orientation versus resource orientation, will be discussed in the context of the European microcomputer industry.

Table 3.2: Procurement in Firm B utilising Integrated Linkage

Components	Total Spending (US$ million)
Main Circuit Boards	378.0
Hard Disks	76.0
Monitors	73.0
Packaging	18.0
Keyboards	20.0
Metals	6.5
Cables	5.5
Plastics	3.0
Modems	3.0
Sub-contract Assembly	2.3
Documentation	2.0
Floppy Drives	2.0
Total US$	589.3

Source: Same as Table 3.1.

DISINTEGRATED BACKWARD LINKAGE STRATEGY

Disintegrated linkage strategy relates to microcomputer firms entering into contracts with external suppliers, rather than undertaking captive production within its various subsidiaries. The concept of disintegrated linkage not only refers to firms that procure all the required components from independent suppliers, but also extends to their use of contract manufacturing services to build semi-finished or fully completed microcomputer systems. In both cases, the value of external procurement as a percentage of total hardware components is 100 per cent.

A microcomputer firm who designs its own components may license the technology to supplier firms when adopting disintegrated linkage strategy. In this case, it will undertake procurement from the licensees; an example is Sun's disengagement in microprocessor manufacturing. Even though Sun designed the UltraSPARC, MicroSPARC and MAJC family of microprocessors incorporated in its microcomputers, it has licensed these products to semiconductor firms such as Texas Instruments, Fujitsu and Hyundai. In return, Sun undertook procurement from the licensees and was the largest buyer of SPARC processors during the 1990s.

The disintegrated linkage strategy can be traced back to Apple Computer's early component procurement policy, where its President Michael Scott mentioned that 'Our business was designing, educating and marketing. I thought that Apple should do the least amount of work that it could and that it should let everyone else grow faster. Let the subcontractors have the problems'.[1] As a consequence, it built the early Apple personal computers in Dallas with printed circuit boards assembled by contract manufacturers in Singapore, microprocessors from Synertek, other semiconductors from Hitachi, Texas Instruments and Motorola, display monitors from Hitachi and power supplies from Astec in Hong Kong.[2]

The practice of disintegrated linkage strategy has also been adopted by Gateway who, since the mid-1980s, procured 100 per cent of its microcomputer components externally. Despite its growth, Gateway maintained its disintegrated linkage and refrained from expanding into component manufacturing. Table 3.3 shows the suppliers of higher value components for Gateway's E1200 model that was launched in 1999, which included US firms AMD, Intel, Creative Labs, Microsoft, Western Digital and Quantum as well as Japanese firms Toshiba and Mitsumi. In addition, Taiwanese firms also served as suppliers of lower value items such as metal housings, power supplies and power supply fans. Gateway described its disintegrated backward linkage strategy in terms of 'I buy parts, I sell parts'; in other words, Gateway is a 'cost-plus'; firm where price reduction from suppliers are passed on to the customer.[3]

Table 3.3: Gateway's Supplier for E1200 and Select 1000 Models

Components	Suppliers
Microprocessors	Intel, AMD
Chipsets/main circuit boards	Intel, Kadoka, AMD
Hard disk drives	Quantum, Western Digital
Mice	Microsoft
Graphic cards	nVidia, ATi
Graphic chips	nVidia, ATi
CD-ROM drives	Toshiba, Mitsumi
Sound cards	Creative Labs, Crystal
Speakers	Boston
DVD-ROM drives	Mitsumi
Others...	

Source: PC Advisor August 2000 p. 173 and PC Pro August 1999 p. 76.

Dell whose external procurement spending approached US$20,000 million in 2000 is also well known for its disintegrated linkage strategy. It was reported that its total value of procurement from the Korean firm Samsung was about US$16,000 million in 2001 while that from Taiwanese firms was approximately US$6,000 million.[4] Samsung's supply contract included memory, LCD panels, optical disk drives and display monitors whereas Taiwanese firms supplied Dell components such as keyboards, mice, motherboards, modems... etc.

INTEGRATED BACKWARD LINKAGE STRATEGY

As microcomputers include components that require a different degree of firm capabilities, no microcomputer firm could operate efficiently as a self-contained unit. Indeed, all microcomputer firms have developed some economic relationships with independent suppliers. Integrated linkage strategy therefore encompasses the captive production of certain elements of hardware components, which could be capital-intensive components such as hard disk drives and/or labour-intensive components such as display monitors. To illustrate, Acer's Dutch manufacturing operation received deliveries of partially completed main system units which encompassed captively produced motherboards, monitors, CD-

ROM drives, CD-RW drives, DVD drives, transformers, modems, keyboards and capacitors from various subsidiaries as shown in Table 3.4. This table shows the division of work within Acer; it can be seen that components are manufactured at more than one site. For instance, the production of motherboards takes place at Acer's subsidiaries in the Philippines, China and Taiwan.

Table 3.4: Acer's Integrated Linkage Strategy

Component	Manufacturing Site
Main circuit boards	Acer Information Products (Philippines) Inc.
	Acer Information Products (Zhongshan) Inc., China
	Aopen Inc, Lungtan, Taiwan
Modems	Acer Netxus Inc., Hsinchu, Taiwan
	Ambit Microsystems Corp, Hsinchu, Taiwan
CD-ROM drives	Aopen Inc., Lungtan, Taiwan
	Acer Communication and Multimedia, Taiwan
	Acer Technologies Sdn Bhd, Penang, Malaysia
CD-RW drives	Aopen Inc., Lungtan, Taiwan
DVD drives	Aopen Inc., Lungtan, Taiwan
Display monitors	Acer Periperals Inc., Taoyuan, Taiwan
	Acer Peripherals (Suzhou) Co. Ltd, China
	Acer Technologies Sdn Bhd, Penang, Malaysia
	Acer Peripherals Mexicana, Mexico
Keyboards	Acer Peripherals (Suzhou) Co. Ltd, China
	Darfon Electronics, Taiwan and China
Capacitors	Darfon Electronics, Taiwan and China
CD-ROMs Controller ICs	Acer Laboratories Inc., Hsinchu, Taiwan
Flyback transformers	Darfon Electronics, Taiwan and China

Source: Acer Group (April 2001).

Furthermore, one should also bear in mind that the integrated linkage strategy is sometimes complemented by external procurement for the reasons of technology and market. For instance, Sony (which is the leader of the high end Trinitron display monitors) spent about US$100 million worth of procurement in Taiwan in 1999. The amount included the purchase of low-end display monitors from Lite-On Technology, which served the purpose of complementing the input requirements at its Japanese manufacturing plant.[5] In addition, the market leader of branded liquid crystal display monitors in 1999, NEC, resorted to external sourcing from Taiwan's Compal Electronics and signed an agreement for the supply of 150,000 display monitors in response to the increase in demand. It was reported that 'like many AM-LCD makers[6], NEC is facing a shortage of these products, forcing it to strike a deal with Compal'.[7] As Compal has engaged in a supply contract of LCD flat panels with LG Semicon that lasted until 2001, NEC's procurement of LCD display monitors paradoxically contained its rival's rather than its own flat panels. Microcomputer firms that utilise integrated linkage strategy may also employ contract manufacturing services for partially or fully completed systems. In the case of Japanese firms such as NEC or Toshiba, their integrated circuits products may incorporate the systems produced by contract manufacturers.

RELATIONSHIPS WITHIN BACKWARD LINKAGE

The implementation of backward linkage strategy is represented by the use of spot contract or long-term contract. A spot contract refers to the discrete exchange of components for a competitive price as stated in the spot market that complies with formal written contractual procedure. A long-term contract, on the other hand, relates to sequential transactions that are based on formal written contracts or relational contracts. A formal written contract specifies the terms of the agreement and a non disclosure agreement containing the seller's responsibilities is the standard requirement among US suppliers. Conversely, a relational contract that refers to an implicit understanding between buyers and sellers that is based on trust, and does not contain formal agreements, is common among the 4,000 to 5,000 microcomputer component firms operating in Taiwan.

The procurement of components such as DRAM whose price fluctuates cyclically tends to be handled by a combination of long-term formal contracts and spot contracts. For example, a microcomputer firm that has entered into a contract for the delivery of a specified quantity of DRAMs in six months' time will supplement any shortfall in DRAMs with spot market purchase if there has been a surge of demand for its systems when it receives the contracted DRAMs. In this sense, the contract price and the spot price of the DRAMs it consumes during that particular production period will differ.[8] However, during the recent worldwide shortage of microelectronic components, microcomputer firms have also utilised spot contracts to procure standard items. It was reported that Hewlett-Packard bought 100,000 capacitors for a premium price on the Internet in order to avoid the shut down of a server production line in the US in December 1999.[9]

Prior to the mid-1990s, long-term contracts for microcomputer components were managed in the context of a relatively abundant supply[10]. Microcomputer firms which pursued a build-to-forecast model[11] would enter into a series of contracts repetitively with suppliers over a long period of time. The suppliers would receive relatively accurate forecasts concerning the demand for their products, which they used to organise their production schedules. However, the diffusion of build-to-order model means that firms only assemble the required systems after they have received the orders; hence any shortfall in the forecast among suppliers will inevitably create a market condition with excess demand. Intel, who has underestimated the demand for its microprocessors in 2000 and created severe shortages in the market between February and October[12] acknowledged that: 'the market is stronger than people were anticipating, and it takes time to ramp up production levels'.[13]

Current practices of long-term contracts, as a consequence, are backed up by non-cancellable purchase commitments from suppliers that may involve advanced payments. For instance, Compaq signed a five-year agreement for the supply of DRAMs in 1999 with Micron Technology that was estimated to be US$20,000 million.[14] Meanwhile, Dell purchased US$200 million of bonds from Samsung to obtain a preferred customer status which guaranteed the supply of US$8,500 million worth of liquid crystal display panels for five years; the two firms further reinforced their contractual relationship with a supply contract in association with memory components, monitors, optical disk drives as well as liquid crystal display panels.[15] Dell also signed long-term contracts with Intel to secure the supply of microprocessors in 1999.[16]

THE STRATEGIC PARADIGM OF MARKET VERSUS RESOURCE

Having outlined the two modes of backward linkage strategy in the preceding sections, I will now explain the paradigm of market orientation and resource orientation that supports the alternative backward linkage strategy. In his discussion of the importance of proactive management within the turbulent environment, Morgan (1988) pointed out the importance of a firm's internal rather than external conditions. He explained business strategy that built from inside-out or adopted a resource orientation would approach the environment in a way that appeared rational to internal divisions in terms of resource accumulation. As a contrast, a strategy that tackled the firm from the outside-in was market oriented. It embraced the environment completely and shaped the strategy within the context of the big picture. A representation of the opposing paradigm is shown in Figure 3.1.

Figure 3.1: Intellectual Background of Backward Linkage Strategy

---

Resource Orientation

Firm Capabilities | *Backward Linkage* | Microcomputer Assembly| End Users

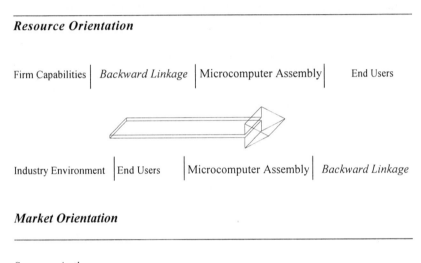

Industry Environment |End Users | Microcomputer Assembly| *Backward Linkage*

Market Orientation

Source: Author.

The dichotomous market and resource based orientations have their origins in the economics of business strategy. Theorists such as Drucker (1954), Ansoff (1988) and Porter (1980) have described market orientation[17] in approaching business strategy whereas Penrose (1959), Wernerfelt (1984) and Hamel and Prahalad (1994) have advocated the use of resource orientation to analyse business strategy. Though the resource orientation has received wide support in the past decade, the importance of the market orientation should also be addressed in detail. In this section, I will first look at writers focusing on the market orientation, then move on to recent writers in relation to resource orientation.

Market Orientation and Strategy

The market orientation is concerned with disintegrated backward linkage strategy built on firms' privileged market positions as advocated by Peter Drucker (1954), who wrote: 'the whole business seen from the point of view of its final result, that is, from the customer's point of view' (p. 39). Drucker (1997) added that managers needed to know what went on outside the firm in order to compete in the highly turbulent and competitive economy, which included information about non-customers, technological development and potential markers. In other words, the opportunities and threats in the markets are important considerations towards a firm's competitive advantage.

Ansoff (1988) also supported a market orientation when analysing the competitive environment during the course of strategy formulation. He began with the assumption that changes in the market environment triggered the need for competitive analysis and then proceeded with the analysis of market potential incorporating factors such as product market structure, technology, conditions for investment and the role of the market. He used the example of Apple technology in operating systems to illustrate the importance of market orientation (ibid. p. 138):

> The traditionally successfully strategy of the Apple Computer Company, based on advanced state-of-the-art computers, which were distinctive and incompatible with IBM computers, was a great success until the mid-1980s. But the changed character of the demand and of industry structure made it necessary to shift to a strategy of market segmentation (Apple has announced that its future focus will be on business and not the consumer market) and of compatibility with IBM.

Another advocate of the market orientation, Michael Porter (op. cit.) identified five important forces within the industry environment that firms should be familiarised with: competition from substitutes, threat of new entry, rivalry between established competitors, bargaining power of suppliers and bargaining power of buyers. Porter's framework addressed the importance of firms' market power during the process of strategic positioning. He also identified two dimensions that firms should consider in selecting business strategy options.[18] The first dimension was related to the pricing of the products while the second one was related to the range of target customers.

The market orientation is further substantiated by Kraljic's (1984) analysis of backward linkage strategy. By concentrating on profit impact and supply risk, Kraljic classified components into four categories: strategic items, bottleneck items, leverage items and non-critical items. Profit impact is associated with the value of the component as a percentage towards the total value of procurement; higher value items such as microprocessors and display monitors will exert greater impact on profitability then lower value items such as mice. Supply risk, on the other hand, can be assessed with the availability of the components, the number of suppliers and the demand conditions.

Figure 3.2: Profit Impact and Supply Risk of Components

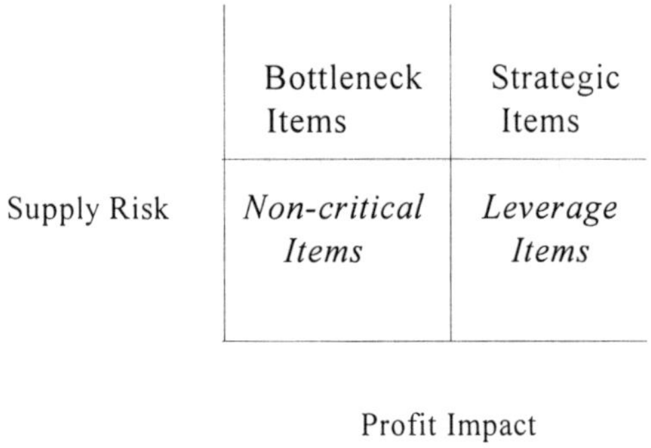

	Bottleneck Items	Strategic Items
Supply Risk	*Non-critical Items*	*Leverage Items*

Profit Impact

Source: Kraljic (1984).

As microcomputer components are highly standardised and generally widely available commodities that can be purchased from alternative suppliers, their supply risks could be considered as low in the long run. Though certain components may be subjected to periodic shortages in supply, microcomputer firms can mitigate the risk with contractual commitments as mentioned earlier (e.g. the recent strategic alliance between Dell and Samsung). According to Kraljic's framework, higher value components such as microprocessors, hard disk drives and CD-ROM drives are therefore leverage items whereas lower value components such as power cords and packaging materials are non critical items. It follows that the disintegrated backward linkage was most appropriate in the European microcomputer industry.

Resource Orientation and Strategy

The premise of the resource orientation is that integrated backward linkage strategy should be pursued as it contributes to the accumulation of expensive and difficult to acquire capabilities[19] that are the ultimate source of competitive advantages. The resource orientation can be traced to the work of Penrose (1959) concerning her theory of firm growth. Penrose interpreted the firm in terms of a broad set of resources such as managerial resources as opposed to the neo-classical economist's model which analysed the firm in terms of factor inputs: land, labour and capital.[20] She argued that as managers standardised their decision making resources, new managerial resources were released and would facilitate growth.

Wenerfelt (1984) emphasised the importance of analysing firms' resources in selecting their market profiles. He wrote that resources and products were two sides of the same coin, and: 'by specifying a resource profile for a firm, it is possible to find the optimal product-market activities' (ibid. p. 171). Hamel and Prahalad took the issue of resource further by looking at the strategic importance of identifying, managing and leveraging a firm's capabilities; in their words (1994 p. 25):

> It is a view of strategy that recognises it is not enough to optimally position a company within existing markets... what is needed is a strategic architecture that provides a blueprint for building the competences needed to dominate future markets... It is a view of strategy that is less concerned with ensuring tight fit between goals and resources and is more concerned with creating stretch goals that challenge employees to accomplish the seemingly impossible. It is a view of strategy as more than the allocation of scarce resources across competing projects...

Hamel and Prahalad further suggested that the more often a capability was reused, the more the capability would be leveraged. They discussed how Toshiba's capability in liquid crystal display flat screen technology was applied in 'everything from pocket diaries to laptop computers to miniature televisions to LCD projection televisions to video telephones' (ibid. p. 218). This, therefore, allowed Toshiba to obtain synergy in flat screen technology in multiple businesses that eventually translated into competitiveness in consumer and professional electronics.

To explain the resource orientation, Fine (1998) compared the decision to integrate the production to a seed planted internally, which might grow, blossom and mature into a valuable capability. Fine depicted this process in terms of a self-perpetuating system where capabilities were fed back into a closed loop that stimulates further utilisation of integrated linkage, which in turn stimulates another cycle of learning and capability acquisition as well as integrated linkage strategy. Figure 3.3 demonstrates the advantages of integrated backward linkage strategy in terms of capability development (p. 161).

Figure 3.3: Firm Resource and Integrated Linkage Strategy

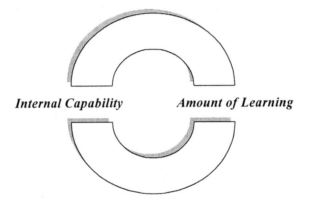

Internal Capability   **Amount of Learning**

Source: Adapted from Fine (1998 p. 160)

BEYOND MARKET AND RESOURCES

It has been assumed that irrespective of their nationalities, firms will comply either with the market or the resource orientations in the strategic paradigm. Nevertheless, the potential of core cultural values in explaining Asia Pacific firms' replication of established US firms' integrated linkage strategy and youthful US microcomputer firms' pioneering of disintegrated linkage strategy has been pointed out in chapter one. Furthermore, US and Asia Pacific microcomputer firms' distinctive pattern of integration in relation to different areas of microcomputer components demands considerable elaboration.

There has been a substantial body of empirical work that has thrown light on the relationship between core cultural values and various systems within business strategy.[21] For instance, studies that related the importance of core values to the seemingly impersonal and mechanical accounting system included Gray (1988), Bloom and Naciri (1989),

Salter and Niswander (1995) and Zarzeski (1996). As microcomputer firms' concept-intensive capabilities, process manufacturing capabilities and people management capabilities are derived from the capabilities of individual designers, engineers and managers, studies concerning the human resource system are of particular relevance to the discussion of backward linkage strategy. Laurent (1983 p. 92) has suggested that the human resource system — selection, appraisal, development, and so forth — can be described as 'institutional preferences for the management of people'. In other words, core cultural values that affected managers' values on how to manage people were translated into human resource strategy.

Prior to the review of recent studies, it should be remembered that Abegglen's (1958) study of Japanese manufacturing firms was a pioneering piece of work in this field. Abegglen undertook personal observation and interviews of 53 Japanese plants[22] and acknowledged the differences of East and West (p. 10):

> In the critical areas of interpersonal relations and group interaction, in the definition of the nature of the relationship between worker and company, and in the way in which skills and energies are mobilised and directed in the group, the Japanese factory is a variant of industrialisation from the American factory. These variations may be seen as essentially from the differences between the broader social systems of the United States and Japan.

Abegglen discussed the implication of the value of collectivism in Japanese human resource strategy. For example, he showed that the Japanese managers' responsibility towards their employees included food, clothing, shelter, medical care and education, which to a great extent was embodied in the value of collectivism. He also wrote that 'the Japanese employee is part of a very much personal system, a system in which his total functioning as a person is seen as management's responsibility and in which his group membership transcends his individual privileges and responsibilities' (p. 66).

Table 3.5 summarises recent empirical studies supporting the relationship of core cultural values with the recruitment, training, compensation, feedback and outcome of human resource strategy. Young and Franke's (2000) study on recruitment practices supported the impact of cultural values. Managers in a US and Korean advertising agency were found to adopt practices influenced by their perceptions of ethical issues. Young and Franke explained that managers with individualistic values would emphasise the role of the individual as the most critical source of ethical behaviour while those with collective values were concerned with the role of the community. As a result, the collective values explained the Koreans' stronger objections to recruiting account executives from another agency. The value of equality among Americans, on the other hand, accounted for their perception that discrimination against women is unethical.

Studies have also looked at cultural influences on training. Earley (1994) surveyed the process through which the value of individualism affected employees' perceptions of self-efficacy (i.e. their abilities to perform certain tasks) after undergoing training. Their laboratory experiments and field experiments in China (low individualism) and the USA (high individualism) involving more than 250 managers suggested that higher self-efficacy could be obtained when those with individualistic values were provided with individualised training, while those exhibiting collective values were given group-based training.

Other studies have supported the association of core cultural values and the content of human resource strategy. Using regression analysis with economic need, cultural value and the desire for control, Sullivan and Peterson (1991) found that the value for loyalty was associated with the prevalence of the lifetime employment system in the Japanese firms they studied. Their finding illustrated that among the causal variables of economic need, cultural value and the desire for control, cultural value was the only one that emerged as significant.

Schuler and Rogovsky (1998) tested the relationship between compensation practices and the cultural values of uncertainty avoidance, individualism and masculinity using three major global data sets, i.e. the IBM-Towers Perrin, International Social Survey Programme and the Price Waterhouse-Cranfield. Their results suggested that nations with higher levels of uncertainty avoidance preferred compensation systems that were based on seniority, skill and individual performance. They have also verified the relationship between individualism and various individualised types of compensation such as tying compensation with individual performance as well as individual bonuses or commissions. In addition, they found positive relationships between masculinity and social benefits plans such as workplace childcare and maternity-leave programmes and negative relationships between masculinity and career-break schemes as well as masculinity and flexible benefit plans.

Oliver and Cravens (1999) examined the 11 most common employee welfare plan within 91 foreign firms in the USA. Their rationale were that 'since all firms are employing US workers and are subject to the same US regulatory constraints for providing benefits in the USA, any differences in managers' provision of benefits should be attributable to their own cultural influences' (p. 749). Indeed, they found the combination of the value of individualism, power distance and uncertainty avoidance affected the discretionary benefits of supplemental unemployment plans, temporary disability plans, vision plans and cafeteria plans[23]. For instance, they explained that the degree of coverage in supplemental plans which provide additional income to employees differed in firms embodying high and low levels of uncertainty avoidance, which was translated into fear of unfamiliar risks. They found that the highest level of coverage was provided by those from cultures with higher uncertainty avoidance and who were uncomfortable with unfamiliar risks.

Bailey and Chen (1997) applied individualism to an examination of national culture and the desire form of performance feedback, which was described in terms of their focus on success or failure. Using a sample of over 200 participants from the USA (high individualism) and Japan and China (low individualism), they found that US participants were more motivated to seek performance feedback that emphasised success while those from Japan and China desired failure feedback. It can be interpreted that individualists' preferences for performance feedback were supported by the emphasis on competition in their culture. In addition, they explained that 'a desire for failure feedback serves the larger purpose of improving the group's welfare' as individual failures might 'put the group in jeopardy'.

A recent study on the leadership style of over 100 managers (which included 39 US managers and 21 Egyptian managers) by Parnell and Hatem (1999) reinforced the effect of national culture on the outcome of human resource system. They defined the outcomes of the system as job satisfaction and effort as well as loyalty and commitment. They found support for the impact of national culture and wrote that US practices such as the solicitation of subordinate participation and tolerance for ambiguity were seen negatively in the Egyptian context. They also stated that participative decision making was associated with job satisfaction, loyalty and productivity in the West. However, as Egyptian managers accepted unequal distribution of power and were risk averse, they viewed participative management 'as a sign of weakness associated with poor leadership skills and low integrity' (p. 413).

The above review has covered the association of core cultural values with human resource component of business strategy; the generalisation that can be made from the studies is that business strategy is embedded in national culture. Nevertheless, these studies did not illustrate the precise mechanism where cultural values impede on human resource strategy. Moreover, as they focus on one specific component of human resource strategy, they lack elaborate and systematic frameworks that explain how values affect strategy.

Table 3.5: Effects of Cultural Values on Human Resource Strategy

Study	Cultural Values	Findings
Sullivan and Peterson (1991)	Loyalty	Lifetime employment in Japan as a natural outgrowth of the desire for loyalty.
Schuler and Rogovsky (1998)	Uncertainty avoidance, Individualism, Power distance, Masculinity	Cultural values were associated with compensation practices concerning status, individual performance, social benefits and programmes as well as ownership plans in more than 20 nations.
Oliver and Cravens (1999)	Uncertainty avoidance, Individualism, Power distance, Masculinity	Cultural values affected the welfare benefits available in 14 nations.
Earley (1994)	Individualism	Individualism determined the effective type of training programme.
Parnell and Hatem (1999)	Distribution of Power	Cultural value influenced the perception of human resource practices and hence the outcome of systems.
Bailey and Chen (1997)	Individualism	Individualism determined the preferred form of performance feedback.
Young and Franke (2000)	Individualism	Managers from individualistic and collective cultures exhibited different business ethics in recruitment practices.

Source: Various.

CONCLUSION

This chapter has clarified the dichotomous concept of integrated linkage and disintegrated linkage strategy. The former relates to a certain degree of internal procurement in terms of firms' total value of procurement while the latter refers to 100 per cent of external procurement in terms of firms' total value of procurement. It then presents the paradigm of market and resource orientation as the strategic basis to complement a cultural theory of backward linkage strategy. The opposing orientations reflect microcomputer firms' underlying differences concerning the fundamental philosophy towards their businesses. The market orientation defines the business in terms of external environmental factors such as customers and technology while the resource orientation defines the business in terms of firms identities such as capabilities. The market orientation which suggests that users' demand for technology and the flourishing market of component supply are the drivers for the disintegrated backward linkage strategy and will be used in conjunction with the concept of isomorphism to explain backward linkage strategy among individualistic US firms in chapter six. Furthermore, the core values of individualism, continuous improvement and flexibility will be utilised to explain US and Asia Pacific microcomputer firms' resource orientations towards component integration. It is suggested that microcomputer firms that possess capabilities derived from the relevant core values will be able to compete in the corresponding component categories, and pursue integration in the long run.

NOTES

[1] Moritz (1984) pp. 200-01.
[2] Apple's disintegrated linkage strategy is quoted in Apple Case Study, Henry Mintzberg and James Brian Quinn (1996) *The Strategy Process: Concepts, Contexts, Cases*, London: Prentice Hall. Despite a temporary diversion towards integrated linkage in the late 1980s with the setting up of a peripherals manufacturing facility in Millstreet, Ireland as well as keyboard production in its Garden Grove facility in California, Apple adhered to the disintegrated backward linkage strategy again in the 1990s.
[3] 'Rodeo disc drive', *Management Today*, August 1996 pp.46–48.
[4] 'Dell to rely on Taiwan', *International Herald Tribune*, 30 May 2001 and PC Direct 'Systems Reviews' January 1999 p. 78.
[5] 'Sony's procurement plans to spell good news for Taiwan', *Electronic Buyers News*, 23 May 2000.
[6] AM-LCD stands for active matrix-liquid crystal displays, the core components of flat panel display screen.
[7] 'NEC strikes LCD deal with Compal', *Electronic Buyers News*, 26 March 1999.
[8] They also sell excess stock in the commodity spot market.

[9]   Charles Haddad, Irene Kunii and Peter Burrows 'Caught With their Chips Down', *Business Week,* 29 May 2000 pp. 46-9.

[10] As DRAM requires advance capital investment, it has been subjected to fluctuation in demand and supply throughout the 1980s.

[11] Nevertheless, the build-to-forecast model with which firms guessed the type of systems customers wanted, and then mass produced them prior to the marketing campaigns became obsolete since the mid-1990s as marketers were unable to sell technically obsolete systems. It was reported that IBM's retailers returned to the firm US$600 million worth of personal computers in 1993.

[12] The survey looked at 200 firms in the US and was undertaken by Computer Reseller News. See 'Solution providers sound off on component availability', *Computer Reseller News,* 11 December 2000 p. 26.

[13] This comment was made by Howard High of Intel Santa Clara, California. See *eWeek,* 'Component shortage plagues IT', 15 May 2000, 17 (20) p. 1.

[14] Arik Hesseldahl, 'Micron inks DRAM deals with Compaq, Gateway', *Electronic News,* 1 November 1999 p. 2.

[15] See 'Samsung Electronics, Dell enter $16 billion alliance agreement', Samsung, *Semiconductor News,* 22 March 2001 as well as 'Dell, Samsung in display deal', *The Financial Times,* 13 October 1999.

[16] Hadad, Kunii and Burrows (op. cit.).

[17] In the domain of economics, the market orientation is expressed in the study of the structure-conduct-performance in relation to firms.

[18] Michael Porter's *Competitive Strategy* (1980) is a classic book in the strategy field.

[19] G.B. Richardson (1972) 'The Organisation of Industry', *Economic Journal,* 82, pp. 883–96 introduced the concept of capabilities as a reflection of the knowledge, experience and skills accumulated by the firm. They differed from activities such as production that were based on firm capabilities.

[20] Accordingly, Penrose explained that once managers have accumulated tacit knowledge to deal with routine tasks, they could direct their attention towards non-routine tasks. This process of new managerial resource creation provided opportunities to solve new problems and hence enhance the growth of the firm.

[21] As pointed out in chapter one, other aspects of business strategy are firm structure and firm culture.

[22] He explained that 19 of these plants were large (i.e. with 2,000–8,000 employees) while 34 of them were small (i.e. with mainly 8–20 employees). The large plants engaged in the provision of chemicals, metal, machinery, ships, electronics equipment, mining and textiles while the small plants focused on textile manufacturing.

[23] Cafeteria plans provide workers choices on how to spend their welfare benefit.

4.   Strategy and Values

Value is the sense of what 'ought' to be. This means that an individual's values do not represent how he or she wants to behave, but represent his or her internalised interpretations about how he or she should behave. Value is a concept that has been applied in anthropology, theology, sociology, psychology, philosophy and politics as well as business; for instance, researchers have focused on areas that cover cultural value, social value, business value, work value, occupational value and individual value (Lipset 1963; Allport et al. 1960; Rokeach 1968 and 1973; England 1975; Hofstede 1980; Inglehart 1981; Peters and Waterman 1982...). Social scientists have also examined the impact of values in the recent past. For instance, Parsons propounded the view that social action could be linked with individual values. He wrote (1960 p. 172):

[that]... a system of value-orientations held in common by the members of a social system can serve as the main point of reference for analysing structure and process in the social system itself may be regarded as a major tenet of modern sociological theory. Values in this sense are the commitments of individual persons to pursue and support certain directions or types of action for the collectivity as a system and hence derivatively for their own roles in the collectivity.

Cross-cultural psychologists have generally agreed that the acquisition of individual values takes place primarily through an early socialisation process during childhood and other formative processes that are conditioned by cultural values (Winterbottom 1958; McClelland 1961; Whiting et al. 1973). Whiting et al. (ibid. p. 185) pointed out that 'certain dominant values of a culture influence the way in which a parent responds to his or her child. If love and warmth are an important positive value for social interaction, this may govern a mother's behaviour toward her child... '. Moreover, in his discussion of achievement values, McClelland (op. cit.) discussed the effect of child-rearing practices on the value of achievement. He also pointed out that parental behaviour was affected by social class as well as religion.

The theme concerning the implication of cultural values and business strategy that has been highlighted in the preceding chapters will be continued in this chapter. The plan of this chapter is as follows: first the concept of values will be elaborated as seen in the social science literature. Then I will discuss how value affects perception and subsequently managerial conceptual maps and firm capabilities; by doing so, I will illuminate the theoretical underpinning for the cultural theory based on backward linkage strategy.

THE CONCEPTION OF VALUES

Kluckhohn (1951) described values embedded in a culture as the conceptions of the desirable that influenced the ways individuals selected or evaluated behaviour and events. He elaborated as follows:

> Values are not directly observable any more than culture is. Both values and culture are based upon what is said and done by individuals but represent inferences and abstractions from the immediate sense data... any given value is in some sense 'built into' the appreciative mass or neural nets of the persons who hold that value — in the same way that a culture is 'built into' its carriers.
>
> A value is not just a preference but is a preference which is felt and/or considered to be justified — morally or by reasoning or by aesthetic judgements, usually by two or all three of these. (ibid. pp. 395-6).

Values have been used interchangeably with attitudes and beliefs, yet one can argue that there is a fine distinction among these terms. At the individual level, beliefs are non-evaluative and simply represent one's knowledge about the world. Attitudes, on the other hand, are evaluative statements concerning the objects, people or events one has knowledge about; they can be considered as a blend of beliefs and values. Rokeach (1968) pointed out '... a value, unlike an attitude, is a standard or yardstick to guide actions, comparisons, evaluations, and justifications of self and others' (p. 160); in addition, he stated that an individual 'probably has tens or hundreds of thousands of beliefs, thousands of attitudes, but only dozens of values' (p. 124).

In his landmark study of individual values that is known as the Rokeach Value Survey, Rokeach (1973) distinguished values in terms of terminal values and instrumental values. Terminal values were self-sufficient end-states of existence that an individual strives to achieve during his/her lifetime. Instrumental values, on the other hand, related to modes of behaviour; in such a sense, they were similar to Kluckhohn's definition of values. In addition, terminal values were desirable in themselves whereas instrumental values were desirable as the means to attain instrumental values.

Table 4.1 shows the terminal and instrumental values developed by Rokeach. The former encompass person-centred values (e.g. a comfortable life, freedom and inner harmony) and society-centred values (e.g. a world at peace and equality) while the latter includes moral-centred values (e.g. helpful and responsible) and competence-centred values (e.g. capable, independent and logical). These values could be discussed in the light of Spranger's (1928) work[1], who discussed six types of basic values: theoretical values, economic values, aesthetic values, social values, political values and religious values. For instance, Rokeach's values concerning a world at peace, national security and equality could be grouped under Spranger's social values whereas pleasure, a comfortable life and an exciting life could be classified under his economic value. In addition, logical, capable and intellectual values could be regarded as theoretical.

Table 4.1: Value Classification in the Rokeach Value Survey

Terminal Values	Instrumental Values
a comfortable life, an exciting life, a sense of accomplishment, a world at peace, a world of beauty, equality, family security, freedom, happiness, inner harmony, mature love, national security, pleasure, salvation, self-respect, social recognition, true friendship, wisdom	ambitious, broad-minded, capable, cheerful, clean, courageous, forgiving, helpful, honest, imaginative, independent, intellectual, logical, loving, obedient, polite, responsible, self-controlled

Source: Rokeach (1973).

Rokeach (1973) reported the values of over 1,000 Americans via self-report questionnaires and highlighted their broad implications. He found that both terminal values and instrumental values, referred to as 'guiding principles in their lives'[2], and were significantly related to behaviour embedded in issues confronting the USA in the 1960s such as the civil rights movement, the war in Vietnam and the hippie life style. In particular, he concluded that the terminal values of a comfortable life, equality and salvation contributed to at least half of the studied behaviour.

A number of studies have used the Rokeach value classification as an instrument for research. For example, Howard et al. (1983) compared the values of Japanese and American managers with the value survey; their findings suggested that Japanese managers attached greater importance to socially beneficial values such as being helpful and forgiving while American managers emphasised individuality and straight-forwardness. Bigoness and Blakely (1996) investigated the differences of managers' instrumental values; they found that broadminded, capable and courageous were ranked as the most important guiding principles among 567 managers from the 12th nations they studied. In addition, their results indicated that managers from the US assigned less importance to these three values than managers from Germany, Holland, Denmark, Italy, Sweden, Brazil and Norway. They also found that Swedish and Brazilian managers considered these values as being more important.

There are obvious advantages in the Rokeach Value Survey, which include its ease to administer and its practical application to a wide range of situations. In addition, respondents generally found it interesting. Nevertheless, the Rokeach Value Survey also has its weaknesses. Most important, the measurement of individual values such as the terminal value, a sense of accomplishment, or responsibility were rated as single items rather than as multiple items. The point of departure for the Rokeach instrument, moreover, was developed predominantly with a focus on Western values. It contains certain values such as salvation that can be considered as culturally biased. Parallel to this, it can be argued that it might have omitted important values within Oriental societies such as Confucian dynamism (a value reflecting the teachings of Confucius which emphasises social hierarchy, protecting the status quo and personal virtue) as found by the Chinese Culture Connection.[3]

VALUE AND PERCEPTION

Perception is a process by which individuals organise and interpret their sensory impressions in order to give meaning to their environment. As McCaskey (1982 p. 17) wrote

> At any moment, we have only a limited, tangible, physical reality around us
> — the office, the hallway and the elevator, for example. We see chairs, walls,
> lights, colour and other people... Our sense of reality, however, is not limited
> to the world immediately before us. We can visualise buildings, spaces,

people, and events beyond our eyes. We can picture current and historical events around the world and use tools to extent our senses.

Perception and Culture

Perception can be related to people perception, event perception and visual perception. Individuals' perceptions of a targeted person, event and visual stimuli, however, can be quite different. In his discussion of knowledge acquisition, Polanyi (1962 p. 96) implied that there is a subjective element within perception and stated that 'perception is manifestly an activity which seeks to satisfy standards which it sets to itself'. The idea that perception varies from individuals was first suggested by Plato who pointed out that prisoners who could only see shadows and reflections inside a cave would perceive the shadows as reality. If they were released and directly witnessed the objects that cast the shadows, the objects would appear less real than their reflections.[4]

There has, however, been comment on the clustering of perception across nations or regions. Whiting et al. (1973 p. 185) discussed a ready-made and culturally acceptable form of self-perception among Texans who undertook agriculture in semi-arid land:

> The principal economic activity — growing pinto beans in this semi-arid area — is not likely to satisfy anyone with a strong need to succeed, and failure is in fact the common lot. Texan culture, however, provides its members with two modes of escape. It permits them to boast of their 'metropolis' as 'Homestead — Pinto Bean Capital of the World', and it permits them to attribute failure to some external source, such as the weather or bad luck. If the rules of culture required each individual to admit to himself and to others that failure was due to his own bad judgement, lack of skill, or laziness, life would be intolerable.

The above quotation illustrates that perception of events is, to a considerable extent, conditioned by the culture of a group. The cultural relativity of perception is due to mainly shared values. Meglino and Ravlin (1998 pp. 356-7) pointed out that individuals sharing similar values tended to perceive external events in similar ways; they wrote: 'among other things, this similarity in interpreting and classifying environmental events serves to clarify their interpersonal communications.... value similarity produces a social system or culture that facilitates the interactions necessary for individuals to achieve their common goals'.

In the area of visual perception artists tend to agree that all portraits make use of cultural codes underlied by the values of the culture. As

Berry et al. (1995 p. 145) stated, 'pictures are perceived in a certain manner mainly because of cultural traditions about how to represent an object or scene'. Research has provided substantial evidence to support the notion that individuals' visual perceptions are shaped by the inferences they acquired in their specific national cultural context (e.g. Segall et al. 1966; Winter 1963; Berry 1971 and Jahoda 1971). In fact, Winter's (1963) study highlighted that cultural idiosyncrasy could lead to discrepancy in communicating the intended and perceived messages in pictures. He reported that a group of workers in South Africa perceived a person holding out a hand as an act of giving (rather than the intended message of receiving something) in conjunction with the local custom.

Perception of people also carries certain cultural overtones; cultural values give specific meanings to individuals that are regarded as national heroes. There are, for instance, contrasting images of popular heroes in nations with individualistic and collective values. American heroes are cowboys, truck drivers, entrepreneurs... who fought the existing system independently; their successes will enable them to stand out and be elevated to the status of stars. Heroes in Chinese culture, on the other hand, are admired leaders of national groups or gangs who strive for the welfare of the collective. Their eventual success will enable the continuity, survival or prosperity of the collective.

Value, Perception and Firms

Managers' values determine what they regard as relevant or irrelevant information within the environment. For instance, managers that are more collectively inclined will aware of working conditions that are not conducive to team work; as a contrast, managers with individualistic values will be keen on talents and achievements among individual subordinates. Postman et al. (1948) wrote 'what one sees, what one observes, is inevitably what one selects from a near infinitude of potential precepts'; Weick (1979) concurred with this view and suggested that a manager 'sees what he wants to see' and 'hears what he wants to hear'. A concrete example of how perceptual filters distort raw data has been provided by Starbuck and Milliken (1988 p.40).

> Someone who perceived without any distortion would hear background noise as loudly as a voice and music, and so would be unable to use an outdoor telephone booth beside a noisy street, and would be driven crazy by the coughs and chair squeaks at symphony concerts... Effective perceptual filtering amplifies relevant information and attenuates irrelevant information, so that the relevant information comes into the perceptual foreground and the

irrelevant information recedes into the background. The filtering information is less accurate but, if the filtering is effective, more understandable.

England (1967 and 1975) acknowledged this selective perceptual process where values influenced the way managers perceived the situations and problems they faced as a type of perceptual screening. The roles values play in perception are critical as individuals consider stimuli that are consistent with their values as relevant, accurate or even superior. Feather (1995 p. 1136) explained how values enable one to construe a reality:

> Values affect the way a person construes or defines a situation so that some objects, activities, and potential outcomes are seen as attractive, or positively valent[5], whereas others are seen as aversive, or negatively valent... Just as a hungry person sees food as attractive or an anxious person sees an unfamiliar situation as threatening, so a person who values honesty sees an honest course of action as attractive and a person who values equality sees forms of discrimination that restrict equal opportunity as aversive.

The impact of a culturally driven perceptual process extends to the domain of business. When individuals take up work roles they inevitably bring along their core values to firms. As Frederick (1995 p.xx) wrote, 'if one wants to understand the value system of the modern corporation, one turns attention to the kinds of values carried in the psyche and projected onto the corporate scene by the firm's chief managers'. It can further be asserted that values are the foundations of managerial perception on strategic variables.

Values enable managers to filter the information they receive: they selectively amplify some strategic variables and attenuate others. Hambrick and Mason (1984) propounded that business strategy is embodied in the values of top managers. Their upper-echelon theory stated that the firm was a reflection of the values and cognitive bases[6] of its powerful actors; they confined the number of stimuli within the environment that is to be perceived by managers during the process of business strategy.

In a similar fashion, the impact of values can also be discussed at the national level where they shape social perception; in other words, national cultural values define the relevance and importance of issues or events. Inkeles and Levinson (1954) suggested that there were three main issues confronting nations worldwide, which were dealt with differently in accordance to their values. These issues that could be qualified as universal problems were relation to authority, conception of self and ways of handling conflicts. The relationship between cultural values and social perception put forward here therefore argues that nations which value collectivism will be more averse to anti-social behaviour which is a threat to cohesion. Nations embodied with the value of continuous improvement, on the other hand, will be more amenable to gradual change. To reiterate, values enable individuals within the same territory such as a modern nation to construct consensual interpretative frameworks to define common problems and then generate capabilities to solve them. In this sense, cultural values contribute to the accumulation of a firm's capital, as Casson (1995 p.89) pointed out:

> since different values legitimate different objectives, and different objectives generate different kinds of problem, societies with different cultures will tend to focus on distinctive types of problem solving. 'Learning by doing' is an important aspect of problem solving and so learning effects will give each culture a distinctive kind of problem-solving expertise.[7]

CONCPETUAL MAPS AND STRATEGY

Maps are diagrammatic representations of routes that enable us to get from one place to another. Conceptual maps are mental maps that lay out the components of business strategies that managers choose in order to achieve corporate objectives. For example, they can represent a general classification of external events as threats or opportunities or a detailed categorisation of product features with some well defined criteria such as technicality or profitability. Perception enables managers to construct their conceptual maps. Perception also endorses a self-corrective mechanism and allows managers to revise their existing maps so as to eliminate any perceived discrepancies. Polanyi (1962 p. 103) expressed the realignment of perception and conceptual maps follows:

> The power of our conceptions lies in identifying new instances of certain things that we know. This function of our conceptual framework is akin to that of our perceptive framework, which enables us to see ever new objects as such, and to that of our appetites, which enables us to recognise ever new things as satisfying to them...
>
> Owing to the unceasing changes which at every moment manifestly renew the state of things throughout the world, our anticipations must always meet things that are to some extent novel and unprecedented. Thus we find ourselves relying jointly on our anticipations and on our capacity ever to re-adapt these to novel and unprecedented situations...

Values are important in the process of backward linkage strategy as they affect managers' perceptions and subsequently their conceptual maps. Studies that highlighted the impact of managerial perception on conceptual mapping included Donaldson and Lorsch (1983) and Dutton and Jackson (1987). The former stated that managers' values about firms' self-sufficiency would influence their perceptions of financial matters and hence indirectly determine their strategic inclinations. Top managers who believed in the no-debt principle were likely to relegate information concerning lending and would, therefore, be less informed about the available financial options. Dutton and Jackson (ibid.) reinforced the notion that managers' conceptualisation of strategic issues in terms of threats or opportunities would affect the way these issues were handled within an industry and eventually the actions taken in response to them. They wrote that, 'when decision makers label issues as opportunities, involvement in the process of resolving the issues will be greater and participation will take place at lower levels of the organisation, compared to when issues are labelled as threats (ibid. p. 83).

National Differences in Conceptual Maps

One of the intriguing aspects of managerial conceptual maps, however, are the exhibited differences across nations. Abramson et al. (1994) found that the process of conceptual mapping among Japanese and Canadian managers were very different. The Japanese managers' processes were more feeling oriented than the Canadian managers. In addition, the two groups also differed in the dimensions of sensing-intuiting as well as judging-perceiving. They stated that the Canadians in their samples tended to be logical, impersonal and objective while the Japanese emphasised the human element in problem solving. Abramson et al. (ibid. p. 581) further discussed the implication of conceptual maps and suggested that the style of the Canadians was associated with 'quick, impersonal, analytically based decisions and impose closure on fact-finding as soon as there is enough objective information for a decision'. As a contrast, the style of the Japanese 'has a concern for group harmony and a tendency to be sympathetic and friendly in human relations. They focus on the facts and seek to remain open to as much data as is available with no need to find closure to make a quick decision' (op. cit.).

Another study by Sullivan and Nonaka (1988) that examined Japanese and American managerial conceptual maps also suggested the presence of national differences. They found that Japanese managers tended to interpret issues embedded in strategy as problems whereas American managers tended to view them as opportunities. They suggested that 'the dramatic emphasis of Japanese senior managers on strategic issues as problems may be rooted in Japanese interpretation of their history as a long series of natural disasters, wars, economic depressions and social catastrophes. Japanese tend to see themselves as people who must overcome problems' (ibid. p. 9). It can, therefore, be said that the cultural value of overcoming adversity was a major influence on Japanese managers' overwhelming view of strategic issues as problems.

Other studies have investigated the implications of cross-cultural conceptual maps for business strategy. Calori et al. (1992) examined conceptual maps among French and British managers within brewing, car manufacturing, retail banking and book publishing and found systematic differences between the two nations. They found that French managers were concerned with product, technical virtuosity and style while the British mangers focused more on short-term revenue within the brewing industry. They added that French managers pursued a broader export strategy, considering Germany, Benelux and South Europe as potential export markets and the UK as an important market. As a contrast, British managers focused narrowly on the home market. They suggested that the business strategy of the UK brewers could be seen as indicative of British insularity. Calori et al. (ibid. p. 75) further discussed cultural influences on managerial conceptual maps in the retail banking as follows:

> French *cloisonnment* may account for French managers' emphasis on the segmentation of the market; and the importance of improvements of products and services they stress is again in line with this cultural characteristic noted elsewhere. The British, on the other hand, are more reserved, tending to talk more reflectively and historically about their firms, but do stress the importance of selecting growth segments.

The theme of divergence in business strategy as a result of cultural variation in values and hence conceptual maps was also of interest to Schneider and De Meyer (1991). They found variations in the classification of strategic events concerning deregulation within the US banking industry among managers from nations classified under Anglo, Latin European, Northern European, Nordic and North American. They noted that Latin European managers that were characterised by the value of uncertainty avoidance were more inclined to categorise deregulation as a threat; accordingly, they recommended a proactive strategy that involved greater investment of resources.

A recent study by Geletkanycz (1997) explained the impact of cultural values on top management's open-mindedness to changes in business strategy. They suggested that the value of individualism contributed to managers' attachment to the status quo and were less inclined to alter existing policies. He explained that individualist nations tended to promote individual decision making, and there were stronger attributions of a firm's performance and leadership. Managers, would, therefore develop a vested interest in existing policies as they regarded changes as an admission of the inappropriateness of earlier decisions.

Though the above studies have examined individual conceptual maps of managers, they are relevant to the current discussion as business strategy is simply a representation of the collective interpretation of individual managers' conceptual maps. Writers such as Daft and Weick (1984) have pointed out that social exchanges among managers created the collectively shared conceptual maps. The findings from the above studies coupled with the fact that microcomputer firms are dominated by headquarters' nationals establish the ground for investigating the influence of national cultural values on conceptual maps, which ultimately shape backward linkage strategy among US and Asia Pacific firms.[8]

FIRM CAPABILITY AND STRATEGY

Firm capability refers to the ability to make effective use of various types of capital so as to facilitate the productive activity that underlie the offering of low-cost or product differentiation. As individuals are the basic units of a firm, the concept of firm capability is entwined with individual capability. Individual capability can be divided into three areas: intellectual, emotional and physical. Cross-cultural writers have implied that individual intellectual capability is a result of a different emphasis of values across nations. Cole et al. (1971 p. xi) proposed that 'people will be good at doing the things that are important to them, and that they have occasion to do often'. In other words, social perceptions regarding the importance of capabilities will create a selective process through which nations will accumulate them.

Social perception allows nations to endorse certain firm capabilities through economic and non-economic means. Economic means relate to the provision of greater economic rewards for firms possessing limited supply capabilities. Economic rewards can be seen in the supranormal profits[9] obtained by firms offering creative products or services in individualistic nations. Non-economic means refer to public approval or recognition for those possessing certain desirable capabilities. Casson (1997 p. 165) elaborated this point and explained the cultural origin of innovation within firms as:

> Many societies confer status on originators to compensate them for their inability to appropriate rents from imitators... an alternative system of rewards is necessary if an efficient level of origination is to be sustained. To address this issue, leaders of societies commonly offer originators public recognition and honorific titles to generate emotional rewards as a substitute for the missing material rewards.

Firm Capability and Integration

Capability is an extremely valuable asset that firms acquire gradually over time; it enables them to pursue component integration on the basis of their competitive advantages (Richardson 1972; Wernerfelt 1984; Langlois 1992; Teece and Pisano 1994; Hamel and Prahalad 1996 and Barney 1997). Richardson (op. cit.) suggested that firms would undertake integrated backward linkage strategy when performing production activities that drew on the same firm capabilities; the rationale is that firms would 'specialise in activities for which their capabilities offer some comparative advantage' (p. 888).

Barney (op. cit.) analysed the logic of integrated backward linkage in terms of rare and difficult to imitate firm capabilities. He stated that as long as the number of firms that possess a particular capability was less than the number of firms needed to generate a perfectly competitive market, the capability could be considered as rare and was a source for competitiveness. He also explained that a firm's capability would be costly to imitate if its development depended on certain unique historical conditions, if there was no clear association between a firm's capability and its competitive advantage, if it involved certain interpersonal relations among managers or reputations among suppliers and customers, and finally, if there was a legal safeguard that restricted direct duplication of the capability.

Langlois's (1992) example of Henry Ford's innovative moving assembly line indeed demonstrated this point; Langlois stated that the innovation which was not available to other firms initially gave Ford a cost advantage over outside suppliers and therefore contributed to the use of integrated linkage strategy. Nevertheless, the evolution and the diffusion of technology over time not only enable the possibility of imitation, they also reduce the cost of imitation. As a result, the logic of integrated linkage in the car industry diminishes.

Argyres (1996) examined the relationship between firm capability and backward linkage strategy of an industrial goods manufacturer with a detailed case study analysis. He found that the firm undertook integrated linkage strategy in the design and development of a mold for cable connectors as well as in the stages of extrusion and initial compounding[10] of wire and cable insulation systems on the basis of its superior capabilities relative to external suppliers. Nevertheless, he also addressed the importance of asset specificity and the potential leakage of proprietary knowledge as reasons for adopting integrated linkage for the wire and cable insulation systems.

Values and Capabilities across Nations

The variation of firm capabilities across nations is associated with the stock of capital within firms as well as firms' strategic manoeuvre of these capital. Hamel and Prahalad (op. cit.) have discussed the manoeuvring of firm capital in terms of leveraging resources[11]; I will elaborate this idea in chapter ten on Taiwanese and Korean firms' capabilities. I will, for the time being, proceed to look at different types of firm capital and their association with cultural values.

Human capital refers to the skills of individuals that facilitate the performance of productive activities within firms and includes management or craftsmanship. Examples of human capital are the entrepreneurial skills of managers such as Apple's Steve Jobs or Microsoft's Bill Gates. Intellectual capital is the stock of knowledge which resides in firms such as the manufacturing process technology shared by engineers within semiconductor production. Financial capital relates to capital funding by venture capitalists for the establishment of microcomputer firms such as Sun and Compaq. Social capital, on the other hand, refers to co-operative networks and can be found within supplier relationships among Taiwanese microcomputer component firms. Physical capital includes tangible items such as plant, machinery and technology whereas organisational capital is derived from qualities of individuals such as commitment and trust.

The national variation of firm capabilities can be traced to the cultural factor. In his discussion of culture as an economic asset, Casson (1996 p. 49) suggested that culture which comprised moral and technical values could be considered as critical in the formation of human capital. He explained that: 'workers with similar technical skills may be more productive in one country than another because the moral content of the local culture makes them better motivated'.

It has been suggested that the cultural values of industrialism, asceticism and individualism as embodied in the Protestant work ethic fostered firm capital in Western Europe during the 18th century (Weber 1958). As Protestants worked hard and systematically accumulated wealth and refrained from the consumption of worldly pleasures, they allowed the accumulation of financial capital for firms' re-investment and expansion. Moreover, Wollack et al. (1971) pointed out that the Protestant value emphasised the intrinsic value of work; in other words, 'work is to be valued because it represents the best use of a man's time, not merely because it is instrumental to the attainment of external rewards' (p. 332). Hence, it can also be argued that the value of industrialism contributed to organisational capital such as commitment and loyalty.

In addition, the cultural values of high achievement, collectivity and Confucianism are sources of firm capital. In his study of the value of achievement, McClelland (1961) found that nations with a higher level of achievement value had a greater supply of human capital endowed with entrepreneurship[12] which was associated with rapid economic development. He explained the importance of the value of achievement among those leading firms or economic organisations as 'in the long run it is they, and their primary concerns, whether for achievement, affiliation, power or something else, that determine the rate at which the economy develops' (ibid. p. 300).

On the other hand, the value of collectivism which binds employees together and inculcates their sense of community contributes to the acquisition of organisational capital. In his discussion of Theory Z firm, Ouchi (1981 p. 50) said that 'collectivism is economically efficient. It causes people to work well together and to encourage one another to better efforts'. The value of Confucian dynamism, which incorporates orderly hierarchical relationships, respect for tradition and personal virtues such as perseverance, thrift and sense of shame have been associated with firm capital. For instance, the Confucian dynamism contributes to financial capital as the value of thrift encourages savings (as high as one-third of disposable income in Taiwan), which in turn channels funding into the business sector. The sense of shame also supports inter-relatedness during the course of business, and enhances the development of social capital that is important in sub-contracting networks that are supported by informal contractual arrangements. The respect for hierarchy allows the founders of entrepreneurial firms to lead with legitimate power in accordance with his/her intuition. This accelerates the speed of decision making in a rapidly changing environment.

Writers such as Shapero and Sokol (1982), Wallace (1970), Shane (1993)... etc. have also discussed the importance of cultural values for the accumulation of intellectual capital, and specifically within the technological domain. Shane (ibid. p. 59) suggested that the values of uncertainty acceptance, individualism and low power distance were associated with the rates of innovation. He concluded that:

> An acceptance of uncertainty appears to be necessary, probably because innovation requires a tolerance of risk and change. Individualism seems to be important, perhaps because of its association with autonomy, independence, and freedom. Lack of power distance appears important, perhaps reflecting the role that tolerance of change in the social order and distribution of power play in the innovation process.

Firm Capital and Firm Capability

Hampden-Turner and Trompennars (1995) wrote about cultural values and areas of firm capabilities. They suggested that one's knowledge about the cultural strengths of various nations might lead to combining firm capabilities internationally. They considered that a car manufacturer might best obtain the steel from Korea, its engines from Germany, its electronics from Japan, and its safety system from Sweden. They further wrote (ibid. p. 6): 'to understand how cultural values influence economic choices, we must first look more closely at the processes by which value systems are constructed. How do organisations make the judgements necessary to create the systems that create products and services that are the basis of economic activity?' This is indeed an interesting question that requires elaboration; a detailed treatment of cultural values will therefore appear in the next chapter.

The widely cited model of heterogeneous firm capability, Porter's (1990) diamond which encompasses factor conditions, demand conditions, related and supporting industry as well as firm strategy and rivalry is based on the interaction of firm capital and various factors at the industry and national level.[13] Though values underlie the elements within the diamond, Porter stated that his framework was created through a highly localised process incorporating economic structures, institutions, history ... In this way, Porter placed greater emphasis on the importance of tangible factors of the nations and their industries than on the cultural values that underlie them. Nevertheless, as multinational firms are not bound to their home bases, the diamond model cannot fully justify the origin of a national pattern of firm capabilities. Indeed, it has been shown that firms can derive their capabilities from locations other than their home bases. For example, a number of US, European and Japanese semiconductor manufacturers have managed to accumulate firm capabilities deriving from the Singaporean diamond in the last decade.[14]

As national cultural values extent in the nations from which managers originate will influence their perceptions, managers' discretion as regards the development of firm capital, will therefore foster a national pattern of firm capability. Among the different types of firm capital, human capital and intellectual capital are of critical importance in microcomputer component capability. The importance of intellectual capital was recognised by early economists such as Alfred Marshall who viewed the firm as the institutional context for the development of intellectual capital. He stated that 'capital consists in a great part of knowledge and organisation... Knowledge is our most powerful engine of production'.[15] Knowledge has been discussed in the literature and can be separated into tacit knowledge and explicit knowledge[16]. Tacit knowledge is difficult to communicate and difficult to imitate while explicit knowledge can be codified in the format of facts, concepts and frameworks. As the type of knowledge within intellectual capital is similar to tacit knowledge, it is therefore difficult to articulate and costly to transmit. Polanyi succinctly summarised the tacit element of knowledge as we knew more than we could tell.

Drucker (1994 p. 22) highlighted the role of managers in developing human capital and wrote: 'The manager works with a specific resource... 'Working' with the human being always means developing him or her. The direction which this development takes decides whether the human being — both as a person and as a resource — will become more productive or cease, ultimately, to be productive at all'.

A firm's capability to manage human capital, according to Drucker's point of view, represents managers' innate qualities to develop their subordinates; he also stated that these qualities must be brought to the job and cannot be acquired on the job. Drucker (ibid. p. 23) stated that these managers: 'command more respect than the most likeable person ever could. They demand exacting workmanship of themselves and other people. They set high standards and expect that they will be lived up to. They consider only what is right and never who is right'.

CONCLUSION

Every nation has some values that are more central and important; these values are core values as they take priority among the values that the nation possesses and permeate aspects of business strategy. The theme that can be identified from the material in this chapter is that managerial conceptual maps and firm capabilities across nations are predominantly cultural phenomena, and are shaped by core cultural values. Managerial perception underlies the representation of conceptual maps and therefore affects the choices of backward linkage strategy. Social perception determines the individual capabilities which in turn are foundations of firm capabilities; different firm capabilities support different areas of component competitiveness which shapes the pattern of integration. The interaction of core cultural values and backward linkage strategy as embedded in the cultural theory will be presented in chapter six. But first I will discuss the core values in the US, Japan, Korea and Taiwan that impinge on microcomputer firms' backward linkage strategy.

NOTES

---

[1] Researchers that applied Eduard Spranger's typology in research included Allport et al (1960) and Guth and Tagiuri (1965).

[2] Rokeach instructed the respondents to rate the 36 terminal and instrumental values in order of importance.

[3] The Chinese Culture Connection is a group of researchers assembled by Michael Bond to examine core values in Chinese culture.

[4] This analogy is quoted from The Simile of the Cave in Plato's book *The Republic*.

[5] Valent refers to one's preferences for the outcomes.

[6] Cognitive base refers to managers knowledge or assumptions about future events, knowledge of alternatives and knowledge of consequences attached to alternatives.

[7] Pascale and Athos (1981) further elaborated this point and stated that managerial reality was culturally determined. They wrote that culture affected how managerial problems were perceived and how they were resolved.

[8] Indeed, headquarters nationals tend to be the Managing Directors of the European operations even though they are stationed at the headquarters. In addition, a number of microcomputer firms pointed out that they communicated frequently with the headquarters by telephone or by E-mail during personal interviews in the late 1990s.

[9] Supranormal profits are economic rents that arose from the limited supply of superior productive resources.

[10] Extrusion refers to applying a copper conductor to the wire while compounding relates to the mixing of the chemicals.

[11] Hamel and Prahalad (1996) stated that the Vietnam War provided a case for the importance of resource leverage; they succinctly pointed out that 'although an abundance of resource, or slack, enables firms to be strategic in an investment sense, it does nothing to enhance the wisdom of strategic decisions' (p. 168).

[12] McClelland defined entrepreneurs as men who organised the firm and/or increased its productive capacity.

[13] According to Porter, four characteristics of a firm's home environment are instrumental to its competitive advantages. The first characteristic is factor conditions or the nation's position in factors of production such as skilled labour or the

infrastructure necessary to compete in a given industry. Second, demand conditions or the nature of home demand for the industry's product or service is also important. Third, the presence or absence in a nation of related and supporting industries that are internationally competitive also affect competitiveness. Finally, firm strategy, structure and rivalry or the conditions in the nation governing how firms are created, organised, and managed and the nature of domestic rivalry are also critical characteristics. Porter added that chance and government could influence the national diamond.

[14] Leading semiconductor firms operating in Singapore since the 1980s included SGS-Thomson, Hewlett-Packard, Lucent, AMD, NEC, Hitachi, Nippon Steel and Canon.

[15] Marshall (1961 p. 115).

[16] Michael Polanyi (1962) introduced the tacit component of knowledge.

5.   Nations and Values

The impact of national culture is so widespread that it permeates a nation, including its industries, corporations and people. Hofstede's (1980) study illustrated the effect of national culture on the values of individuals. Trompenarrs (1993) highlighted the diversity of corporate culture that emerged from different national systems whereas Gray (1988) and Perrera (1989) discussed the impact of national culture on accounting culture. In the context of the software industry, Carmel (1997 p. 135) also pointed out a process of assimilation: 'these talented, educated immigrants self-select into the American culture of software and assimilate many of its values'.

As values are the deepest manifestation of a nation's culture, the divergence of national culture will be conceptualised as the differences between the core values among representative samples of members from the USA, Japan, Korea and Taiwan.[1] Core cultural values can be considered as indicators of the four nations' culture as the value variations between individual members of their total population and the representative samples are rather narrow. This is supported by the fact that Japan, Korea and Taiwan are composed of heterogeneous groups that have shared a common historical and cultural heritage. Though the USA consists of a considerable number of immigrants from more than 20 nations, which were about ten per cent of its total population, the value variation between individual members and representative sample is not wide. The reason is that the USA is a melting pot[2] where its core values are acquired by all its citizens without exception.

The preceding chapter delineated the strategic implications of core cultural values which affect managerial conceptual maps and firm capabilities; this chapter will further explore the issues revolving around the concept of core national cultural values. There are three main sections, the first of which reviews value typologies across different nations. I will then elaborate on the core cultural values of individualism, continuous improvement and flexibility among US and Asia Pacific microcomputer multinational firms. I will end this chapter with a discussion of the infiltration of core cultural values within US and Asia Pacific firms.

TYPOLOGIES OF VALUES IN NATIONAL CULTURE

Values are products of national culture or 'the collective programming of mind'[3] which distinguishes the members of one cultural group from another. Culture affects the values of business and play an important role in the understanding of national differences in managers' conceptual maps as well as in the composition of firm capabilities. Though the Rokeach Value Survey provides a useful instrument to explore individual values, it was pointed out in the preceding chapter that its conception was associated with values in America and therefore cannot be employed satisfactorily in nations such as Japan, Korea and Taiwan. In this section, I will review the prominent typologies that have been designed to elicit values across different nations, in particular, those typologies applicable to business firms and their managers. An early comparison of managerial values is Haire, Ghiselli and Porter's (1966) study of 3,600 managers in 14 nations such as the USA and Japan; they found that about three-quarters of the managers they studied exhibited similar managerial maps. Their findings implied that cultural value was not a critical factor concerning managers' conceptual mapping of business strategies. Nevertheless, they found that Japanese managers were very different from other managers; for example, they exhibited reciprocal values to a greater extent than managers from other nations. The major weakness of Haire et al.'s study, however, was the unrepresentative nature of their sample which was drawn 'impressionistically and sometimes opportunistically' (ibid. p. 6).

England's Pioneering Work

England's (1975) profile of values comprised 66 concepts that impeded on managers' acceptance of firm's objectives or their views on groups and individuals. The value profiles were derived from more than 2,500 managers from the US, Japan, Korea, India and Australia who answered his personal value questionnaires. The reasons for this work, as explained by England, were to investigate the important implications of values, which: 'influence a manager's perceptions of situations and problems he sees', 'influence a manager's decisions and solutions to problems' as well as 'influence the extent to which a manager will accept or will resist organisational pressures and goals' (ibid. p. 1). Examples of England's concepts within the five areas of value profiles are:

- *Firm objectives* — organisational stability, high productivity, organisational efficiency, organisational growth.

- *Personal goals* — achievement, creativity, success, job satisfaction.
- *Groups* — my company, me, customers, employees, my boss, my subordinates.
- *Interpersonal relationships* — loyalty, ambition, trust, skill, co-operation.
- *General ideas* — rational, competition.

England asked the managers to judge the value concepts in terms of high importance, average importance and low importance. Value concepts that were rated as high importance and corresponded to managers' primary value orientations (i.e. pragmatic, moralistic, affective and mixed)[4] were most central to managers and therefore would exert the greatest impact on their behaviour in their firms.

England found that national culture (as approximated by nationality) accounted for 30 to 45 percent of the variations in managers' values.[5] His summary of primary orientations across Japan, the USA and Korea is shown in Table 5.1. The figure shows that 52.9 per cent of all managers studied were pragmatic, 24.4 per cent were moralistic while 5.1 per cent were affective. In addition, 17.6 per cent of the managers exhibited a combination of the three primary orientations. It can therefore be said that Japanese managers exhibited a very high level of pragmatism, US managers were moralistic and perceived what they considered as high in importance as right while Korean managers combined pragmatic, moralistic and affective orientations.

Table 5.1: England's Findings on Primary Orientations

	Pragmatic	Moralistic	Affective	Mixed
Japan	67.4%	9.9%	6.9%	15.8%
USA	57.3%	30.3%	1.2%	11.2%
Korea	53.1%	9.0%	8.5%	29.4%
International Sample	52.9%	24.4%	5.1%	17.6%

Source: England (ibid. p. 20)

The mean of the scores for the value concept in the five main areas provides a further analysis of US, Japanese and Korean managers' values. Table 5.2 shows the major differences of managers' value scores regarding the area of firm's objectives. As higher value scores correspond to the greater behavioural relevance of the concepts, it can be said that Japanese managers have internalised firm objectives in conjunction with high productivity, organisational growth, organisational stability and industry leadership to a greater extent than their US and Korean counterparts.

Table 5.2: England's Value Scores on Selected Firm's Objectives

Values concerning firm's objective	International Sample	US Managers	Japanese Managers	Korean Managers
High Productivity	68	63	79	67
Organisational Growth	51	50	72	61
Organisational Stability	46	41	58	55
Industry Leadership	40	43	50	30

Source: England (ibid. p. 30)

Though England's work demonstrated the commonality of managers' values in the US, Japan, Korea, India and Australia, it is important as it it is the first study that has highlighted differences of managerial values across nations; in addition, the study is also constructive in terms of generating further research in cross-cultural comparison of individual values, in particular, values among managers.

Hofstede's Classic Study

Hofstede (1980) reviewed the result of his value surveys carried out around 1968 and 1972 which covered over 100,000 IBM employees in 40 nations, and found that these nations could be differentiated in terms of four core values:

• *Individualism* is related to how one defined his/her identity, whether it was by personal choices and achievement or by the groups to which he/she is permanently attached.

- *Power distance* describes the extent to which a culture accepted that power in institutions and organisations is distributed unequally.
- *Masculinity* measures the extent to which a society endorsed work goals that are more commonly viewed as masculine (e.g. assertiveness, earnings and advancement).
- *Uncertainty avoidance* expresses the extent to which a culture felt threatened by ambiguous situations and tried to avoid them.

The national scores for the four values were obtained from respondents' answers to 20 specifically constructed questionnaire items designed to tap into the values. The level of individualism, for example, was measured with Likert scale ratings of 1 (of utmost importance to me) to 5 (of very little or no importance) with items such as:

Personal time Have a job which leaves you sufficient time for your personal or family life.
Freedom Have considerable freedom to adopt your own approach to the job.
Challenge Have challenging work to do — work from which you can achieve a personal sense of accomplishment.

It was found that nations that were characterised by high levels of individualism rated the above items as relatively important while those with collective values rated them as of little importance. Overall, Hofstede found that nationality accounted for half of the differences in the four values. Table 5.3 shows the scores of cultural values for the USA, Japan, Korea and Taiwan. It can be seen that the US and the Asia Pacific nations differ markedly in the area of individualism, uncertainty avoidance and power distance.

Table 5.3 highlights that the cultural value of individualism varied from 2 to 91 with a mean of 51. The table shows that the USA (with a score of 91) was the most individualistic nation in Hofstede's sample. The scores for Japan, Korean and Taiwan were 46, 18 and 17 respectively and could be considered as relatively low. In addition, it can be observed that the scores for power distance and uncertainty avoidance among the Asia Pacific nations were greater than the means of the sample (i.e. 51 for power distance and 64 for uncertainty avoidance) while those for the USA were lower than the sample means. As a generalisation, the USA is highly individualistic whereas the Asia Pacific nations can be characterised by collective values, large power distance, and strong uncertainty avoidance.

Table 5.3: Selected Scores on Hofstede's Cultural Values

	Power distance	Uncertainty avoidance	Individualism	Masculinity
USA	40	46	91	62
Japan	54	92	46	95
Korea	60	85	18	39
Taiwan	58	69	17	45
Sample mean	51	64	51	51
Sample range	11-94	8-112	2-91	5-95

Source: Hofstede (1980).

Hofstede and Bond (1988) supplemented the four value dimension with the Confucian dynamism (also known as the Time dimension), This dimension embraces the long-term and short-term orientation within cultures. The former involves perseverance, thrift and sense of shame while the latter includes personal steadiness and stability, respect for tradition and the reciprocation of favours.

Studies undertaken by the Chinese Culture Connection (1987) and Schwartz (1992) have suggested that Hofstede's four value dimensions were relatively culturally-robust.[6] As values are the foundations for perceptions, it can be understood that individuals possess self-serving biases toward their national cultural values. Hofstede (1994 p. 71) wrote about this absolutist view regarding the level of individualism:

> Most Americans feel that individualism is good, and at the root of their country's greatness. On the other hand, the late Chairman Mao Tse Tung of China identified individualism as evil. He found individualism and liberalism responsible for selfishness and aversion to discipline; they led people to placing personal interests above those of the group, or simply devoting too much attention to one's own things.

Hampden-Turner and Trompenaars' Cultures of Capitalism

Trompenaars (1993) developed the work of Parsons and Shils (1951) as well as that of Kluckhohn and Strodtbeck (1961) and proposed a dichotomous set of cultural values; five of these values were based on relationship between people while the remaining two were based on how people relate to time and environment.

- *Universalism versus particularism.* This dimension represents how the culture confronts the expectation that priority will be given to standards defined in generalised terms as opposed to differential treatment.
- *Individualism versus collectivism.* This is similar to Hofstede's dimension.
- *Analysing versus integrating.* This refers to analysing the parts as opposed to the whole.
- *Inner-directed versus outer-directed relationships.* This value dilemma consists of using one's inner-directed judgements versus signals in the outside world in decision making.
- *Achieving versus ascribing.* This value dimension examines individuals' status in terms of what one can do versus who one is.
- *Perceptions of time* as sequential versus synchronous.
- *Equality versus hierarchy.*

Hampden-Turner and Trompenaars (1995) applied their value questionnaires to 15,000 managers from seven advanced nations, which included the USA and Japan. Some of their questions elicited managerial values by analysing their responses in certain imaginary situations while others provided a polarised choice between value statements describing certain aspects of their behaviour or general issues. For instance, their instruments for individualism included the respondent selecting from the following options (a) or (b) under the specified situation:

> A man had a fire in his shop and lost most of his merchandise. His store was partly destroyed by the fire. He and his family had to have some help from someone to rebuild the shop as fast as possible. There are different ways of getting help.
>
> (a) It would be best if he depended mostly on his brothers and sisters, or other relatives, to help him.
>
> (b) It would be best to borrow some money on *his own* in order to get some construction people to rebuild this store.

Hampden-Turner and Trompenaars found that managers' values clustered along their national cultural origins. For example, they found the US managers were individualists that believed in upholding universal rules whereas Japanese managers believed in the communities and the operation of customised rules. They pointed out different perspectives on contracts would arise from these opposing values; the Japanese might expect to rewrite or scrap the contract when the situations change so as to maintain a mutuality of benefit for both partners while Americans would consider such practice as illegal and immoral. They added that the American managers 'regard the individual as the basic unit and building block of the enterprise and the origin of all its success... they locate the source of the organisation's purpose and direction in the inner convictions of its employees' (ibid. p. 48). As a contrast, Japanese managers view themselves as part of the larger systems, to the extent that, they 'see capitalism as a system in which communities serve customers, rather than one in which individuals extract profits' (ibid. p. 167).

They proposed that each of the seven nations they studied have a unique combination of values, which could be considered as an economic fingerprint and had profound performance implication. They wrote (ibid. p. 6) that 'wealth creation requires, at a minimum, that an organisation successfully originate and bring to market products and services that all groups who share these processes work together energetically and effectively... '.

Casson's Cultural Asset

Writing on national culture as an economic asset, Casson (1996) provided the following classification of five characteristics of cultural values that affect the economic development of nations:

- *Scientific differentiation* describes the adoption of science as the basis for decision making as opposed to experience.
- *High tension* is the continual engagement on projects in order to explore the limits of human capability.
- *Atomism* corresponds to the extent of individualism. It supports individual rights and the private appropriation of resources.
- *High trust* describes the honouring of contracts even though they are not accompanied by material well-being.
- *Judgement* is how managers arrive at decisions; it ranges from the reliance on knowledge to reliance on experience.

Table 5.4 compares the cultural values of the USA and Japan using Casson's typology; it can be seen that American and Japanese managers are both strong in terms of scientific differentiation, high tension and judgement; however, they differ in terms of atomism and trust. Casson wrote (ibid. p. 49) that 'different groups have different characteristics and hence different levels of performance. It is the interaction between these characteristics, and not just their additive effects, that are important'.

The significance of Casson's typology is its interpretative power; in particular, it provides an explanation of the different paces of economic development in the USA, Japan and other less developed nations. He wrote that less developed nations, in general, seemed to lack the basic ingredients for development in terms of the five cultural values listed in Table 5.4 and pinpointed that (ibid. p. 62):

> Their political organisation often reflects an organic view of society in which dissent is identified with factionalism and suppressed in the interests of maintaining a fragile national unity. Networks of trust are confined to extended families and to religious groups, with considerable suspicion existing between members of different groups. Because scientific and moral issues are not clearly distinguished, the quality of judgement used in decision-making is relatively poor.

Table 5.4: Casson's Factors for Economic Development

	USA	Japan	Less-developed nations
Scientific differentiation	Strong	Strong	Weak
High tension	Strong	Strong	Weak
Atomism	Strong	Weak	Weak
High trust	Weak	Strong	Weak
Judgement	Strong	Strong	Weak

Source: Casson (1996 p. 62).

Contrary to England, Hofstede and Trompenaars' empirical approaches, Casson adopted a theoretical approach to construct his typology. This illustrates, therefore, that there is a lack of consensus on the conceptions of national cultural values, which can be further observed in the operationalisation of values. There have been, for example, more than one hundred different questionnaire-based instruments to capture the value of individualism in the past two decades.

A CONTRAST OF CORE CULTURAL VALUES

So far, I have made the point that core cultural values are central to a nation and take priority over the values it possesses. With a departure from the quantitative measurement of values, writers such as Lipset (1963) McClelland (1961) and Said (1993) examined cultural values with content analysis of relevant documents. Lipset (op. cit.) compared the values of achievement, universalism and specificity[7] in the USA, Australia, Canada and the UK with in-depth analysis of historical writings. In a discussion of the high level of achievement value in the US, he wrote (ibid. p. 178):

> In a country which stresses success above all, men are led to feel that the most important thing is to win the game, regardless of the methods employed in doing so. American culture applies this norm of a completely competitive society to everyone. Winners take all...
>
> A study of a Boston election in the 1940's in which James Curley was re-elected mayor while under a charge of fraud (for which he was subsequently convicted) reported that there was a general image among his supporters, who were aware of the charges of dishonesty, that he 'gets things done'.

Based on the analysis of translated literature, McClelland (1961) examined the values of achievement (among other values) across 41 nations. McClelland adopted content analysis of children's literature for the reason that their themes reflected the cultural values of their nations.[8] His measurement of the achievement value was whether the character in the selected story was able 'to change one's rank in the social order, relative to other persons, or to gain recognition, by accomplishing some end' (ibid. p. 465). By analysing the character of his sample stories, McClelland found that the value of achievement differed in more than 30 nations, which included the USA, Japan, Italy, Turkey and Poland at periods around 1925 and around 1950. He found the value of achievement varied from 0.43 to 3.38 with a mean of 1.83. The achievement value of the USA, for instance, was 2.24 and could be considered as relatively high.

In the light of the aforementioned qualitative work, I will present the cultural products that illuminate the core values of individualism, continuous improvement and flexibility. I will refer to historical documents and seminal literature that are of contemporary significance; in addition, I will include prevailing customs and proverbs as well as collective policies adopted by firms. Customs and proverbs that mirror common sense thought on life may, at first glance, seem a rather remote reference for core cultural values. Nevertheless, as Geertz (1983) pointed out, common sense was in fact 'a loosely connected body of belief and judgement' that 'differs from one place to the next' (p. 11), hence it is justifiable to say that customs and proverbs which constitute the core values of the four nations should be included in the discussion.

The Core Value of Individualism

Individualism denotes that each human being is unique, equal and independent; it is manifested in loose human relationships and is fostered by individual freedom. The behaviour of those within an individualistic culture is predominantly governed by personal needs and perceived rights. The core value of individualism encourages individuals to be competitive in order to achieve their goals. Hence, one's personal goals within group situations tend to conflict with other group members. Consequently, work roles tend to be specific in an individualistic culture. The reason is that as individual competition is the foundation of career advancement; the specific work role enables individuals to be accurately assessed and provides a justification and basis for promotion.

Individualistic values are entrenched in the American culture; indeed the Declaration of Independence and the US Constitution explicitly stated that the individual is a separate entity. In addition, prominent American economists (and, of course, their British counterparts) have long advocated that the aggregate of individuals' self-interests and independent decisions will contribute towards the most efficient allocation of resources.

As a contrast, low individualism (or collectivism) places strong emphasis on the inter-dependent relationships among people as well as the socio-economic units they create. In collective cultures such as Japan, Korea and Taiwan, social behaviour is dictated by norms, duties and obligations. Accordingly, members of these cultures consider the family, the work group or the nation state to be above themselves; personal goals therefore tend to correlate with those of the collectives.

Collective values support the concept of sharing, hence inter-personal relationships are tighter in Japan, Korea and Taiwan. Collective culture tends to have ambiguous demarcation of work as employees are more willing to carry out diverse duties, as opposed to the norm of performing narrowly defined work roles in individualistic cultures. This broader concept on work roles, to a great extent, enhances the firms' prosperity as a whole. Indeed, employees are expected to adjust their roles for the welfare of the firm. In addition, collective practices such as open-plan offices are usual in Japan, where junior and senior employees sharing the same office space. The year-end bonus where all employees sharing the prosperity of firms is also an entrenched practice among overseas

Chinese firms. In addition, inter-personal relations are considered more important in Korea than task-related relations in the work environment.

As a result of different emphasis on inter-personal relationships, individualistic and collective cultures also exhibit their own distinctive views on harmony and justice. The former places strong emphasis on justice, where individuals or groups who suffer injustice will initiate a conflict to resolve any unfair treatment. In collective cultures such as Taiwan, Korea and Japan, individuals or groups tend to bear injustice in order to preserve the harmony of the group. Korean firms such as Goldstar, in particular, have advocated the importance of harmony; its basic philosophy was depicted as 'harmony for the benefit of the society as well as for the employees of the company'[9].

Ouchi (1981 p. 48) contrasted the collective value in Japan with the US value of individualism using the following illustration concerning the practice of a new US manufacturing subsidiary:

> In the final assembly area of their new plant long lines of young Japanese women wired together electronic products on a piece-rate system: the more you wired, the more you got paid. About two months after opening, the head foreladies approached the plant manager. 'Honourable plant manager', they said humbly as they bowed, 'we are embarrassed to be so forward, but we must speak to you because all of the girls have threatened to quit work this Friday'. (To have this happen, of course, would be a great disaster for all concerned.) 'Why,' they wanted to know, 'can't our plant have the same compensation system as other Japanese companies?... The idea that any one of us can be more productive than another must be wrong because none of us in final assembly could make a thing unless all of the other people in the plant had done their jobs right first. To single one person out as being more productive is wrong and is also personally humiliating to us'.

The Core Value of Continuous Improvement

Japan and Korea have traditionally looked to the historically more successful nations (e.g. China and America) to acquire the appropriate social, economic and political characteristics that could be assimilated into their own culture. Continuous improvement or *kaizen*, the constant step-by-step improvement towards perfection, supports this gradual learning process.

Kaizen takes into account the accumulated power of insignificant details that contribute to incremental improvement; it flourishes in Japan and Korea where attention to detail and self-discipline is viewed as advantageous to one's well being. For instance, it can be considered in the light of Japan's warriors, the samurai, who undertook an unending quest for self-improvement in their pursuit of honourable objectives. The philosophy of *kaizen* sees life as a journey towards perfection emphasing the process rather than the result. It recognises that, in reality, perfection may not be attainable and continuous improvement simply represents one's effort towards the ideal of perfection. In this sense, it is supported by the philosophy of Zen Buddhism in Japan and Korea which views life as a never-ending search for enlightenment.

At the industry level, Imai (1986 p. 3) described the Japanese core value of *kaizen* as 'ongoing improvement involving everyone, including both managers and workers'; he added that 'the *KAIZEN* philosophy assumes that our way of life — be it our working life, our social life, or our home life — deserves to be constantly improved'. The Japan Human Relations Association found that the average number of suggestions for improvement per employee was also substantially high among Japanese firms. For example, firms such as Matsushita, Hitachi and Canon received over 50 suggestions per employee.[10] In fact, continuous improvement can be seen in the pursuit of quality among Japanese and Korean firms in areas such as quality control, where employees voluntarily perform activities to improve quality. Similarly, Hayes (1981 p. 61) stated that 'to the Japanese, quality is a way of thinking'; he also quoted a Japanese scholar's comment that illustrated the importance of continuous improvement in the pursuit of quality:

> If you do an economic analysis, you will usually find it is advantageous to reduce your defect rate from 10% to 5%. If you repeat that analysis, it may or may not make sense to reduce it further to 1%. The Japanese, however, will reduce it. Having accomplished this, they will attempt to reduce it to 0.1%. And then 0.01%. You might claim that this obsession is costly, that it makes no economic sense. They are heedless. They will not be satisfied with less than perfection.

The practice of quality control was introduced to Japan by the US occupation forces 'Training Within Industries' in the late 1940s. Quality control and its variants such as statistical quality control, quality control circles, total quality control and company-wide quality control has been practised by Japanese firms such as NEC, Fujitsu, Toshiba, Toyota and Matsushita enthusiastically since then. The emphasis on quality has become the integral part of the Japanese production system since the 1980s.

The importance of quality has also been spread to Korea, and has been taken up seriously since Korea lost labour-cost competitiveness to neighbours such as Malaysia, China and Thailand. Korean firms such as Samsung, Sunkyong, Daewoo and Hyundai maintained in the late 1980s a strong focus on quality. In particular, the Korean firm Samsung announced a quality-oriented management in 1993 to emphasise the importance of quality. The quality concept is also supported by the continuous improvement aspect of Korean cultural values. According to Lee (1989) the leading values in Korean firms were harmony, diligence and development, embodied in the practice of gradual consensus and constant improvement. The value of continuous improvement as exhibited in Samsung's drive for perfection has been observed in its founder Byung-Chull Lee's desire to be the best through continuous improvement; he once commented that 'Money is not what I pursued. Instead I have only striven to be the best in whatever business I choose'.[11] Moreover, the Korean proverb 'know new facts by reviewing old ones' suggest the importance of incremental improvement in all aspects of life.

Paradoxically, the US government's 'Training Within Industries', which had been successfully adopted across America during the early 1940s, was abandoned immediately after the war. The importance of quality which was advocated and practised in the USA by consultants such as Deming and Juran in the 1940s, was only accepted by US managers in the 1980s. In fact, it should also be remembered that the re-introduction of continuous improvement in the US manufacturing industries had mixed results. As Robinson and Schroeder (1991 p. 73) wrote, 'not all of these programmes have been successful, leading some critics to argue that they are inappropriate outside of Japan or cannot be effectively introduced into ongoing US manufacturing operations'.

The Core Value of Flexibility

Flexibility refers to the willingness to take action so as to maximise the benefits derived from altered conditions; it arises from being able to perceive the situation from divergent or even dichotomous perspectives. A higher degree of flexibility tends to be reflected in nations that are more inclined to use non-standardised rules and differential treatments.

Flexibility is entrenched in the philosophy of Taoism that is deeply ingrained in Korean and Taiwanese society. Taoism is fatalistic and believes in sequential chains of events. One of the key works the *Book of Changes*, places much emphasis on chaos and constant evolution in life and hence emphasises the importance of flexibility within the Chinese and Korean minds. Taoism has intermingled with Chinese customs and religions and is practiced by the Koreans and the Overseas Chinese. The Korean national flag carries the symbol of *yin-yang*, a symbol of Taoism, which refers to the co-existence of lightness and darkness or in analogy good and bad. Interestingly, at the societal level, both Korean and Chinese families adopt dual approaches in dealing with children's behaviour. The father's role is usually strict and autocratic, and he is a strict disciplinarian in the family. The mother's role is benevolent and is opposite to that of the father's; she is known for spoiling the children.

The strong Confucian legacy in the two cultures also demands individuals to establish their identity differently in relation to appropriate levels within the social hierarchy. Indeed, individuals fulfil their obligations in relationships such as father and son, husband and wife, elder brother and younger brother, distant relatives and close relatives... with varying etiquette. The value of flexibility within the Chinese and Korean cultures enable individuals to accept intrinsic differences among people and, as a consequence, they relate to others within the culturally-conditioned perception of equitable manner.

The Chinese proverb 'riding on an ox to look for a horse' indeed implies that when striving for ultimate goals, one should temporarily settle for the next best option. Hence, it suggests the importance of flexibility in difficult situations which may require the use of relatively less appropriate options in the short run (such as the slow moving and bumpy ride on the ox). Another Chinese proverb teaches: 'to be successful in life and to achieve greatness, one must be flexible'. Successful individuals can be compared to the clay that is expected to adapt to different sizes and shapes as required.

Flexible thinking has also been the main theme in military strategy; Sun Tzu, utilised the concept of flexibility in *The Art of War* and stated that 'just as water shapes itself according to the ground, an army should manage its victory in accordance with the situation of the enemy. Just as water has no constant shape, so in warfare there are no fixed rules and regulations. Therefore, do not repeat the tactics that won you a victory, but vary them according to the circumstances' (Wang 1976 p. 201).

At the economic level, flexibility is exhibited by Korea and Taiwan's industralisation and the re-structuring of their economies. As Redding (1990 pp. 221–2) pointed out, the large-scale shifts in an economy reflect 'the aggregate result of myriad strategic changes by single companies carried out without crisis, with little bankruptcy, and with often complex internal adjustments such as those of technology and labour skills'. Indeed, the rise of Taiwan's personal computer industry was associated with the government's banning of video game manufacturing in the late 1970s.

The transition of the Korean economy from a natural resource and commodity trading basis to the current export-led bias also suggests the flexibility of its large business groups. A review of Samsung's corporate history reflects its ability to upgrade itself from trading to high technology manufacturing in five decades. Samsung was founded in 1938 as a small agricultural trading business. Over time, it maintained its commodity trading origins but also acquired high technology manufacturing in semiconductor, electronic components, chemicals and shipbuilding. The economic crisis in Asia in the late 1990s has reiterated Korea firms' swift restructuring as compared to their Japanese counterparts; the flexibility of Korean firms, to a great extent, therefore, demonstrates the core value of the nation.

Another interesting observation of the core value of flexibility is that it enables Chinese and Koreans to incorporate individualism within their predominantly collective culture. Song (1990 p. 199) observed that 'while Koreans are relatively group-oriented, they also have a strong individualistic streak like most Westerners. Koreans frequently joke that an individual Korean can beat an individual Japanese, but that a group of Koreans are certain to be beaten by a group of Japanese'. Similarly, Winckler (1987) registered the following comment made by a Chinese-American scholar concerning the co-existence of collectivism and individualism as the core Chinese values:

> Americans' primary values are individualistic and underneath, most of their secondary values are individualistic as well. The primary values of Japanese are communitarian and, underneath, so are most of their secondary values. However, the primary values of Chinese are communitarian, but, underneath, most of their secondary values are highly individualistic.

The inflexibility of American culture has been pointed out by European and Japanese firms operating in the USA in terms of their managers' unduly strong focus on the home market. Rosenzweig (1994) gathered comments from French managers such as: 'The horizon of Americans often goes only as far as the US border. As a result, Americans often don't give equal importance to a foreign customer. If a foreign customer has a special need, the response is sometimes: 'It works here, why do they need it to be different?'.

CULTURAL VALUES AND BUSINESS VALUES

Business values are the essence of a firm's business culture and tend to be highly visible among firms that managed to attain market shares in competitive industries such as the microcomputer industry. As the top management of US and Asia Pacific microcomputer firms is dominated by their headquarters nationals, the collective managerial conceptual maps of these firms, to a considerable extent, reflect the values of the nations they originated from.

The impact of headquarters' managers on the European subsidiaries is reflected in a recent personal interview with a General Manager of a Japanese information technology product manufacturing firm in Europe. This information technology firm, which was a division of a wholly owned US subsidiary of a Japanese parent, had expanded in Europe via a number of acquisitions. The General Manager explained that the Board of Directors of the US subsidiary consisted of two Japanese nationals, i.e. the Managing Directors of the US subsidiary and the European operations, based primarily in Japan. Hence, they tended to adopt 'an outsider perspective'; for instance, they insisted on centralised warehousing destinations in Europe using a US mentality of the East, the West and the Middle location.

In their discussion on Japanese management, Pascale and Athos (1986) explained how the cultural values of individualism are displayed by Japanese and US managers; they stated (pp. 118–9):

> As every infant is dependent on others, so every executive has known dependencies... American executives traditionally have been taught to become independent of others, separate, self-sufficient. Japanese executives traditionally have been taught to become interdependent with others, integral parts of a larger human unit, exchanging dependencies with others...
>
> In each society there is a range in the degree to which individuals proceed from being dependent to becoming independent or interdependent. Those with less success are disapproved of in both societies as "too dependent". They do not tend to become executives.

Various writers have suggested that cultural values run through the business values of US and Asia Pacific firms. Schein (1985) explained how founders defined the culture of their firm with culturally derived values such as the role of the firms and then reinforced it by the subsequent recruitment and socialisation process; he stated that the ideas of the founders were 'based on their own cultural history' (pp. 212–3).

The CEO of Silicon Graphics McCraken, who was a former manager in Hewlett-Packard, discussed the impact of its founder in an interview as: 'Hewlett and Packard, both wonderful people, came out of the World War II generation, that had a different set of values — perhaps including a little bit more institutional responsibility for the individual'.[12] Burck's (1940) description of IBM's culture supported this point; he interviewed some senior managers and reported one of their views: 'Mr Watson gave me something I lacked — the vision and the foresight to carry on in this business, which from that day forward I have never had any thought of leaving (p. 40). Humes (1993 pp. 287–8) also pointed out how Samsung selected, developed and promoted the 'Samsung man'[13]. He wrote:

> Almost without exception they are Korean, and they are recruited directly from the top universities in South Korea. Those selected are chosen by means of a Samsung written and oral examination system, in which the Samsung Group founder/chairman was often personally involved. Once when asked why he spent his precious time in this activity, he is reported to have replied, 'because hiring future leaders is the most important way I can spend my time'. After an initial three to six months of a rigorous indoctrination and education programme, the trainees select the company with which they wish to spend their careers; transfers are rare, but do occur. The emphasis on education and training continues through an employee's career. Even the overseas Korean staff must return once a year for 'spiritual renewal'.

As individualism, continuous improvement and flexibility are critical in the current discussion of backward linkage strategy, I will provide a review of these core values operating among US and Asia Pacific firms. US firms such as IBM has always emphasised the importance of individualism in business operations. It was reported that Tom Watson Junior 'had spent a fair proportion of his time preaching the virtues of individualism'.[14] Indeed, he even dedicated a whole book to the importance of business values in the success of firms.[15] Individualism underpinned practices and policies in IBM. Rodgers (1986) recalled that IBM sales representatives were told that they were recruited for their individual talents, expected to use their own methods and rewarded on their own merits.[16] IBM's former president Thomas Watson also publicly discussed the value of the firm as respect for the individual.[17]

Hampden-Turner and Trompenaars (1995) mentioned that the values of American firms were embodied in individual business practices such as Management by Objectives, which assumed a free commitment by individuals to an objective deemed important to the firm. They (ibid.

p. 56) wrote: 'you are rewarded according to your performance of a contract freely entered'. Deal and Kennedy (1982) who wrote one of the leading books on the culture of firms also found that successful US firms generally exhibited clear business values shared by all the employees. More specifically, they provided a typology of their values which were supported by American values. For instance, the tough-guy, macho culture was full of individualists (i.e. stars) who regularly took high risks and obtained short-term and immediate feedback on their actions. The work hard, play hard culture, on the other hand, reiterated the respect for individualism where the needs of customers were catered for. The bet your company culture, which focused on 'big-stakes' decisions, was subordinated by the entrenched value of achievement.

Similarly, the value of collectivism strongly underlied the culture of Asia Pacific firms. Chang and Chang (1994 p. 132) claimed that 'in the Japanese management system, team spirit or group consciousness is more important than individualism. The term individualism is a contemptuous one in Japanese society. Individual aspirations must subjugated to team efforts in order to maintain group spirit'. The collective corporate culture taken to the extreme, however, will be evolved into a kind of favouritism. As Hampden-Turner and Trompenaars (ibid. p. 168) stated that 'you over-indulge your best customers. Japanese scandals often demonstrate this tendency taken to excess, since the money has to come from other, less-favoured customers or from shareholders'. Indeed, nepotism does poses a problem in the differentiated treatments among the in and out groups in Korea and Taiwanese firms.

The value of continuous improvement is a central theme of Japanese and Korean firms. The rationale for continuous improvement has been explicitly described by the president of the Japanese firm Suntory in terms of tackling the inherent complacency among individuals:

> Because human beings are, in a sense, weak and become complacent, continually new challenges are, therefore, very important.
> It is necessary to have some tension or feeling of crisis within the organisation. That tension arising from the need to learn many new things will pervade the organisation and contribute to the driving force for making it successful.[18]

The essence of continuous improvement can be summarised in the values of Japan's Nissan, which pointed out in its *Kaizen Leader Training Manual*: 'our world is far from perfect and we are not going to change it overnight. But, step-by-step, we can improve that small part with which we come into contact. Whether it is at home, at work or in our social activities, the principles of *kaizen* apply'.[19] In their study of Matsushita, Pascale and Athos (op. cit. p. 51) also pointed out that 'struggle for betterment' as a value of the firm. The value of continuous improvement can also be seen in the Korean firms who undertake daily meetings in their manufacturing plants that aim to improvise the manufacturing process.

Finally, the core value of flexibility can also be observed in Korean and Taiwanese firms. The flexibility of Korean firms have been recognised by their counterparts in Japan. Mangers from Hitachi America commented that 'the Koreans are more flexible than we are... The Japanese are from a homogenous society, so they are less accepting of anything that is not Japanese. Korea is a land of division, so the people are willing to listen and not get their feet stuck in concrete'.[20] Similarly, the flexibility of Taiwan's small businesses have been commented on by industry observers. T.C. Tu, Director of the Market Intelligence Centre in Taipei, commented that Taiwanese computer firms' short product cycles were related to their 'flexibility in moving from one right choice to another quickly'; it was estimated that the best Taiwanese manufacture could proceed from a concept on the drawing board to the production line in 90 days in the early 1990s.[21]

The value of flexibility has also been widely acknowledged by overseas Chinese firms that tend to blend with the local culture wherever they operate. They adopt local names, local technology and human resource practices. The Taiwanese firm Acer's strive for flexibility was reflected in its mission to balance 'global brand and local touch'. Acer aimed to build up a federation of publicly listed subsidiaries in its target markets in order to attain this balance.

Korean firms have demonstrated their flexibility by combining family management with large business. Traditional management theory suggests an elaborated style of management that comprises the separation of ownership and management when an organisation grows in size. However, Korean multinationals still adhere to family management, where the sons of the owner-founders or other close relatives typically manage the firms by acting as Chief Executive Officers (CEOs) as well as representing on the management boards. In the case when non-family members serve as CEOs, the families tend to maintain important positions and therefore can influence important strategies. For example, the current chairman of Samsung Electronics Kun-Hee Lee[22] is the son of Samsung's founder Byung-Chull Lee. There was a widespread consensus in Samsung Group when Kun-Hee Lee succeeded his father in 1987.

Taiwanese and Korean firms have also demonstrated flexibility in their arrangement of work roles. In US and Japanese firms, job rotations are regular and incorporate periodic shifting of work tasks from one to another. Though Korean firms utilise job rotations, they are on an ad hoc basis and correspond to the core value of flexibility where ability to adjust with the constant change of environment is emphasised. This parallels the overseas Chinese firms which do not implement formal job rotation, but believe employees could be assigned to another job area if needs arise.

CONCLUSION

This chapter has introduced the major typologies of national cultural values; it illustrates diversity as the salient feature in the conceptualisation and operationalisation of core values. Most importantly, it has been shown that values vary across nations and that core cultural values influence the formation of business values through founders and top management. This is particularly applicable to the microcomputer industry, where Japanese firms and established US firms have a strong culture defined by the founders and continued by the headquarters nationals. Similarly, youthful US firms, Taiwanese firms and Korean firms are predominantly run by the entrepreneurial founders whose visions shape the values of their firms. For instance, Acer's CEO Stan Shih reflected on the development of the firms in books such as *Re-engineer Asia*, which the firm distributed to its employees for reference. Shih explained Acer's business values as being closely associated with Taiwan and traditional Chinese culture and also with the vision of its co-founders.

The lack of consensus on the nature of core values and the measurement of them has underpinned the difficulty in achieving objectivity in examining core values. A possible route is to concentrate on deeper cultural products such as historical documents, seminal literature, customs and proverbs that embrace the core values of nations. Adhering to a qualitative approach, this chapter has discussed the value of individualism in the USA, the value of continuous improvement in Korea and Japan as well as the value of flexibility in Korea and Taiwan that will contribute towards the cultural theory on backward linkage strategy. The next chapter will continue with the cultural selectivity theory.

NOTES

[1] Every nation has some values that are more central and important; these values are core values as they are priorities among the values that the nation possesses and permeate families, work organisations and socio-political institutions.

[2] Hampden-Turner (1991 p. 94) expressed the concept of the melting pot in terms of 'the conviction that principles of general validity can be discovered that apply to all people everywhere'; he wrote that 'universalism colours the American approach to everything from politics to sports to business'. Trompenarrs added (1993 pp. 21–2) that universalism allowed the USA 'to play host to people from so many lands without substituting a universal code for many particular customs'; he added that 'you must teach children American habits of mind of which their foreign parents may be ignorant. For this reason the American way is codified to an extent that other nations regard as strange'.

[3] This is Hofstede's (1980) widely quoted definition of culture.

[4] The pragmatic managers are those that adopt evaluative frameworks that are guided by success and failure considerations; the moralistic managers are those whose decisions' are judged by right or wrong. The affective managers are guided by hedonism, i.e. one aims to increase pleasure and decrease pain. Finally, the mixed type refer to a combination of pragmatic, moralistic and affective modes.

[5] The importance attached to individual differences could be expected as England (1975 p. 13) utilised a sample that was 'roughly comparable'. The managers were from small, medium and large businesses of more than eight different industries; in addition, they were from different functional areas and management levels.

[6] Hofstede's value typology is comparable to that obtained from the Chinese Culture Connection (1987) and Schwartz (1992) as shown in the following table. For example, collectivism, masculinity and high power distance were presented in all three typologies. In addition, Schwartz's typology which consisted of values in seven domains corresponded to Hoftstede's values with only one exception of high uncertainty avoidance.

Hofstede	Chinese Culture Connection	Schwartz
Collectivism	Integration	Collectivism
Individualism	-	Affective Individualism
Masculinity	Human-heartedness	Mastery
Femininity	-	Harmony
High power distance	Moral discipline	Hierarchy
Low power distance	-	Social concern
Low uncertainty avoidance	-	Intellectual individualism

[7] Lipset defined these values in accordance with Talcott Parsons' pattern variables, i.e. achievement-ascription, universalism–particularlism and specificity-diffuseness. The achievement-ascription distinction relates to a society's value in terms of the emphasis on individual performance as opposed to inherited qualities. The universalism–particularism distinction relates to whether individuals should be treated with the same standard or according to differences in individual qualities. The specifity–diffuseness distinction refers to the difference between treating individuals in terms of the specific positions they are in or diffusely as individual members of the collectivity.

[8] He pointed out the advantage of children's literature was that it has been read by all segments of the population. In addition, as the writing style was explicit, its message could be easily identified.

[9] Quoted in Lee (1989) 'Management Styles of Korean Chaebols' in Kae H. Chung and Hak Chong Lee (eds) *Korean Managerial Dynamics* p. 187.

[10] In comparison, the average figure for leading US firms was about 23 suggestions per employee. See *The Power of Suggestion*, Japan Human Relations Association, April 1988.

[11] *Business Korea* 1987 p. 47.

[12] McCracken has worked in Hewlett-Packard for 16 years before joining Silicon Graphics. Interview by Jager and Oritz (1997 p. 194).

[13] The recruitment practice in large Korean firms, to a great extent, parallels that of large Japanese firms.

[14] McClelland (1984) p. 232.

[15] Thomas Watson Jr (1963) 'A Business and its Beliefs', McKinsey Foundation Lecture, New York: McGraw-Hill.

[16] Buck Rodgers was a former IBM manager.

[17] Thomas Watson Jr (op. cit.)

[18] This statement was made by Keizi Saji of the Suntory Company, and was quoted in J.J. Sullivian and I. Nonaka's article 'The application of organisational learning theory to Japanese and American Management' in the *Journal of International Business Studies,* Fall 1986, p. 130.

[19] Garrhan and Stewart (1992) p. 61.

[20] L. Baum, 'Korea's newest export: management style', *Business Week,* 19 January 1987.

[21] Louis Kraar, 'Your next PC could be made in Taiwan', *Fortune,* 8 August 1994, p. 51.

[22] Kun-Hee Lee has also become the Chairman of Samsung Electronics since 1997.

6.   A Theory of Cultural Selectivity

The preceding chapters have laid the theoretical ground work for the present one. The aim of this chapter is to investigate the essence of the cultural selectivity theory which argues that the core cultural values of individualism, continuous improvement and flexibility will determine the backward linkage strategies pursued by US and Asia Pacific microcomputer multinational firms within Europe. The first part of the cultural theory explains the diffusion of the contrasting backward linkage strategy in the European microcomputer industry. It argues that the resource-oriented integrated linkage strategy utilised by established US firms since the mainframe computer era will be received differently by managers in youthful US firms and Asia Pacific firms, who operate on culturally diverse conceptual maps. The collective value will contribute to Asia Pacific firms' replication of the integrated strategy; far from conforming to the existing practice, the individualistic US firms will pioneer the market-oriented disintegrated linkage strategy. The second part of the theory further considers the pattern within the integrated linkage strategy among US and Asia Pacific firms, it focuses particularly on the national pattern of firm capabilities that contribute to component integration. It is suggested that the core cultural values of individualism, continuous improvement and flexibility which impede social perceptions of the desirability of firm capabilities, will determine microcomputer firms' competitive advantages in concept-intensive, capital-intensive and labour-intensive areas respectively.

CULTURAL REPLICATION OF INDUSTRY STRATEGY

The backward linkage of the successful firms IBM[1] and DEC in the mainframe and mini computer era was integrated strategy. They designed the computers, manufactured most of the components and then performed the final assembly. IBM has been and is well known for its remarkable marketing and technology capability. It engaged in early digital electronic computer production in 1953 and then became involved in mainframe computers after the invention of integrated circuits by

Texas Instruments in 1961. IBM emerged as the leader within the computer industry by the 1960s. Indeed, its System 360 and System 370 became the architectural standard for large computer systems until the 1980s. With the expansion of the supercomputer market in the late 1990s, IBM is well positioned to lead in the world market and had approximately one-third of the worldwide market share in 1999.[2]

The rationale for integrated linkage strategy in the microcomputer industry is to build on firms' rare and difficult to imitate capabilities such as process technology and management skills in order to compete with superior cost structure; it places strong emphasis on capturing firm capabilities in the production of components such as printed circuit boards, hard disk drives, liquid crystal displays and semiconductors. For example, Acer's CEO Stan Shih commented in an interview that Acer had a built-in edge over competitors pursuing disintegrated linkage strategy on the grounds that it manufactured components that fed into its systems[3].

Figure 6.1: Resource Orientation and Backward Linkage Strategy

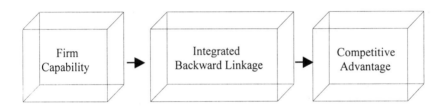

Source: Author.

IBM shared nearly 80 per cent of the total volume of personal computer market sales in its third year of operating in Europe. Though its total sales had declined throughout the 1980s, it still shared approximately 10 per cent of the European market in terms of sales volume by the mid-1990s. IBM's strong presentation in the corporate segment meant that it actually offered higher value personal computers than majority of its competitors. In the UK market, for instance, Amstrad had taken 19 per cent of total personal computers sales by volume while IBM shared only ten per cent in 1991. A comparison of their market shares by sales revenue, on the contrary, reveals a very different picture: it shows that IBM had a 15 per cent share of the market in 1991 while

Amstrad who targeted the low end of the personal computer market had eight per cent. The integrated linkage strategy as followed by IBM has been admired by a number of participants in the European microcomputer industry. IBM's Greenock plant in Scotland engaged in the assembly of display monitors, keyboards, power supplies and personal computers, and spent £103.5 million in 1983 for parts and services with over 4,000 firms, of which 40 per cent were Scottish.[4]

The notion of integrated linkage strategy, which has been imitated by Asia Pacific firms through an isomorphic process, can be referred to as the industry recipe. The concept of an industry recipe was created by commonalties among managerial interpretation of strategic issues; it suggests that managers within the same industry have similar conceptual maps that are conducive to business success. Though the industry recipe originated from individual firms, Spender (1989 pp. 193–4) pointed out that 'analysts and other newcomers to the industry can pick up the recipe directly without being concerned about the individual corporate events and experiences on which it is based'.

Grant (1998) elaborated on the implication of industry recipes, suggesting that in a sense, they could condition managers' perceptions concerning the competition and create blind spots. He stated that: 'Industry-recipes may limit the ability of a firm, and indeed an entire industry, to respond rationally and effectively to external change' (p. 98). For example, industry recipes that were prevalent among the three leading manufacturers General Motors, Ford and Chrysler in the US car industries during the 1970s and the early 1980s represented an underestimation of the potential of the small car segment. As a result, Japanese and European firms were able to penetrate the US market with imports.

The first part of the cultural selectivity theory is derived from the idea of conforming to the industry recipe. It proposes that Asia Pacific firms from cultures with collective core values are more susceptible to the influence of reputable and historic US firms such as IBM, and therefore will replicate the perceived norm of integrated backward linkage strategies. Kelly and Keeble (1990 p. 20) wrote about how IBM was the focus on the computer industry prior to the onset of the 1990s: 'IBM dominates the information technology (IT) industry in a way which few companies in other markets can claim to match. It is a market leader, a trend-setter, a model employer, and an innovator, but above all, a superb marketer'.

As a contrast, the individualistic youthful US firms pioneer the disintegrated linkage strategy despite the prevalence of the integrated linkage strategy.[5] The adoption of disintegrated linkage strategy can be explained by the technology and supply characteristics of the market orientation discussed in chapter three. The technology driver in relation to microcomputer components implies that firms that need to undertake product development at an ever accelerating pace will encounter high costs associated with internal administration among various functions such as research and development, production and marketing. The supplier driver suggests that the availability of industry standard component suppliers will contribute to low market transaction costs. Both these considerations therefore provide incentives for youthful US firms to pursue disintegrated backward linkage strategy.

Figure 6.2: Market Dynamics of Youthful US Firms' Strategy

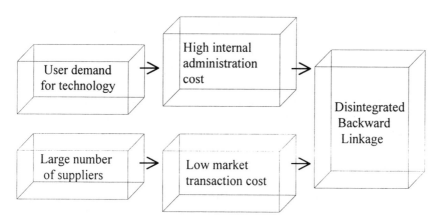

Source: Author.

Conformity to the industry recipe refers to replicating the perceived best practice of integrated linkage strategy from the established US firms; the reason being that managers wanted to demonstrate their awareness of best practice. Conformity is the tendency of people to adopt the behaviour of members in a reference group and has been demonstrated by experiments in industrial settings. Elton Mayo's Hawthorne Studies revealed that workers conformed to an informal group norm of output.[6] In one of the experiments concerning productivity, Mayo observed the emergence of informal norms among small groups of workers engaged in wiring work even though they were under formal supervision. Such informal group norms affecting productivity included 'not turn out too much work' and 'not turn out too little work'. Mayo (1945 p. 79) concluded that 'the working group as a whole actually determined the output of individual workers'.

The landmark study on conformity undertaken by Solomon Asch in 1952[7] further echoed the individual's conformity to the norm of a group. Asch designed an experiment where subjects were asked to compare straight lines of unambiguous length; the subjects were tested in small groups made up of members who had been briefed to provide inaccurate answers. He found that individuals conformed to group judgements that were in conflict with their own. Numerous studies conducted across nations replicated Asch's findings (e.g. Milgram 1961; Claeys 1967; Chandra 1973; Perrin and Spencer 1981), while some studies further demonstrated that individuals or groups generally conformed with those who displayed competence over specific tasks (e.g. Rosenberg 1963; Huang and Harris 1973).

Deutsch and Gerard (1955) suggested that individuals' compliance to the majority view was motivated by the desire not to appear deviant; this suggests that conformity will be greater in cultures that place more importance on groups than individuals. It follows that the strong emphasis on co-operation in collective cultures will create pressure for individuals to conform to prevailing group norms. As a contrast, the emphasis on independence in individualistic cultures generates variations within groups and approves non-conformists. Triandis (1999 p.129) explained the importance of attention to group norms among people in collective cultures as 'well-beings for collectivists depends on fitting in and having good relationships with the in-group which requires close attention to the norms of the in-group'. In an earlier article, Triandis (1990 p. 42) stated that 'social behaviour is determined largely by goals shared with some collective', and 'if there is a conflict between personal and collective goals, it is considered socially desirable to place collective goals ahead of personal goals'.

Indeed, researchers support the variation across cultures as regards what is an acceptable degree of conformity. Bond and Smith's (1995) survey of more than 100 Asch type conformity studies undertaken in 17 nations revealed that the core value of individualism is negatively correlated with conformity. In other words, the core value of individualism is linked to non-conformity whereas the core value of collectivism is associated with conformity. Using other types of conformity measurement, Huang and Harris (1973) as well as Meade and Barnard (1973) indicated that Chinese were more conforming than Americans to the opinions of the group in controversial issues. They also reported a greater tendency to non-conformity among Americans than among the Chinese, which Hsu (1953) termed a 'backlash' effect where one becomes even more convinced of the correctness of one's position in the face of overwhelming pressure from the group.

Though early studies in Japan failed to substantiate the relation between industry and conformity, it was later found that the inconclusive result could be explained by the nature of in-group and out-group conformity. Williams and Sogon (1984) noticed a higher level of conformity among Japanese with the Asch procedure when the majority were friends than when they were strangers, and thereby pointed to the importance of in-groups within cultures embracing collective values as discussed by other theorists. For example, Triandis et al. (1988 p. 333) concluded: 'People in collectivist cultures *do not* necessarily conform more, feel more similar to others, and/or uniformly subordinate their goals to the goals of others. Such responses are more selective... One may be a collectivist in relation to one in-group but not in relation to other groups'.

The cultural selectivity theory expands on the similarities of conceptual maps adopted by managers embodying the same cultural values and argues that the tendency to replicate the industry recipe of integrated backward linkage strategy is correlated with the value of individualism. Building on the variation of conformity across nations with varying degrees of individualism, it is suggested that Asia Pacific firms and youthful US microcomputer firms will respond differently to the perceived best practice of integrated linkage strategy endorsed by established US firms such as IBM. Managerial conceptual maps employed by collective Asia Pacific firms who aspire to the historic US firms, will be inclined to replicate the integrated backward linkage strategy while managerial conceptual maps used by youthful US firms from an individualistic culture will focus on the alternative disintegrated backward linkage strategy.

CULTURAL DIFFERENTIATON OF CAPABILITY OF FIRMS

Ferguson (1956) wrote that 'cultural factors prescribe what shall be learned and at what age; consequently different cultural environments lead to the development of different patterns of ability'. Building on the theme that microcomputer firms' competitive advantages in component production are associated with culturally constructed firm capabilities, it is argued that the core cultural values of individualism, continuous improvement and flexibility will enhance microcomputer firms' acquisition of product design, manufacturing process capabilities and people management capabilities, which in turn will shape their resource orientation in concept-intensive, capital-intensive and labour-intensive components. Figure 6.2 summarises the relationship between core cultural values and the pattern of integration among US and Asia Pacific firms undertaking integrated linkage.

Figure 6.3: Resource Orientation and Microcomputer Components

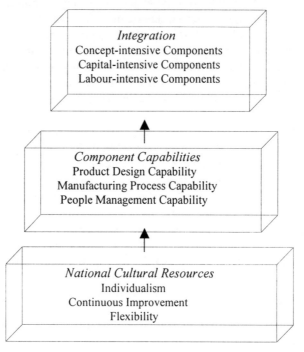

Integration
Concept-intensive Components
Capital-intensive Components
Labour-intensive Components

Component Capabilities
Product Design Capability
Manufacturing Process Capability
People Management Capability

National Cultural Resources
Individualism
Continuous Improvement
Flexibility

Source: Author.

Concept-intensive Components and US Firms

The cultural selectivity theory states that US microcomputer firms will integrate into concept-intensive components where competitive advantages are consistent with their product design capabilities deriving from the core American value of individualism. Product design capability represents an abstraction of ideas with existing information; individualism encourages uniqueness and creativity and therefore enhances the production of concept-intensive components such as software.

Hudson (1966) examined creativity in terms of two different types of cognitive styles, convergent thinking and divergent thinking. Convergent thinking follows strict logic and is directed towards a single right answer to a problem while divergent thinking is intuitive, unconventional, and involves sudden ideas. He suggested that the latter style was associated with creativity. As individualistic nations tend to encourage divergent thinking, individual creations that critically contribute towards product design capabilities are much respected.

The inventor of the Linux[8] operating system, Linus Torvalds explained the creative aspect of software in an interview as 'when you program, you create your own world, and the source code is the blueprint to that world. You're creating new laws. You're creating new laws of physics within the computer...'.[9] He elaborated on his personal experience of creating Linux in 1991 as follows:

> I basically sat around in my room for six months, very much the typical hacker. Lonely guy. It doesn't matter if the sun was shining outside. The shades are hiding the fact, and I am just sitting there programming. That was actually fairly normal for me, because that's what I'd been doing for most of my life, since I started getting into computers.[10]

Marc Andreesen and Eric Bina's writing of the first internet program Mosaic also illustrated the enthusiasm associated with creative experience. As Freiberger and Swaine (2000 p. 409) wrote 'They coded like mad. Between January and March of 1993, they wrote a 9,000-line program called Mosaic... It displayed graphics, it let you use a mouse and click on buttons to do things — no, to go places... using Mosaic, one had a compelling sense of going from one location to another in some sort of space. Some called it cyberspace'.

America's core cultural value of individualism is exhibited in the centre of software development, the Silicon Valley. The extreme aspect of individualism in the Silicon Valley has been captured by Castells and Hall (1994) in terms of devious aggressive competitive behaviour. They reported that more than half of the high-technology workers considered that 'some people would do anything to get ahead', and commented that 'there is an all-out struggle to keep ahead, leading to loose moral standards in professional relationships'.[11] A recent survey on social involvement in the Silicon Valley reiterated this extreme aspect of individualism.[12] It stated that the Silicon Valley was a place where people lived in isolation in terms of informal relationships, where people were less likely to help the poor and the elderly or to join a neighbourhood or civic group when compared with other demographically similar communities. In addition, residents of the Silicon Valley were also 22 per cent less likely to socialise with colleagues outside the office, 27 per cent less likely to visit relatives, to serve as community leaders, join clubs or even attend public meetings when compared with overall US statistics. The report concluded that: 'Silicon Valley, where networking relationships have given rise to great innovations, is inept at building social networks to build a healthy society...'.[13] Individualism has been applied by US software firms in a constructive manner. For instance, Microsoft's ethos of encouraging 'people to speak out, take risks and challenge conventional wisdom' [14] enables it to foster a creative corporate culture that channels into innovative software products. IBM also described itself as 'At IBM, we strike to lead in the creation, development and manufacture of the industry's most advanced information technologies, including computer systems, software...'.[15]

As a contrast, collective nations emphasise harmony and tend to perceive unique patterns of behaviour as deviant. For example, there is a consensus on the importance of group harmony in Japanese, Korean and Chinese culture, which is at the expense of individuality. The management principle of harmony is '*wa*' in Japan, '*inhwa*' in Korea and '*wo*' among overseas Chinese. Japanese firms have designed a well structured organisation (such as the consensual decision making system) to maintain harmony. Korean firms are noted for their strong emphasis on harmony in their corporate culture. It is expected that by being loyal to the firms, the employees' well-being will be taken care of. This is of particular importance as a substantial number of Korean senior managers within the *chaebols* are related to the owners' families. Within overseas Chinese businesses, harmony is also implicitly maintained, in the sense that opinions different from the top management tend not to be appreciated and considered. The notion that collective value is not conducive to product design capability has been widely commented on:

Shimada, a Japanese government research agency official considered that potential whiz-kid scientists were culturally discouraged from expressing their creativity in Japan. In his opinion, 'geniuses aren't so shy' to challenge authority in the US, and this was the reason why major ideas always come from America.[16]

Sandoz's (1997) interview with employees in Canon (which is widely regarded as an innovative Japanese firm) provided some insights into Asia Pacific firms' lack of product design capability embodied in concept-intensive components. One of his interviewees stated that: 'Canon has been very successful developing hardware, but the market now is demanding more and more sophisticated software. The company needs to allow individuals of both sexes much more freedom and responsibility. Only then we can expect to get some really meaningful technological breakthroughs' (ibid. p. 104). Another interviewee also recalled his own experiences of working in the USA and commented: 'when I was in America, I wasn't part of the mainstream operations, but worked on my own and had to make all my own decisions. It was free and very enjoyable. But when I came back to Japan there was a problem. At first I continued to work in my American way, but eventually had to change to a more consensus style so that I didn't stick out too much from my colleagues'. (ibid. p. 103).

Yamamoto (1992) observed that 'the researchers employed by Japanese companies are well-versed in the objectives of their firms, and are highly unlikely to take off in unexpected and unrelated directions' (p.139). He put forward a cultural-historical perspective on the lack of creativity in Japan and considered that entrenched values such as 'humility as a virtue' and 'culture of co-operation' manifested in the view that 'the emergence of anything new or out of the ordinary' is disruptive to the existing organisation and hence 'leading to its denunciation or outright rejection'. In fact, one of the laws in Japan's Edo period was 'it is a crime to do things that others do not' (pp. 144–5).

Mashima (1996) also quoted the Japanese proverb 'A nail that sticks up is hammered down' to demonstrate that individualism is far from encouraged in Japan.[17] This proverb expresses the belief that an individual should always maintain harmony with its group; in other words, individual achievement should be embedded in the context of the group and individual ambition should promote the interest of the group.

Spence (1985 p. 1288) reiterated this theme and explained: 'Social organisation in Japan centres on the genealogical family and kinship group but also includes the neighbourhood and often by extension other groups such as the company by which he is employed and the nation itself. Socialisation involves the development of a strong identification by each individual with the group and a continuing sense of mutual obligation among its members in which the desires of the individuals are subordinated to the needs and expectations of the larger community... Pressures toward conformity that exist in all levels of Japanese society, including the schools, may create a climate that is less conducive to scientific creativity than exists in the individualistic West'.

Capital-intensive Components and Labour-intensive Components among Asia Pacific Firms

The cultural selectivity theory also proposes that Japanese and Korean microcomputer firms' integration in capital-intensive components such as memory integrated circuits is derived from their process manufacturing capabilities which are obtained from their core values of continuous improvement. Finally, it suggests that the core value of flexibility among Taiwanese and Korean microcomputer firms enables them to undertake integration in labour-intensive components such as display monitors where competitive advantages are drawn from people management capabilities.

Cultural Legacy in Korea

The cultural selectivity theory suggests that Korean firms that share the relevant core values with Japan and China will integrate into both capital-intensive and labour-intensive microcomputer component areas. The historical links between Korea and China and Japan can be traced back to both ancient and recent history. From 109 BC to AD 735 China ruled the territory currently known as Korea. Chang and Chang (1994 p.9) explained that Korea 'has been under the influence of the Chinese culture for more than a thousand years... All aspects of the Chinese culture spread into Korea through Chinese books, traditions, customs, and the value system'.

Indigenous Chinese philosophies Confucianism and Taoism were introduced into Korea through exchanges of envoys and subsequently evolved into part of Korean thinking and behaviour. Confucianism, the dominant philosophy in Korea, reached the peak of its influence during the Yi Dynasty (1392–1910) when it became the state ideology. Lee and Yoo (1987 p. 69) stated that 'Confucianism has been the dominant philosophy behind the Korean culture' and they wrote that its impact on Korean management included paternalism, loyalty to the organisation and respect for the hierarchy of occupational ranking.

Japan's influence upon Korea began in 1904 during the Russo-Japanese War and was formalised after its annexation of Korea in 1910. Its impact upon Korea was highly visible; it built schools, highways, railroads, ports, communications facilities and even elaborated a government bureaucracy.

Moreover, some early Korean businesses had their roots in this colonial period. Japan withdrew from Korea after its defeat in the Second World War.

The legacy of China and Japan in modern Korea can be observed in various aspects of Korean firms. Fukuyama (1995 p. 127 and p. 133) regarded Korean firms as 'the Chinese company within... beneath the imposing exteriors of corporate behemoths like Hyundai and Samsung lie familistic interiors that are slowly and grudgingly accommodating themselves to professional management, public ownership, the divorce of management and ownership, and an impersonal, hierarchical corporate form of management'. Indeed, both Samsung's founder and former chairman Byung-Chull Lee as well as his son, the current chairman of the group, Kun-Hee Lee were educated in the elite Waseda University in Japan. Though Byung-Chull Lee failed to complete his education, he was described as 'the most pro-Japanese of Korea's tycoons'; he was also reported to have 'adopted Japanese tactics of putting new employees through strenuous and sometimes bizarre training programs to instil company loyalty'.[18] Others have also commented that the composition of Samsung's corporate philosophy at the same time reflected the 'Confucian tradition'.[19] Indeed, the present corporate philosophy of Samsung which has embodied the creation of a society where people lived in harmony also reflects the Confucian ideal of a harmonistic world.[20] In addition, Korean firms' typical inheritance systems that unduly favoured the eldest son of the family as well as their practices of benevolent authoritarian style management are drawn from Confucianism.

Japanese and Korean firms also resemble each other in their structure. Korea is dominated by the *chaebols* and Japan by the *keiretsu* within the large firm sector that engage in diversified businesses. Cross-shareholding is common among member firms within the *chaebol* or the *keiretsu*. In addition, the Korean consensus decision making system, the *pumui* system came from Japan and is basically similar to the *ringi* system. Interestingly enough, both *pummi* and *ringi* adopt the same Chinese character to represent the concept of consensus decision making. Nevertheless, there is an observable degree of difference in relation to the decision making among Japanese and Korean firms. Within the Japanese system, proposals work their way up from the bottom to the top of the hierarchy and therefore tend to have gathered wide support by the time they reach senior management. However, the Korean system seldom follows any strict direction compared to the Japanese one and, as a consequence, is used to provide documentation to new ventures or other programmes.

Process Manufacturing Capabilities in Japanese and Korean Firms

I will now explain the importance of process manufacturing capabilities for capital-intensive components such as memory integrated circuits. Process manufacturing capabilities are tacit in nature; in other words, they are difficult to impart as well as to imitate. By constantly refining the work procedures associated with the quality of products during the manufacturing process (i.e. learning by doing), firms can maximise the quantity of output for each unit of input employed in a production cycle. As a senior manager from Matsushita commented, 'the front line in the semiconductor war today is the battle of TQC', i.e. the ability to undertake total quality control.[21] Fruin (1997 p. 54) wrote that 'at the blueprint level, there is little apparent difference among leading chipmakers in Japan. They all produce state-of-the-art engineering drawings and the most recondite points of hardware and software design are quickly diffused among elite computer engineers'. However, he pointed out that process manufacturing capabilities differ among plants.

The value of continuous improvement or *kaizen*, which generates process-oriented thinking, reinforces Japanese and Korean microcomputer firms' capabilities in refining the process of integrated circuits manufacturing. Two Japanese academics pointed out the importance of continuous improvement towards the Japanese semiconductor industry as follows:

> In greatly simplified terms, nearly all major innovations that determine the direction of future product and process development originate in US firms. Japanese display their strength in incremental innovations in fields whose general contours have already been established... A dominant design is an authoritative synthesis of individual innovations formerly applied separately in products... Since a dominant design synthesises past technologies, after its appearance major innovations no longer occur frequently. From then on, the centre stage is occupied by incremental innovations aiming at product refinements and at improvements in the manufacturing process. The innovations conceived by Japanese firms correspond exactly to these incremental innovations. The reputation earned by Japan's 16K RAMs when they captured a large share of the American market was precisely one of high performance and low price.[22]

In fact, researchers at IBM recognised in the early 1980s that the scientific process control techniques as advocated by Shewhart (1931) and Deming (1950) were necessary for the control of quality, reliability and yield of integrated circuits. Furthermore, Melan et al (1982 p. 613) wrote 'process-sensitive technologies generally have an exposure to quality and reliability effects that are potentially detrimental in terms of device yields, quality levels, and reliability performance of the product'. Rosenberg and Steinmueller (1988 p. 233) also stated that 'innovations in the IC industry have been strongly influenced by the incremental improvement of process technology... Recent successes of Japanese IC firms in international competition have been dependent upon success at manufacturing improvement. In IC production, the proportion of workable devices emerging from the production process, production yield, is the most important manufacturing cost factor...'

In particular, Cole (1998) pointed out that quality was a crucial factor determining the competitive stance in integrated circuits such as dynamic random access memories. Kimura (1988) pointed out that the abilities to continuously adjust and re-coordinate the repeated steps of etching circuitry designs onto a silicon wafer, as well as modifying the assembly techniques that were developed at the research stage of the DRAM production, could sharply improve the quantity of output per production cycle. Furthermore, Sieling (1988) wrote that learning by doing provided the first important source of production cost dynamics in semiconductor technology. She added that the complexity and sensitivity of the dynamic random access memory manufacturing process made small variances in chemical solutions or minor pollutants in plant surroundings capable of damaging the product quality within a production cycle. Indeed, the second clean room in Toshiba's Yokkaichi plant has a total floor area of 60,000 square metres; the stringent requirement for air purity is less than 0.05 microns diameter particle per cubic foot of air.

The value of continuous improvement supported the attention to quality and hence process-improvement which enable the Japanese and Korean firms to compete with lower cost structure. Indeed, personal interviews with Firm C and Firm D that originated from cultures with the core values of continuous improvement illustrated their process manufacturing capabilities. Both firms engaged in arrays of capital-intensive components for external and internal users. They implemented continuous improvement within their global structure, and were credited with their emphasis on product quality.

Firm C has been, and is, one of the top ten DRAM manufacturers in the world, and was widely associated with continuous improvement. It had, in fact, diversified in the 1960s from telecommunications into computing and semiconductor production, gradually improving its products to the current high standard. Its early semiconductors were directed towards the Japanese market and were below international quality and product configuration. Nevertheless, it initiated product-reliability campaigns as well as research and development activities to continuously improve the design and the quality of semiconductors. In addition, Firm C had publicly stated that it admired IBM's expertise in marketing during the 1980s, and had endeavoured to nurture such capability. It was eventually acknowledged for its sales prowess within Japan after its persistent efforts in marketing.

Firm D was a youthful firm that had endeavoured to continuously improve on its component technology. It participated in a wide range of information technology products after the 1970s, including printers, word processors and personal computers. It had a relatively low market share in personal computers and had eventually withdrawn from the market by 2000. As for its laser printer business, it acquired during the 1990s the engine technology as well as other component technology. Its European Marketing Manager recalled that in its early stage of production, it constructed the systems around the engines, controllers and software that it procured from established suppliers. Then it acquired the manufacturing skill and obtained a license for some elements of the engine technology from an established market leader. To assure the quality of its products, it worked closely with its suppliers on a long term basis. It even assigned two employees permanently to one of its UK suppliers' manufacturing premises; this meant that when problems concerning component quality arose, it would not abruptly end its relationship with the suppliers. Instead, it would utilise its resources to solve the problems with them.

The core value of continuous improvement supports the importance of quality control in the manufacturing process, which results in the superior quality of the final product. An example can be seen in Toshiba's total productivity campaign (TP). The total productivity concept was developed by Yamamoto, who implemented a programme to reorganise the shop floor and the entire factory from 1978 to 1982 at Toshiba's electric motor factory in Mie, near Nagoya. The key points of total productivity were: '1) to set clear goals for the entire organisation; 2) to provide mechanisms whereby every department and section reviews the goal in light of their own means and ends; 3) to create the tools and standards of comparison for setting appropriate targets and rewards; 4) to train leaders for TP campaigning in local units and provide them with structures for integrating employee efforts' (Fruin 1997 p. 224). Toshiba formalised total productivity in 1985 and had adopted it over 27 factories in Japan by 1991. It was no coincidence that Toshiba was able to achieve a reputation in manufacturing process capability which led Fruin (op. cit.) to describe its factories as Knowledge Works.

People Management Capabilities in Taiwanese and Korean Firms

Management capabilities have been discussed in conjunction with the structural context of Japanese firms and US firms in the use of temporary labour or flexibility manufacturing; however, people management capability in labour-intensive components is associated with the softer aspect of management. People management capabilities can be seen in managerial expertise to extract the maximum productivity from a semi-skilled workforce usually in the context of developing economies or the less prosperous regions of developed economies. The ability to manage with flexibility is critical for labour-intensive components as the supply conditions of the work force and the operating environment of the assembly plants are rather unique in most low-cost localities.

The operating environment in low-cost localities can be illustrated in problems encountered by Toshiba's Northern China operation during the 1990s, which included constant changes of government policy, the increasing threat of labour disputes over pay and living conditions as well the rapacious lefy of fees and charges by local officials.[23] Another issue associated with investment in China is the legacy of the command economies. Warner (1999 pp. 12-3) reported that leading computer manufacturers such as Legend and Founder still provided accommodation or housing subsidies for employees. 'Legend laid on dormitory accommodation for young unmarried workers... Most firms provided housing for key workers such as managers and technical experts, but some (for example Ufsoft) provided housing only for 'high-performing' staff. Founder provides a two-bedroom flat for every worker who has worked for the company for more than two years'.

In addition to the unique operating environment, managers also need to understand the variation in the skill of the workforce as well as their work ethics in the context of economic, political and cultural backgrounds of low-cost localities; this implies that the standard practice in the headquarters may need to be refined or redesigned. For instance, observers have commented that the three entrenched rituals among Chinese factory workers encompass drinking tea, reading government newspapers and attending party meetings and as such were ingrained work behaviour in industrial firms.[24] Recent reports on microcomputer firms' Chinese operations did suggest that they had to deal with idleness on the factory floor.[25]

Korean and Taiwanese firms that are endowed with the core value of flexibility, are more able to exercise people management capabilities to handle unique operating environments of low-cost localities. For example, Samsung managed to embark on indirect trade through Hong Kong with China as early as 1979.[26] By 1994, its exports to China amounted to approximately US$1,100 million while its imports were US$300 million.[27] In addition, Samsung further demonstrated its ability to cultivate '*guanxi*' with top Chinese officials. The practice of '*guanxi*' or connections is generally considered as important for business operations in China where economic and legal infrastructure have not been properly established. It was reported that Samsung's Chairman Kun-Hee Lee were greeted by China's President Jiang Zemin and his 107 officials during a recent tour of the firm's Ki-Heung Semiconductor Plant in China; the incident demonstrates the connections Samsung has with central government officials.

The following field study observation from Beck and Beck (1990) in relation to a Japanese operation in China, on the other hand, demonstrates people management capability among overseas Chinese managers. In their observations of a Japanese electronics firms' operations in China, Beck and Beck (ibid. p. 95) highlighted that workers' motivations were higher when managers exercised a greater degree of flexibility in management. They cited the rather controversial 'slipper only' corporate policy within the Japanese firms to demonstrate this point. This policy required workers to wear slippers rather than shoes within the factory premises, and replicated the headquarters policy which derives from social practices in Japan. Beck and Beck observed that overseas Chinese and Japanese managers within the firms interpreted the policy rather differently. The overseas Chinese managers that supervised workers assembling radios and portable cassette players enforced the wearing of slippers loosely since it was not compatible with local practice. The Japanese managers that were responsible for the electronic components section, on the other hand, adhered strictly to it and even built a raised platform to help workers conform to it. Using both questionnaires and interviews, Beck and Beck concluded that the overseas Chinese management style resulted in higher job satisfaction among workers. As a contrast, the workers resented their treatment by the Japanese managers. Commenting on the workers' feelings, Beck and Beck (ibid. p. 102) wrote: 'it seemed to them that the Japanese managers' exhortations for them to remove their shoes to avoid bringing dust into the work area were flimsy — they realised that dust came in on their clothes and often blew in through the open doors of the room. To them, the Japanese managers' insistence on maintenance of the rubber slipper rule seemed arbitrary and irritating'.

CONCLUSION

Chapter one highlighted the economics, social, historical and strategic perspectives on backward linkage strategy. This chapter has presented something quite different; it builds on the theoretical underpinnings concerning the isomorphic process and firm capability to propose a cultural theory that can justify the diverse pattern of backward linkage strategy within the European microcomputer industry. The cultural selectivity theory has integrated the concept of national culture into the domain of business strategy and argues for the importance of the core value of individualism towards the replication of the industry recipe. It also attempts to illuminate the impact of the core values of individualism, continuous improvement and flexibility on the component capability of microcomputer firms, which subsequently determine US and Asia Pacific firms' area of specialisation within the integrated linkage. In such a sense, the cultural theory is arguably antithetical to the bounded rational framework that draws upon the assumption of managers as economic men/women; it continued with the studies by Mintzberg (1976 and 1994)[28], Hamel and Prahalad (1989 and 1994) as well as Knights and Morgan (1991) that involved intuition and feeling in the discussion of business strategy formulation. The next few chapters will proceed to examine the validity of the cultural theory with evidence from the European microcomputer industry.

NOTES

[1] Even by the end of the 1980s, IBM held over 50 per cent of the mainframe computer market in Western Europe. The national champions were still far behind its market shares. See 'Europe: a crisis that knows no national boundaries', *The Financial Times*, 23 April 1991. International Data Corporation estimated that IBM still dominated the supercomputer market by 1999, with a 30 per cent share. See William Bulkeley 'NEC and Cray Research Agreement on Sales of Supercomputers in US', *Wall Street Journal Europe*, 1 March 2001.

[2] See William Bulkeley 'NEC and Cray Research Agreement on Sales of Supercomputers in US', *Wall Street Journal Europe*, 1 March 2001.

[3] Louis Kraar, 'Acer's edge: PCs to go', *Fortune*, 30 October 1995 p. 65.

[4] Kelly (1987 p. 62).

[5] Though the integrated linkage strategy has been continually practised by established US firms and Asia Pacific firms during the 1990s, the use of disintegrated linkage strategy had been legitimised in the 1990s as a result of the meteoric rise of firms such as Dell and Sun.

[6] The Hawthorne Studies were a series of studies concerning productivity and issues such as social relationships at work and the impact of work groups carried out at the Hawthorne works of the Western Electric Company in Chicago between 1924 and 1932.

[7] Reported in S.E. Asch's study (1952) 'Effects of group pressure upon the modification and distortion of judgements' in H. Guetzkow (ed.) *Groups, Leadership and Men*, Pittsburg, US: Carnegie Press.

[8] Linux is a variation of the Unix operating system. Other variations include IBM's AIX, Compaq's Ultrix, Hewlett-Packard's HP/UX, Silicon Graphics' Irix and Sun's Solaris.

[9] Software programs contain codes (i.e. a series of written commands). Source codes are the written out version of an entire program in its original programming language. This quote is from an interview by Moira Gunn in 'Pragmatism, ethics and beautiful codes' SiliconValley.com site 2 July 2001.

[10] Ibid.

[11] A survey in *San Jose Mercury New,* August-September 1984 as reported by Castells and Hall (1994 p. 23).

[12] The Social Capital Community Benchmark Survey in 2000 as reported in 'Valley residents network but don't connect', *San Jose Mercury News,* 1 March 2001.

[13] Ibid.

[14] From a Microsoft advertisement in 2000.

[15] IBM.com site September 2001.

[16] *Business Week*, 15 June 1990.

[17] There was an anti-merchant decree that stated that 'You must not invent anything new' in the Kansei Reforms period in Japan (1789–93).

[18] *Business Week*, 23 December 1985 p. 41.

[19] *London Times,* 18 October 1994.

[20] *Samsung.com site*, 28 March 2002.

[21] The comment was made by Hajime Karatsu, Managing Director of Matushita Communication Industrial in Imai (1986) p. 216.

[22] Comment made by Professor Ken'ichi Imai and Akimitsu Sakuma at Hitotsubashi University in *Economic Eye* June 1983 as quoted in Imai (1986 p. 35).

[23] Tony Walker and Michiyo Nakamoto, 'Japanese companies take stock of investment in China', *The Financial Times*, 18 April 1995 p.7.

[24] Richard Tomlinson, 'China's reform: now comes the hard part', *Fortune*, 11 January 1999 p.54

[25] Neel Chowdhury, 'Dell cracks China', *Fortune,* 21 June 1999 p. 50.

[26] At the time, most western and newly industrialised nations tended to refrain from trading with China due to ideological differences.

[27] *Samsung News*, 23 March 1996.

---

[28] Mintzberg's (1976) study of managers in fact suggested that they did not manage from the left hemisphere of their brains (i.e. the part of the brain that is associated with logical thinking processes). As an anti-thesis to rationalism in business strategy, Mintzberg found that managers utilised their right hemisphere (i.e. intuition and judgement) in choosing strategic business choices.

7. US and Asia Pacific Multinationals Backward Linkage Strategy

This chapter will investigate the choices of integrated linkage strategy and disintegrated linkage strategy among microcomputer firms headquartered in nations with different degrees of individualism. It was proposed earlier that the integrated linkage strategy advocated by established US firms such as IBM would be prescribed by managers of collective Asia Pacific firms whose conceptual maps were inclined to conform to the industry recipe. Managers from individualistic US firms, on the contrary, would pioneer the disintegrated backward linkage strategy.

The integrated linkage strategy can be conceived as building on the resources of firms while the disintegrated linkage strategy can be seen as exploiting the market dynamics. The early entrant in the personal computer industry, Apple, explained the disintegrated linkage in terms of complying to the rules in the market:

> The old paradigm was that you had as much self-sufficiency as possible... When you do everything yourself, in the short term you may get better margins, but also lose tremendous flexibility to change. And as hard as we work to define what the information technology industry might look like in the beginning of the next century, we still can't do it with much accuracy. We want to retain that flexibility of being able to change as circumstances change.[1]

The disintegrated backward linkage strategy was regarded by Rappaport and Halevi in their controversial article in Harvard Business Review as the appropriate strategy for US computer firms. They (1991 p. 70) wrote that 'implicit in most discussions of US high technology is the assumption that a true computer company is one that manufactures systems hardware'. They also pointed out that 'so long as companies have reliable supplies of adequate hardware – and this seldom means the most advanced hardware – there are fewer advantages and a growing number of disadvantages to building it... A computer company is the primary source of computing for its customers.' (ibid. pp. 69-70).

Indeed, they had (op. cit.) rightly predicted the trend of disintegrated linkage strategy as irreversible at the time:

> By the year 2000, the most successful computer companies will be those that buy computers rather than build them. The leaders will leverage fabulously cheap and powerful hardware to create and deliver new applications, pioneer and control new computing paradigms, and assemble distribution and integration expertise that creates enduring influence with customers... The future belongs to the computerless computer company.[2]

Though the disintegrated linkage strategy has gathered supporters, its advantages had been commented on sceptically by a number of managers, academics and policy advisors prior to the early 1990s. It has been referred to as 'a dangerous recipe for an industry', 'a hollow victory' or has been equated to the 'loss of leadership in manufacturing and technology'. Rappaport and Halevi's article in particular has been widely attacked[3]:

> Articles like 'The Computerless Computer Company' (July-August 1991) make me nervous. Andrew S. Rappaport and Shumel Halevi's underlying thesis is one that we have heard many times in many different guises for over two decades: US companies should abandon highly competitive manufacturing businesses for more specialised niche markets that have higher profit margins. And since the United States is uniquely innovative and entrepreneurial, other countries will not be able to challenge us in these new markets as easily as they can in manufactured goods.[4]

> Rappaport and Halevi develop a convenient division of labour where US companies are the 'best' software producers and Japanese companies are the 'best' hardware producers. The real world, however, is not so simple... Rappaport and Halevi perpetuate a fundamental American myth: the hard and fast distinction between innovation and production, intellectual and manual labour. Indeed, the twenty-first century will see the divisions fade between knowledge-intensive and physical production, the R&D lab and the factory, intellectual and manual labour.[5]

> To be competitive, the United States must manufacture with zero defects, develop critical products and technologies on short schedules, and aggressively market those products with impeccable service.[6]

The first part of the cultural selectivity theory does not attempt to argue for or against the disintegrated backward linkage strategy; instead it argues that microcomputer firms' backward linkage strategy is relative to the core cultural values of individualism which they originated from.

It subscribes to a view that there is no one single industry economic logic in the choice of backward linkage strategy, and suggests that the extent of individualism will evoke opposing managerial conceptual maps in relation to the industry recipe of integrated backward linkage strategy. More specifically, it is suggested that Asia Pacific microcomputer firms with collective values will conform to the integrated backward linkage strategy while individualistic youthful US firms will pioneer the disintegrated backward linkage strategy. In this chapter, I will first elaborate on the two opposing backward linkage strategies with industry examples of firms from nations with the core values of individualism and collectivism. Then I will examine the pattern of backward linkage strategy exhibited by US and Asia Pacific microcomputer firms in Europe. Finally, I will examine further evidence that supports this cultural theme of backward linkage strategy.

THE OPPOSING BACKWARD LINKAGE STRATEGY

Figures 7.1 and 7.2 reviews the organisation of backward linkage strategy graphically[7]. Figure 7.1 illustrates a US firm, Firm E, that set up in the early 1990s; its European facility had eight assembly lines and a daily capacity of 8,000 desktop personal computer systems in 1996. At full capacity, it operated three shifts (i.e. 3 x 8 hours) a day. Firm E prescribed disintegrated backward linkage strategy in relation to desktop personal computer system; it procured capital-intensive and labour-intensive component inputs externally and concentrated on the product design, materials handling and customer processing aspects of its business.

Firm E's European plant utilised multiple sourcing for component parts which means that a single component would be sourced from a number of global suppliers simultaneously. For example, it purchased DRAMs from Samsung, Hyundai, Toshiba, Oki and Motorola which resulted in 42 per cent of the delivery within Europe, 38 per cent from the Far East and 20 per cent from the US in the first quarter of 1996. The percentage of procurement from Samsung and Hyundai was approximately 50 per cent; while that from Toshiba, Oki and Motorola was 20 per cent, 15 per cent and 5 per cent respectively. Its Commodity Manager stated that the practice created competitive pressure amongst suppliers and would provide them with incentives to minimise costs. He also quoted that 20 per cent of the operation's power supplies was procured from Taiwan's Lite-On while 80 per cent was from its counterpart High Pro. As a result, Lite-On would have incentives to strive for a larger share of its account.

Firm E also had international purchasing offices in Taiwan and Japan to collect up-to-date component marketing intelligence. Its Taiwan office acted as advisor to the European manufacturing plant on the eligibility of prospective Taiwanese suppliers. This procedure was important as most Taiwanese suppliers were very small firms and operated within a different legal system. The Japan office, on the other hand, facilitated the plant's procurement of memory integrated circuits. In the product areas of notebook computers, Firm E took advantage of Taiwanese contract manufacturers' capabilities and had most of its products built under original equipment manufacturing contracts by firms such as Quanta.[8]

Figure 7.2 depicts the integrated backward linkage strategy within Taiwanese Firm F's European subsidiary in 1997. Firm F was one of the leading notebook computer firms in Taiwan. This subsidiary was established in the early 1990s and had expanded since then. Firm F engaged in both own brand manufacturing and contract manufacturing of notebook computers at the time. Its customers in conjunction with the contract manufacturing business included leading Japanese and US microcomputer firms. Firm F's Managing Director mentioned that the sales of own brand models as a proportion of the total sales were approximately 60 per cent; he added that as the firm's strength was in manufacturing rather than marketing, it aimed at the shorter term objective of creating general awareness of its brand name in Europe.

The European operation undertook the purchase from its headquarters of partially finished notebooks that required microprocessors, hard disk drives and memories for completion. Firm F employed external procurement from the USA and Japan as regards these components. The European subsidiary also purchased power cords, packaging materials and manuals locally. In addition, the firm established a warehouse in Europe that could carry as many as 20–30 days stock of partially finished notebooks. The Managing Director stated that its component manufacturing division in Taiwan served as the supplier of various labour-intensive components to its assembly division. The component manufacturing division in turn relied on an extensive network of suppliers for inputs. He also depicted the supplier relationship practised by its headquarters as Taiwanese style, where written contracts were seldom enforced and verbal commitment was taken as contractually binding.

Figure 7.1: Firm E's Disintegrated Linkage Strategy

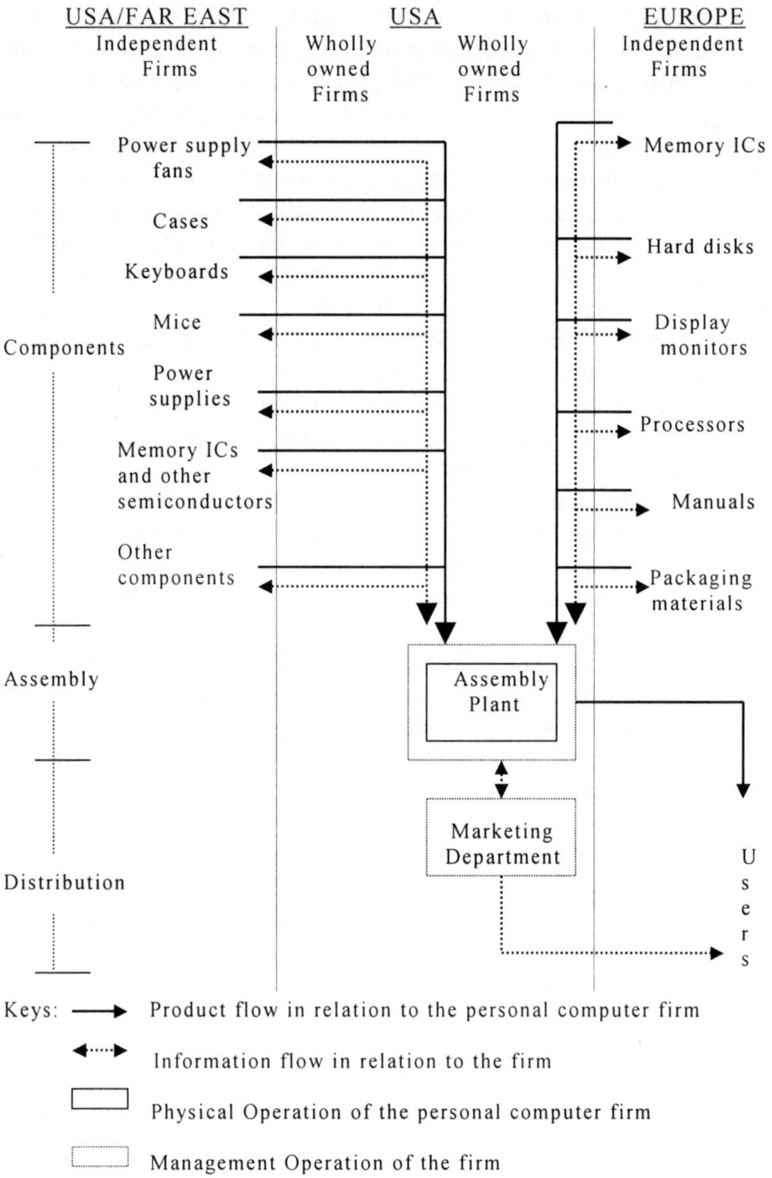

USA/FAR EAST — Independent Firms
USA — Wholly owned Firms
USA — Wholly owned Firms
EUROPE — Independent Firms

Power supply fans
Cases
Keyboards
Mice
Power supplies
Memory ICs and other semiconductors
Other components

Components

Memory ICs
Hard disks
Display monitors
Processors
Manuals
Packaging materials

Assembly

Assembly Plant

Marketing Department

Distribution

Users

Keys:
→ Product flow in relation to the personal computer firm

◄·····► Information flow in relation to the firm

▭ Physical Operation of the personal computer firm

▭ Management Operation of the firm

Source: Author.

Figure 7.2: Firm F's Integrated Linkage Strategy

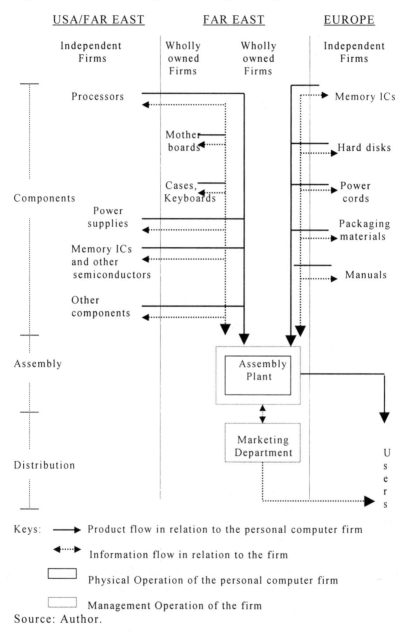

Keys: ──▶ Product flow in relation to the personal computer firm

◀┈┈▶ Information flow in relation to the firm

▭ Physical Operation of the personal computer firm

▭ Management Operation of the firm

Source: Author.

CULTURE IMPLICATION ON BACKWARD LINKAGE

Table 7.1 shows the various locations such as Greenock and Essones[9] that were responsible for IBM's component manufacturing within Europe in the early 1980s. IBM assigned its Greenock plant in Scotland to undertake the project of manufacturing the IBM PC for the European market in 1982. Though IBM initially adopted disintegrated linkage strategy in its new business, the microcomputer business reverted to the entrenched practice of integrated linkage strategy characterised in its mainframe and minicomputer segment by the mid-1980s.

Table 7.1: IBM Component Manufacturing within Europe, 1984

Location	Component Type
Germany	Disk File Units (Berlin)
	Power Supplies (Hanover)
	Memory Modules (Hanover)
	Semiconductors (Singelfingen)
	Printed Circuit Boards (Hanover)
UK	Hard Disk Drives (Havant)
	Keyboards (Greenock)
	Display Monitors (Greenock)
France	Circuit Packaging (Brodeaux)
	Semiconductors (Essones)
	Data Processing Accessories (Boign)

Source: Kelly 1987 p. 56.

The Greenock plant drew on the internal resources of IBM and procured hard disk drives, monitors, memory chips, keyboards and power units from internal subsidiaries; in addition, it spent £500 million per year on some 300 firms that provided it with electronics and electro-mechanical components[10] in relation to the PS/2 personal computer systems and IBM workstations by the late 1980s. Most of the suppliers delivered their components to the plant at least several times per week. It should, nevertheless, be recognised that IBM had developed the Scottish supplier bases over the years. Its UK manager commented that European sourcing was important for IBM on the grounds that it allowed for shorter lead times and flexibility in the supply chain and eliminated the cost of currency transactions. It also satisfied trade and tariff regulations, which enabled IBM to balance its earning and spending in Europe.[11]

One of IBM's suppliers' Fullarton, which was founded in Scotland in 1978, specialised in sheet metal fabrication, plastic injection mouldings and cables. It expanded into sub-assemblies in the early 1990s as the Greenock plant abandoned the manufacturing of sub-assemblies and focused on the final assembly of display monitors. Fullarton is now one of the largest fabricators and assemblers of electro-mechanical products in the electronic, telecommunication and computer industries, with manufacturing facilities in the USA and China. Its total number of employees in these global locations has also grown to about 2,000. IBM has also attracted component input suppliers such as Philips, who supply colour display tubes, to locate in Durham in order to shorten the supply chain. In fact, Philips has been and is one of the market leaders in the cathode ray tubes across Europe and globally.

The integrated linkage strategy in microcomputers has been perpetuated by other US entrants such as Digital, Hewlett-Packard, Compaq and Texas Instruments which were associated with minicomputer businesses during the 1980s. A reporter commented in 1993 that 'IBM, Hewlett-Packard and Digital — produce a slew of parts in-house, including disk drives that provide the company's memory and microprocessors that furnish its speed and power'.[12] Most notably, Digital's Professional series of personal computers has a considerably high value of internal procurement. Langlois and Robertson (1995 p. 95) wrote: 'except for the hard disk and the line cord, DEC designed and built every piece of the Professional. The company tooled the sheet metal and plastics, manufactured the floppy drive, and even developed the microprocessor'.

The integrated linkage strategy propounded by IBM has been diffused and maintained over time. Table 7.2 summarises the backward linkage strategy among microcomputer firms in 2000. Asia Pacific firms Fujitsu, Toshiba, NEC, Samsung, Acer, Mitac and Twinhead have all replicated the integrated linkage.[13] For example, Toshiba's manufacturing investment in Germany, which was established in 1990, practised integrated backward linkage strategy and internally procured component inputs such as hard disk drives, printed circuit boards, memories and batteries despite the growing trend for disintegration in the Japanese computer industry. Another example can be cited from Samsung's Teeside plant which procured components such as display monitors, hard disk drives and printed circuits broads internally during the late 1990s.

Table 7.2: Patterns of Backward Linkage Strategy, 2000

	Disintegrated Linkage	Integrated Linkage
Youthful US firms	Dell, Gateway, Sun, SGI	
Asia Pacific Firms		Fujitsu, NEC, Toshiba, Acer, Samsung, Mitac, Twinhead

Source: Author.

The propensity of collective Asia Pacific firms to conform to the industry recipe of integrated linkage strategy adopted by established US firms can be seen in their admiration of IBM in the wider industry context. IBM has always been a model firm in the computer industry. Though it suffered historic losses in the early 1990s, it repositioned itself and turned around under the leadership of Louis Gerstner[14] after 1993. It was regarded as 'a growth company again' by Business Week in 1996.[15]

A senior official from Japan's Ministry for International Trade and Industry stated in the early 1990s that the IBM model was a yardstick for comparing performance and Japanese firms 'are still trying to catch up with IBM'.[16] In fact, Canon Europe's President Takeshi proclaimed in 1989 that 'our model is IBM', i.e. IBM was a model for the development of a global organisation.[17] The importance of IBM was reiterated by the comment of Taiwanese firms such as Acer. For instance, Acer's CEO stated that, 'in 1989 I thought IBM was the best-managed company in our field. I supposed that Liu (a 20-year-old IBM veteran) was more experienced and capable than I'.[18] Such strategic inclination demonstrating conformity to the industry recipe is a characteristics of managerial conceptual maps in Asia Pacific firms.

In addition, Japanese business consultants such as Mochio Umeda pointed out that Japanese management was incapable of articulating a clear vision or providing leadership in the style of a US chief executive for competing successfully in the computer industry. He argued that 'for Japanese companies to succeed in the computer industry, they will have to achieve this type of profound vision. This will require significant changes in the style of management practised in Japan'. He added that Japanese management would have to give up 'its parochialism, its perverse egalitarianism, its in-group orientation and its tendency to suppress individuality and creativity' in order to achieve success in the computer industry.[19]

Nevertheless, the integrated backward linkage strategy has not been taken up by the market orientated individualistic US firms Dell, Sun, SGI and Gateway. As component technology evolved at an ever accelerating rate, these US firms maintained leadership in product innovation by exploiting the strengths of independent suppliers. Indeed, Methé et al. (1997) described a domino effect of technological advances in personal computer components. They wrote 'innovation in one sub-technology is likely to stimulate and may require innovation in another sub-technology', and 'advances in the OS technology can only provide real value to the final end user of the PC when it is combined with a more powerful MPU. These changes in turn require better memory capacity and higher resolution displays' (ibid. p. 326).

The disintegrated linkage strategy was legitimised by the success of Dell's operation in the 1990s. Michael Dell started his firm and offered customised IBM PC-compatible under the brand 'PC's Limited' in 1984, he then changed its name to Dell Computer. Dell entered Europe with a marketing subsidiary in the UK in 1987. It escalated its commitment in Europe with manufacturing investment in 1991. It also undertook further investment in 1997 and 1999. As a result, Dell employed five per cent of the 68,000 strong labour force in Limerick. Kevin Ryan, the Dean of the College of Informatics and Electronics at the University of Limerick, commented that 'any young person with reasonable ambition and high school education can get work here now, because of Dell. And indeed, that did not used to be the case'.[20] Dell's Irish plants purchased all the required component inputs from independent firms, which included Intel, Maxtor, Microsoft, Sony, 3Com, Ati, Phoenix and Crystal.[21] On two separate occasions, Michael Dell commented on its unconventional backward linkage strategy:

> The low cost way to support European customers is from a single site. This enables overheads, inventory and accommodation costs to be minimised. Dell pioneered the trend by central European logistics and customer support in Ireland, which offers one of the lowest cost and most flexible working environments in Europe.[22]

> If you look back to the industry's inception, the founding companies essentially had to create the components themselves. They had to manufacture disk drives and memory chips and application software; all the various pieces of the industry had to be vertically integrated within one

firm... As the industry grew, more specialised companies developed to produce specific components. That opened up the opportunity to create a business that was far more focused and efficient. As a small start-up, Dell couldn't afford to create every piece of the value chain. But more to the point, why should we want to? We concluded that we'd be better off leveraging the investments others have and focusing on delivering solutions and systems to customers.... It's a pretty simple strategy, but at the time it went against the dominant, 'engineering-centric' view of the industry. The IBMs and Compaqs and HPs subscribed to a 'we-have-to-develop-every-thing' view of the world. If you weren't doing component assembly, you weren't a real computer company.[23]

Another youthful US firm echoed this view during a personal interview in 1996 and pointed out that microcomputer firms would not be able to compete with specialist suppliers such as Intel or Seagate, and those that attempted to possess captive capabilities on all core components would be distracted from the logistics of the business. In fact, a close scrutiny of research expenditure in specialist suppliers Intel in Table 7.3 strongly supported this view. Intel was able to maintain its market position by continually investing in research and development, which was approximately ten per cent of its sales revenue throughout the 1990s.

Table 7.3: Intel's Research Expenses, 1991–2000   (US$ million)

Year	Sales	Research Expenditure	R&D as % of Sales
1991	4,799	680	14.0%
1992	5,844	780	13.3%
1993	8,782	970	11.0%
1994	11,521	1,111	9.6%
1995	16,202	1,296	8.0%
1996	20,847	1,808	8.7%
1997	25,070	2,347	9.4%
1998	26,273	2,509	9.5%
1999	29,389	3,111	10.6%
2000	33,726	3,897	11.6%

Source: Intel (2001).

Moreover, comments made by the youthful US firm Sun served to illustrate non conforming as a feature of its managerial conceptual maps. One of Sun's founders, William Joy, acknowledged the importance of disintegrated linkage in workstation business as: 'The technological change in the computer industry is continually accelerating. No single company can be at the forefront of every important breakthrough, and those that try doing it all themselves — the classical vertical integration route — inevitably fall behind'.[24] He stated that Sun could maintain its market position in workstations by co-operating with the technology leaders. Scott McNealy, Sun's founder and President commented in 1987 that 'with 20 per cent to 30 per cent growth per quarter, for a company our size it's a nontrivial manufacturing ramp-up while maintaining quality... We're not looking to get sophisticated right now in terms of integration strategy or anything like that'.[25]

Sun's Vice President of Manufacturing, James Benn, also declared at the time that Sun was consciously pursuing the disintegrated linkage strategy that fits into the product characteristics of the industry, hence he commented that 'if we were making a stable set of products, I could make a solid case for vertical integration' (op. cit.). Sun's reliance on external suppliers had allowed the introduction of four major product generations in its first five years of operations. McNealy remarked five years later that the company's focus on designing microprocessors, writing software and marketing workstations was 'the only way to run a computer business'.[26] Sun even phrased the corporate commandment of 'thou shalt not do thyself what others can do better' to depict its strong belief in the disintegrated backward linkage strategy (op. cit.). Sun's relationships with contract manufacturers Flextronics and Solectron in the Silicon Valley demonstrated the advantages of disintegrated linkage strategy. 'Flextronics developed internal engineering services and gradually took responsibility for the initial design and layout of Sun's printed circuit boards as well as the pre-screening of its electronic components' (Saxenian 1994 p. 153). With Solectron, Sun gained tremendously from its early transition towards the surface mount technology in printed circuit board assembly:

> Traditional through-hole assembly involved soldering individual leads from an integrated circuit through the holes in circuit boards. SMT uses epoxy to glue electronic components onto the board. The new process is attractive for two reasons: it produces smaller boards because components can be mounted on both sides of the board, and it is cheaper in high-volume production than the through-hole process... Industry analysts describe SMT as five to ten

times more difficult a process than through-hole. Moreover, a single high-speed SMT production line costs more than $1 million. (ibid. pp. 153–4).

OTHER AREAS OF US NON-CONFORMITY

Youthful US firms have not only introduced the disintegrated backward linkage strategy to the microcomputer industry, they have also exhibited non-conforming practice in other business areas. Dell's unconventional entrance into the European market, for example, was viewed with extreme criticism. It was reported in the late 1980s that 'in early June this year, PCs Ltd set up business in the UK. The company calls itself the Dell Computer Corporation... As in the USA, you can't walk into a dealer in the UK and buy a Dell machine — you have to order it over the phone and it will be delivered by courier to your door.'[27] Dell's UK operation was received negatively by the 22 British journalists who attended its first European press conference in June 1987; 21 of them predicted that Dell would fail.[28]

Dell challenged the concurring practice in the industry and insisted on tackling the market with its innovative toll-free telephone marketing and internet sales, e.g. individuals contact Dell for product enquiry or order placement. Dell's prospective customers in Europe could contact its European telephone marketing team 12 hours a day during the week, nine hours on Saturday and six hours on Sunday in the late 1990s. They can also utilise the internet and order from the firm 24 hours a day. Michael Dell considered internet sales as 'zero-variable-cost transactions' and rightly predicted in 1997 that half of the firm's revenue would come from internet sales in the next two to four years[29]. Overall, Dell obtained US$1 million sales per day from its web site in the middle of 1997; its internet sales in mid-1999 represented 40 per cent of its sales revenue.[30] Europe has grown into a large market for Dell by 2000, generating a fifth of its total revenue.

Dell also entered the Asian market and even the Chinese market in the late 1990s with its 'all-American model' of direct selling as opposed to established US firms IBM, Hewlett-Packard or Compaq's reliance on resellers. Critics stated sceptically that Asia's low internet penetration and the emphasis on personal relationships would not be conducive to Dell's marketing strategy. The Chief Financial Officer of the indigenous Chinese firm Legend commented negatively that Dell's telephone marketing operation (which was established in 1998) would not be appropriate for local tastes: 'It takes nearly two years of a person's savings to buy a PC in China, and when two years of savings is at stake, the whole family wants to come out to the store to touch and try the machine'.[31] Nevertheless, Dell gained market shares in China shortly after its participation in the market. Its telephone marketing has proved to be workable and gradually introduced changes to the distribution channels in China.

Dell reiterated its non-conforming managerial conceptual maps when it entered the server sector in the mid-1990s. Unlike its competitors that adopted intermediaries to resolve after sales problems and cultivate customer relationships, Dell adhered to the direct sales of a narrowly defined ranged of systems that are backed by efficient procurement and assembly processes. In the face of industry analysts' doubts, it proved that its insight was accurate and had improved its market shares from two per cent in the USA in 1996 to 22 per cent in 2001[32].

In order to counteract the weakening demand of its core product area of mid-range desktop business systems, Dell has recently reduced its profit margins in the segment against industry analysts' recommendation of improving third-party customer support and service. One of the analysts commented that: 'Look at the small- and medium-sized business market. SMEs accounted for almost 40 per cent of western European PC sales in the fourth quarter and if you don't have intermediaries you don't have the same ability to resolve problems and develop customer intimacy'; another analyst echoed this view and stated that 'companies now want services and support when equipment is installed. Having channel partners helps address customer security'.[33]

I will now turn to other youthful US firms Apple, Sun and Gateway's non-conforming managerial conceptual maps. Apple, which operated a manufacturing operation in Cork, Ireland between 1980 and 1998, exhibited certain non-conforming practices. Apple Computer founded in California by Steve Jobs and Steve Wozniak on 1 April 1976 did not follow the prevailing industrial product conception of the computer, when launching the Apple II in 1977 as well as the Machintosh in 1983.[34] Instead, it skilfully extended the status of computers from industrial products to consumer products through mass marketing campaigns. Apple developed extensive distribution networks comprising approximately 2,500 channel members in the USA as well as abroad by the early 1980s. Apple reinforced the image of personal computers as consumer products with novel approaches in marketing. For example, it launched the 'Apple II Forever' conference in San Francisco in April 1984 and held a preview of its new television commercials in New York, October 1986. It also managed a number of Macintosh showrooms directly or indirectly through authorised dealers in the late 1980s. Apple opened a number of Apple Stores throughout the UK in 1986; Personal Computers plc was one of the firms that obtained the contractual rights to operate 'The Macintosh Centre' in London and Leeds. Indeed it wrote in its marketing material that 'there's a place where you can buy a Macintosh, choose Macintosh software, consult with Macintosh experts, see the latest Macintosh add-ons, join Macintosh training courses, rent a Macintosh system and arrange a Macintosh maintenance contract'.

The technology incorporated in Macintosh also transformed the personal computer into a consumer product. Its graphical user interface, which allowed its user to interact with the system by moving and pointing to positions on the screen via a mouse, was distinctively user friendly. It was described as:

> If you wanted a friendly machine and could afford a premium price, you bought an Apple Macintosh. It came with Apple's software, which transformed the screen into an electronic desktop with nifty icons to help you keep track of data programs, and pull-down menus to help you select and issue commands.[35]

The youthful US firm Sun also challenged the conventional wisdom of the computer industry with powerful yet affordable computers. Sun Microsystems was incorporated in California in 1982 by Andreas Bechtolsheim, Vinod Khosla, Bill Joy and Scott McNealy. The name Sun is an acronym for Stanford University Network; the original S. U. N. workstation was a generic workstation designed by Bechtolsheim to run on the Stanford University Network project. Its CEO Scott McNealy once stated that: 'I want Sun to be controversial. If everybody believes in your strategy, you have zero chance of profit'.[36]

Sun's success was due to its conviction that there was a demand among engineers and scientists for workstations with higher performance relative to the personal computer and lower price when compared to the minicomputer network. It pioneered the concept of affordable and powerful workstations based on an open system, i.e. the adoption of standard hardware and software components such as Motorola's microprocessor and the UNIX operating system. Sun's later innovation included workstations that were equipped with communications networks — the advantages of these systems were they could attach to any computer systems. It was reported that 'from the outset, the computer workstation was designed to be affordable... Sun was the start-up company that came to symbolise the rise of the workstation... The market for powerful workstations exploded, taking Sun to a turnover of over US$31,000 million, with 550,000 units shipped in under a decade'.[37] Indeed, Sun had approximately one-third of the worldwide workstation market share in 1991, and was ahead of established US firms such as IBM and Hewlett-Packard. Scot McNealy described Sun's achievement in the famous line: 'In the past, computer companies have been able to charge a premium for proprietary technology. In the future they will have to offer a discount'.[38] Sun's ability to clearly differentiate its workstation in terms of price and performance allowed it to become, after a few years, an important player in this segment of the microcomputer market.

Unsatisfied with the performance of the available microprocessors that were incorporated into workstations, Sun designed a reduced instruction set computer microprocessor, the SPARC; nevertheless, it refrained from integrated backward linkage strategy and licensed other firms to manufacture SPARC that is incorporated into its workstations. Sun has successfully expanded the workstation market and established new segments in commerce, by first setting up pilot schemes in prospect operations to demonstrate the advantages of workstations. Sun's effort resulted in its gaining of market shares in banks, insurance and financial institutions, airlines, healthcare, education, government, internet... By the mid-1990s, its workstations were not restricted for scientific use and Sun sold a third of its workstations to the commercial market.

Finally, the marketing of Gateway whose logo is a distinctive black-and white spotted cow, is yet another non-conforming example among youthful US firms. Gateway is found by Ted Waitt in South Dakota in 1985. Although the rural and country symbol projects friendliness and honesty, it is indeed an untypical logo for a high-technology product. In addition, the logic of Gateway's location, which is away from the high technology clusters in California, Texas or Massachusetts, has posed a challenge to the importance of regional agglomeration. In addition, Gateway adopted unconventional working hours in the microcomputer industry; it implemented a 12-hour shift in its manufacturing plant so as to minimise the time workers spent travelling within Dublin.

It should also be pointed out that Sun, Dell and Gateway led in the adoption of efficient contract manufacturing services on fully assembled systems. Dell and Gateway utilised contract manufacturing on a very high proportion of their notebook shipments during the mid-1990s. Such a practice, which was initially not approved of by established US firms and Japanese firms, has also been increasingly popular among the same firms over time. IBM converted to the contract manufacturing services of fully assembled personal computers for the first time in 1997. Japanese computer firms such as Toshiba and Sony were among the last leading firms that eventually converted to the contract manufacturing relationship with a number of Taiwanese firms in recent years.

CONCLUSION

This chapter has shown the distinctive backward linkage strategy pattern among youthful US firms on the one hand, and established US firms and Asia Pacific firms on the other. It supports the notion that the tendency to replicate the industry recipe of integrated backward linkage propounded by established US firms is associated with the degree of individualism. Managerial maps among collective Asia Pacific firms are inclined towards conforming to the industry recipe while those of individual youthful US firms pioneer the alternative disintegrated linkage strategy. As the best industry practice in the microcomputer industry evolved towards the disintegrated linkage strategy in the 1990s, both established US firms and Asia Pacific firms modified their backward linkage strategy. Nevertheless, Asia Pacific firms from nations with the core cultural value of collectivism will exhibit greater conformity towards the new industry recipe. On the other hand, established US firms that are characterised with conceptual maps shaped by individualism will introduce innovation to the new practice.

NOTES

[1] Comment made by Apple's CEO John Sculley (1983–93) in McKenna (1989 p. 157).
[2] This comment generated considerable debate concerning the future of the manufacturing industry in the US, for example, Intel's Andrew Grove and Harvard Business School's Bruce Scott argued against Andrew Rappaport and Shmuel Halevi in the September–October 1991 issue of Harvard Business Review.
[3] See 'Should the United States abandon computer manufacturing?' *Harvard Business Review*, **69** (5), 140-158.
[4] Ibid p. 140. Comment made by Daniel Burton, Executive Vice President of the Council on Competitiveness, Washington D.C.
[5] Ibid p. 148. Comment made by Richard Florida (Associate Professor of Management and Public Policy in Carnegie Mellon University, Pennsylvania) and Martin Kenney (Associate Professor of Management and Public Policy in the University of California).

[6]   Ibid p.143. Comment made by T.J. Rodgers, CEO of Cypress Semiconductor.

[7]   The firm information about the backward linkage strategy was collected in person-to-person interviews.

[8]   Recently, this US microcomputer firm has also begun to utilise contract manufacturing services from Japan.

[9]   IBM disposed both these sites in the 1990s.

[10]   'Procurement tasks require a new way of thinking', *New Electronics,* January 1991 p. 51.

[11]   Ibid.

[12]   Shawn Tully, 'The modular corporation', *Fortune*, 8 February 1993 p. 54.

[13]   It should, however, be noted that IBM, HP, Fujitsu, Toshiba and NEC have all utilised integrated linkage to a lesser extent during the 1990s.

[14]   Louis Gerstner became the CEO of IBM in April 1993 after a 27-year career as management consultant at McKensey, American Express and RJR Nabisco.

[15]   *Business Week's* cover story 'How IBM became a growth company again' described IBM as regaining the respect of Corporate America in its 9 December 1996 issue.

[16]   Jonathan Friedland, 'Disconnected', *Far Eastern Economic Review*, 30 June 1994 p. 46.

[17]   This comment is quoted from Humes (1993) p. 204.

[18]   Louis Kraar, 'Acer's edge PCs to go', *Fortune*, 30 October 1995 p. 72.

[19]   See *'Failing to change: the plight of the Japanese Computer Industry'* as published by Arthur D Little, 2nd quarter, 1994 as well as Alan Cane 'Management: The need for a survival strategy', *The Financial Times*, 19 August 1994 p. 10.

[20]   Rob Norton, 'The Luck of the Irish', *Fortune*, 25 October 1999.

[21]   See *PC Pro* August 1999 p. 76.

[22]   Quoted from the Irish Development Authority.

[23]   Joan Magretta, 'The power of virtual integration: an interview with Dell Computer's Michael Dell', *Harvard Business Review*, March–April 1998 p. 74.

[24]   Stuart Gannt, 'Sun's sizzling race to the top', *Fortune*, 17 August 1987 p. 60.

[25]   'For flexible, quality manufacturing — don't do it yourself', *Electronic Business*, 15 March 1987 p. 60.

[26]   Robert D. Hof, 'Deconstructing the computer industry', *Business Week,* 23 November 1992 p. 46.

[27]   *Personal Computer World*, July 1987 p. 113.

[28]   Michael Dell (2000) *Direct From Dell, London, UK: Harper Collins Business* p. 28.

[29]   *The Financial Times,* 20 August 1997.

[30]   Louise Kehoe, 'Dell claims lead in PC market', *The Financial Times*, 18 August 1999 p. 16.

[31]   Neel Chowdhury 'Dell cracks China', *Fortune,* 21 June 1999 p. 47.

[32]   Carlos Grande 'Facing up to the new computer world', *ft.com site*, 16 February 2001.

[33] The first comment was made by principal PC analyst Bryan Gammage at Dataquest Europe while the second one was made by the managing director of Context, London Jeremy Davies. Both comments were cited from Carlos Grande op. cit.

[34] Of course, there are the intermittent failures of Apple that were less publicised, i.e. Apple III and Lisa.

[35] *Fortune,* 4 October 1993 p. 57.

[36] 'Scot McNealy's Rising Sun', *Business Week,* 22 January 1996.

[37] *The Financial Times Survey*, 26 May 1993 p. II.

[38] Gannt (op. cit.).

8. Creativity in Software

Borland International, established by Philippe Kahn[1] with a personal loan in 1983, grew rapidly with the specialised Turbo Pascal programming language package for personal computers. The birth of the firm was as follows:

> In early 1982, Phillippe Kahn was living on the French Riviera, teaching mathematics by day and playing jazz saxophone by night. But a new passion was beginning to take over his life: the Apple II computer. He began spending hours creating programs for it and soon was hectoring his American-born saxophone teacher to translate articles from US computer magazines. After months of watching Kahn's obsession grow, the teacher said: 'People like you don't live here. They live in California'. By summer, Kahn had arrived in Silicon Valley.[2]
>
> With only $2,000 in his pocket, he landed in the US with no green card and no job. He founded Borland International in an office over an automobile repair shop in 1983. Despite the humble abode, Kahn convinced a BYTE ad salesperson to accept on credit a full-page colour ad for Turbo Pascal. At a ridiculous $49.95, Kahn was swamped with orders.[3]

The above description not only reiterates the self-selection of immigrants into the US culture as suggested in chapter five, but also highlights the entrepreneurial spirit among US software firms formed since the 1980s, and parallels the description of youthful US firms such as Dell, Sun and Gateway as mentioned in chapter one.

There is an observable unique cultural approach in software that emerged from the interplay between the industry's culture and the business culture of different national firms. As Chang and Burgess (1991 p. 4) observed: '... the different image of software engineering around the world. The creative white collar image prevalent in the US clashes with the grind-it-out, blue collar image that prevails in Japan'. Maital (1990 p. 5) further elaborated on the different approach to issues such as delays and cost overruns in software projects. He pointed out that US managers aimed to 'remain flexible highly skilled people, hire or fire as needed, and rely on loosely structured 'job shops' like those used to make fine furniture or Ferraris'. Japanese managers, alternatively, would apply 'tight controls and procedures'.

The part of the cultural selectivity theory that deals with concept-intensive components argues that US microcomputer multinational firms' integration into components such as software are consistent with the product design capabilities derived from the core American value of individualism. In this chapter I will first provide an overview of the software industry, followed by a discussion of the relationship between the core value of individualism and product design capabilities in software. I will then discuss how US and Asia Pacific microcomputer firms' capabilities contribute to their pattern of integration in concept-intensive software. Finally, the impact of the Japanese core cultural value of *kaizen* on firms' unique practices in software development will be highlighted.

AN OVERVIEW OF SOFTWARE

Computer software refers to programs that operate a computer's hardware. It is an important industry that forms the backbone of the new economy and was valued at more than US$260,000 million in 2000. Figure 8.1 shows that software is a component of the computer industry and also highlights that computer services contain some degree of contract programming.

Figure 8.1: Major Segments of the Computer Industry

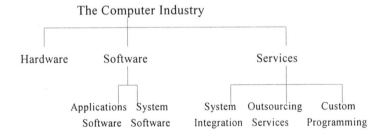

Source: OECD (1991).

Traditionally software has been classified in terms of customised software and packaged software. Customised software relates to the development of software for a specific user, the norm of software development prior to the 1960s. Packaged software, on the other hand, is the standardised production of software for general purposes and represents the majority of software sales. Brooks (1987) explained the substitution of packaged software for customised software in terms of the decline in the hardware/software cost ratio over the past few decades. He pinpointed that 'the buyer of a two-million dollar machine felt that he could afford $250,000 more for a customised payroll program' while 'the buyer of a $50,000 office machine cannot conceivably afford a customised payroll program' (p. 17). Despite this distinction of customisation and standardisation, firms could employ packaged software that incorporated a degree of customisation.

The growth of packaged software is associated with IBM's two strategic moves during the 1960s. The first one being the success of its industry wide standard mainframe System 360 line of computers in 1964, which created a market for standard software packages. The second one is its move towards a separate policy for hardware and software products in 1969 which provided the opportunity for the growth of a software market. Due to the significant costs involved in the development of customised programs, the majority of the software operating on microcomputers nowadays is packaged software. As a matter of fact, the total revenue of the worldwide packaged software market was approximately US$157,000 million in 1999 as compared to about US$54,000 million in custom software.[4] The International Data Corporation has further estimated that the packaged software market will grow to US$310,000 million in 2004.

Figure 8.2 shows that 80 per cent of the packaged software was produced in the US in the late 1990s as compared to 15 per cent from Europe. The first tier US software firms such as Microsoft and IBM, for instance, obtained US$34,000 million from the licensing of their software packages in 1999. The combined licensing revenues of the second tier US software firms Computer Associates, Oracle, Hewlett-Packard, Sun, Unisys, Compaq and Novell were about US$16,000 million. Software licenses are typically granted to individuals, firms or cover specific sites. The sales revenues achieved by European firms, for example, represented Germany's SAP US$2,000 million revenue in software licensing fees.[5] There is, in addition, a cluster of indigenous firms that have grown up in Ireland in the last decade contributing to European software. A recent survey found that 50 per cent of the indigenous Irish firms were set up in the late 1990s; they tend to concentrate in areas such as wireless, e-learning, customer relationship management and enterprise application integration.[6]

Figure 8.2: Production Shares of Packaged Software

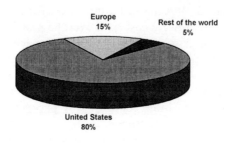

Source: Dutch Ministry of Economic Affairs as quoted in Europe Wall Street Journal 9 April 1997 p. 4.

Software is also differentiated into the major category of operating systems software and applications software; they were estimated at approximately US$31,000 million and US$161,000 million in 2000 respectively.[7] The former controls the primary functions of the microcomputer system, and is defined by its roles such as systems inputs and outputs as well as connections to other computers. For instance, the operating system determines how to obtain materials from the program in which one wants to print through various parts of the system to the printer. The operating systems segment of software has been, and is dominated by, US firms such as Microsoft. Application software, on the other hand, is a program that renders support functions to home, business or institution and performs tasks directly for users. Applications software can be further subdivided into the areas of business or entertainment. Business applications have always been considered as mainstream software and contributes to the majority of software revenue.[8]

BYTE magazine considered the most important business applications software producers in the 1980s, as shown in Table 8.1, were US firms such as Lotus, Novell, Microsoft, Adobe, Autodesk, Norton and WordPerfect. Netscape Navigator, which pioneered the growth of the Internet can be considered as the most important applications software in the 1990s. Netscape was found by Marc Andreessen and Silicon Graphics' co-founder James Clark in 1994; its innovative product Netscape Navigator was the leading web browser among microcomputer users. Other important web software firms that have emerged since the mid-1990s include BEA, i2Technologies, Kana and E.piphany. For example, BEA, which was founded by a former Sun Microsystems manager William Coleman, has designed web software that serves as foundation for E-commerce applications. It gained 8,000 customers including General Electric and Amazon.com in its first five years. The development of the applications software industry discussed so far has, therefore, illustrated the importance of new ideas; successful new firms are able to come up with products that can be considered as critically essential, which improve firm productivity or open new markets. As industry observers commented on the US start-ups: 'out of the hundreds of software companies launched since 1995, 16 stand out as leaders in their markets. Their quarter revenues are growing from 77 per cent to 2,900 per cent over five years, and half of them are--gasp--profitable'.[9]

Table 8.1: Early US Packaged Microcomputer Applications Software

Operating System	*Computer Aided Design*
CP/M 2.0	Autodesk
DOS 2.0	
Novell NetWare	*Wordprocessing*
Unix System V	WordStar
Mac OS and System 7	WordPerfect
Windows 3.x	
	Accounting
Spreadsheets	Quicken
VisiCalc	
Lotus 1-2-3	*Others*
Excel	SideKick 1.0
	Norton Utilities
Publishing	Flight Simulator
PageMaker	Lantastic
Adobe Type	Lotus Notes 3.0

Source: BYTE, September 1995 pp. 99-104.

Table 8.2 shows the predicted growth for segments of business applications software as illustrated in a recent survey by Advanced Marketing Research[10]; it predicted that Enterprise Resource Planning and E-Commerce software would be the main areas for firms' IT spending in 2001. The survey result corresponds to the industry trend where more than one-third of the Software 500 firms in 2000 were in the sectors of Enterprise Resource Planning, Customer Relationships Management, Manufacturing Supply Chain and E-business.[11]

Table 8.2: IT Budget Spending, 2001

Applications Software	Manufacturers	Service Firms
Enterprise Resource Planning	42%	25%
E-Commerce	19%	26%
Supply Chain Management	12%	10%
Customer Relationship Management	11%	17%
Other	16%	22%

Source: AMR Research as quoted in Internetweek 16 October 2000 p. 27.

The aforementioned business applications software generates a substantial amount of sales revenue and is the focal point of the industry. For instance, leading software participants such as IBM's current software strategy incorporates customer relationship management, value chain management and enterprise resource planning. Enterprise Resource Planning software, which manages firms' operational tasks such as human resource management, accounting, production control, materials requirements, has grown from US$5,700 million in 1995 to US$18,400 million in 1999[12]. Table 8.3 shows that the German firm SAP shared 30 per cent of the total revenues in the ERP market while US firms Oracle, PeopleSoft, J.D. Edwards and SCT also had 30 per cent of the market in 1999.

Table 8.3: Leading ERP Software Firms Worldwide (By Revenue)

	Nationality	Market share
SAP	German	30%
Oracle	US	14%
PeopleSoft	US	8%
J.D. Edwards	US	5%
Geac SmartEnterprise Solution	Canadian	5%
Baan	Dutch	3%
SCT	US	3%

Source: AMR Research as quoted in Chemical Market Reporter 25 September 2000.

E-Commerce software is a segment of E-business software. E-business software was worth about US$13,500 million in 2000, and accounted for

13 per cent of the corporate software market.[13] E-commerce is a fast growing segment that has surged from US$1,700 million in 1999 to US$3,900 million in 2000, and is expected to increase to US$6,400 million in 2001 as well as US$14,900 million in 2003.[14] It focuses on the buying and selling activities of firms such as building product catalogues, collecting payments and tracking deliveries. Leading firms in this segment include US firms BEA Systems, BroadVision and IBM. E-Commerce has been employed successfully in the travel industry such as car rentals, airline tickets and hotel reservations. One of the European ventures that has prospered within this new segment is the Irish firm Datalex which specialises in internet air ticket reservation software. Datalex was found in 1985 and by 2000 it had achieved US$33 million in sales revenues. Its clientele includes British Airways, QUANTAS, Lufthansa, Thomas Cook, Air Canada, American Airlines...[15].

Customer relationship management software (CRM), which has been estimated to increase by 50 per cent and with a market value of US$9,800 million in 2001[16], is designed to streamline the contact points between a firm and its customers in both pre-sales and after-sales services (e.g. call centres). The leader in this area is the US firm Siebel, which shared over one-third of this expanding market segment despite competition from firms such as Oracle and PeopleSoft. Siebel had grown faster than any firm in the US software industry by 2000. After merely seven years since its formation, it has attained more than US$1,000 million sales revenues in 2000. An industry commentator, however, recently warned that the biggest threat for Siebel are new Silicon Valley upstarts such as E.piphany and Kana Communications who designed their software from the ground up for the Internet.[17]

Finally, Supply Chain Management software (SCM) which supports both supply chain processes such as ordering, inventory, logistics, transportation and warehousing, has been estimated to be able to reduce at least ten per cent of a firm's expenses associated with price fluctuation in inventory. Leading firms in SCM software for the manufacturing industry include the US firms i2Technologies whose sales revenues were about US$1,200 million in 2000. The advantages of SCM software can be seen in the consumer electronics firm Panasonic's subsidiary in North America. Its implementation of i2Technologies' software has enabled it to reduce the time it takes to order parts from suppliers and then deliver the finished products to retailers by 75 per cent. The software also enables it to collect sales information from retailers and then estimate the demand for its products as well as the appropriate level of inventory[18].

INDIVIDUALISM AND PRODUCT DESIGN CAPABILITY

The launch of software involves three stages: design, production and marketing. The design process is a critical stage and can be defined as the process of applying various techniques and principles for the purpose of defining a process in sufficient detail to permit its physical realisation. Budgen (1993) suggested that the designer's goal was to produce a model or representation of an entity that will later be built. Yet, he pointed out that software design methodology lacked the depth and quantitative nature associated with classical engineering design disciplines. Human capital in terms of programmers that can design a technically sophisticated program rather than one that simply functions, is critical. Brooks (1987) stated that great software designs came from great designers rather than good designers; he wrote that 'the differences are not minor — they are rather like the differences between Salieri and Mozart. Study after study shows that the very best designers produce structures that are faster, smaller, simpler, cleaner and produced with less effort' (p. 18). Other studies that support the importance of talented programmers include Curtis et al (1988) and Blackburn et al. (1996) and it is well established that the work of talented programmers is essential towards success in the software industry. The way established software firms organised their product design activity has been described as follows:

> Many cash-rich technology companies produced software by hiring as many top-level programmers as possible — regardless of how much it cost to recruit and retain them. Once assembled, the programmers were closeted in offices for weeks or months to bang out code. The individual efforts were then glued together and submitted to the long process of debugging[19].

A historical review of successful software has substantiated the importance of human capital in the design of software. A widely discussed successful venture that attests to the significance of individual talents is Adobe Systems' desktop publishing and electronic document software. Adobe was founded by the PhD engineers John Warnock and Charles Geschke in 1982. It developed the PostScript Page Description Language that linked microcomputers to any connected printers. Commenting on the firm's landmark product, John Warnock stated that 'I think meaningful document standards will emerge over the next five years. There is a need for an abstraction layer that is independent of operating systems'.[20] The rise of Adobe was linked to Apple's Steve

Jobs' appreciation of its significance. Warnock described the meeting when Apple agreed to acquire 20 per cent of the firm as well as provide it with an advance against its royalties as follows:

> I remember the contract meeting with Apple CEO John Sculley, board member Al Eisenstadt, and Jobs. Eisenstadt said, 'Let me get this straight. We're giving this no-name company — they haven't even been in business a year — a million-dollar advance plus two-and-a-half-million dollars in cash. We have no guarantee that they can deliver and we're doing this just on pure faith?' And Steve said, 'Yup. That's right'.[21]

Similarly, the Irish firm Iona which was founded in 1991 by distributed computing researchers Chris Horn, Annrai O'Toole and Sean Baker of Trinity College, has demonstrated the importance of human capital in successful software ventures. Horn recalled that Iona faced some opposition from the faculties at Trinity College as well as scepticism from state agencies; he added that 'we literally put about £1,000 each in, and bootstrapped it from there'.[22] In 1992, IONA shipped the Orbix, a product that enabled distributed computers and software systems to work together collaboratively as well as building the foundation for its ascendancy in the software industry during the 1990s.

Other successful software firms were also equipped with human capital. Sun's Chief Scientist Bill Joy, who has always been associated with vision and innovation, has had a profound impact on the industry's development. A recent article published in the Economist provided the following account of Joy:

> As a graduate student at Berkeley in the late 1970s, Mr Joy rewrote AT&T's Unix operating system to give it the strength and reliability demanded by enterprises chaffing at the high cost and inflexibility of mainframes... After becoming a co-founder of Sun Microsystems in his late 20s, Mr Joy wrote an even more robust version of Unix, called Solaris...[23]

Again, Sun's Java was developed mainly by one of its programming talents, James Gosling. Gosling spoke unequivocally of the project work that led to the emergence of Java as follows:

> What we decided to do was to build a prototype remote control home network system for controlling TVs and VCRs. We coined a technique we called 'hammer technology' we would take something, hammer them apart, grab the bits and pieces out of them, then hammer them together... We started

building it using the standard software tools, but the tools we were using just weren't working. It was one of these places where languages came to the rescue. So I went off into a corner and I built this compiler and programming language that eventually turned into Java.[24]

A recent report compiled by the US International Trade Commission also pointed out the role of human capital on the speed of development of packaged applications software and its subsequent impact on firm competitiveness. It used an example in the PC spreadsheet market to demonstrate Microsoft's speed in introducing the Windows-based Excel which enabled it to undermine the dominant position that Lotus 1-2-3 held in the DOS-based spreadsheet market. This report also highlighted that creative individuals working in a team environment was most conducive to the speed of product development (based on expert opinions collected by USITC staff in 1994).[25] Creativity is, without a doubt, an essential attribute evidenced in recruitment among software firms. The following advertisements by Sun and Microsoft underlie the industry's emphasis on creativity:

> Recruiting is Microsoft's No. 1 core competency. We are after smart folks who are fired up about improving people's lives via software, no matter where they live... If you've got the talent, creativity, and experience we're looking for, we put the latest technology and virtually unlimited resources at your disposal. Then we'll give you the flexibility you need to take full advantage of some incredible opportunities. Ready to soar?[26]

> Sun Labs, the research division of Sun Microsystems, is looking for talented, creative individuals interested in setting industry trends and breaking new ground through research, collaboration and implementation of new technologies. Our scientists, researchers, and engineers come to us from all over the world to enjoy an innovative, exciting and fun-filled environment that fosters creativity and incubates their ideas into real products.[27]

Furthermore, software firms have endeavoured to maintain an environment that enhanced individual creativity in order to derive the maximum productivity from their stock of human capital. Matheson and Tarjan (1998) highlighted the need for creative environment in software design as follows:

> Few things are as important to new software ventures as new ideas. To nurture new ideas, especially deep, proprietary ideas, research environments

need to preserve creative freedoms and provide support. Research laboratories are designed to provide this kind of environment. Indeed, many large technology companies, including AT&T, IBM, DEC, Microsoft, and Xerox, have produced a successful research environment.

Microsoft's UK Research Director Roger Needham echoed this view and mentioned that 'the way you get very good ideas is you get the best people and give them the freedom to think and experiment and let their imaginations rip'.[28] For example, Microsoft's new Silicon Valley Campus that was opened in 2000 is employee-focused, it contains private offices, an employee library and an in-house store. This new investment supports the firm's value of providing employees space and encouraging them to challenge conventional wisdom. In terms of the design process, the importance of creativity in software was indicated by Jones (1970):

> Designers are obliged to use current information to predict a future state that will not come about unless their predictions are correct. The final outcome of designing has to be assumed before the means of achieving it can be explored: the designers have to work backwards in time from an assumed effect upon the world to the beginning of a chain of events that will bring the effect about.

So what is creativity? Moustakas (1967 p. 27) explained that 'to be creative means to experience life in one's own way, to perceive from one's own person, to draw upon one's own resources, capacities, roots'. The creativity required in the problem-solving within software design, which has been illustrated by the above quotation from Jones can be contrasted with the analytical technique in the scientific approach to problem-solving. The scientific process focuses on investigation; the researcher constructs a theory and then proceeds to test its validity. As a contrast, the software process concentrates on achieving a goal. The designer specifies the requirement and designs software around it. The designer than builds the software and validates its usefulness against the requirement specification.

In his comment on the early creators of personal computer software, Campbell-Kelly (1995 p. 93) stated that they possessed 'creative flair and the technical knowledge of a bright, first-year computer science student'. Stross (1996 p. 39) also described the human resource criteria for software production as 'conceptual creativity, speed, ingenuity of design or problem-solving ability'. Certainly the most appropriate description of the creativity involved in software development is to compare it to an art. Bill Gates (1996 p. 18) who founded Microsoft in 1975 with his high school colleague Paul Allen described the experience of creating the firm's first product BASIC as a process parallel to creativity in art: 'Sometimes I rock back and forth or pace when I'm thinking because it helps me focus on a single idea and exclude distractions... Paul and I didn't sleep much and lost track of night and day... Some days I didn't eat or see anyone'. As in the arts, the type of creativity required in software writing cannot be taught. Bill Gates commented in 1993 that Microsoft could teach new programmers specific skill areas, but it could not teach them creativity.[29] The difficulty in imparting creativity is due to the elusive nature of the topic. The imagination required in software design described by an official from the Association of Data Processing Service Organisations (ADAPSO): 'You can't pick it up and imitate it so easily. You can't carve it, measure it; you can't even see it'.[30]

Some US firms even adopt an informal practice in the management of software developments so as to harness its creative aspects. Indeed, a recent study by Carmel and Becker (1995) revealed that only one out of 12 US packaged software firms followed the formal step-by-step standard procedure of specification, design, test and prototype in software development. They found that most firms 'allocated little development effort to formal specifications, design, documentation, or formalised testing'; in addition, 'several firms were still dominated or influenced by the 'hacker culture' that is generally averse to many of the formalisms of quality control' (ibid. p. 55). Table 8.4 provides a breakdown of firms' practices and shows that 17 per cent of them did not even have any procedure regarding specifying the requirement of the project.

Table 8.4: Informal Development among US Software Firms

	Formal	Informal	None
Specification	25%	58%	17%
Design	33%	67%	0%
Test	50%	50%	0%
Prototype	58%	8%	25%

Note: Only 11 responses for the prototype stage, hence the total percentage adds up to 91%.
Source: Carmel and Becker (1995 p. 56).

SOFTWARE AND BACKWARD LINKAGE STRATEGY

Table 8.5 shows US and Asia Pacific microcomputer firms' involvement in concept-intensive software. It can be seen that the US firms IBM, Hewlett-Packard, Sun, Compaq and Silicon Graphics have integrated into operating systems and other areas of software such as middleware. IBM has a strong position in software, its 8,000 software sales specialists enabled the firm to generate nearly US$13,000 of sales revenues in software in 2000. An analyst from ABN Amro commented that 'IBM has a database, Lotus, Tivoli and middleware to draw on'.[31] Actually, IBM's software sales accounted for about 15 per cent of its total sales, but about one-third of its profits in 2000. The aforementioned US firms operate their software businesses within internal divisions as well as within various independent wholly-owned or jointly-owned ventures. Sun, however, organised its software businesses under Sun ONE (Sun Open Net Environment), encompassing Solaris, Java, Forte, iPlanet and its alliance with AOL and Time Warner in September 2001.

Table 8.5 also shows that Japanese firms that have acquired experience in mainframe software since the 1960s have established software subsidiaries such as NEC Soft and Fujitsu Support and Service in order to engage in software research. Fujitsu's software development is also undertaken in Glovia[32] and Teamware[33]. Glovia is a Californian firm that specialises in ERP software products for manufacturer's material requirements and stocktaking. Glovia achieved a sales revenue of US$52 million in 1999; its ERP product has been implemented in Fujitsu's manufacturing plants in Thailand, China, Vietnam and Korea. Its Philippines hard disk drive facility reported that the ERP software enabled its 8,000 employee operation to smoothly handle in 1999 an output of 1.6 million disk drives a month.

The overall pattern of integration among microcomputer firms is summarised in Table 8.6. It can be seen that five out of seven US microcomputer firms and three out of seven Asia Pacific firms (i.e. all Japanese firms) have pursued integration in software. An interesting feature of Japanese firms that pursued integration in software is that they had established facilities in the Silicon Valley by 2000. The Japanese firm Fujitsu's presence in the Silicon Valley included Amdahl, Glovia and Fujitsu Software while NEC owns a research laboratory in San Jose that was established back in 1972. By establishing subsidiaries in the Silicon Valley, Japanese firms, in theory, will be able to tap into America's strength in software. In fact, Canon's Director of R&D, Toru Takahashi, also acknowledged the creativity in the firm's US subsidiary; he commented that 'we used to think we should keep research and development in Japan, but that has changed. As for creativity, we have to admit that the Americans are better.'[34]

Table 8.5: US and Asia Pacific Firms and Software, 2001

	Software Segments
IBM	Middleware/ Connectivity/Application Servers/Web Servers/Operating Systems/Infrastructure
HP	Infrastructure/Systems Management/Middleware/ Connectivity/Operating Systems
Sun	Middleware/Connectivity/Application Development/ Operating Systems/Servers Testing Tools
Compaq	Operating Systems/Sourcing
SGI	Operating Systems
Fujitsu	Enterprise Application Suites/ Application Servers/ Network/Systems Management
NEC	Operating Systems/Middleware/Database
Toshiba	Network/Systems Management/Project Management

Source: Software Magazine June 2001 and various annual reports.

Table 8.6: Individualism and Integration in Software

	Individualism	Not individualism
Integration	5	3
Not integration	2	4

Source: Various.

Table 8.7 illustrates the competitiveness of microcomputer firms in software. US firms Sun and Hewlett-Packard attained at least a three-fold increase in software revenues between 1995 and 1998; Sun's revenues grew from US$325 million to US$1,368 million whereas Hewlett-Packard's software revenues increased from USS$782 million to US$1,412 million.

Hewlett-Packard's software revenues as incorporated in the broader classification of IT services was US$7,129 million in 2000. The growth of their software revenues were parallel to the emergence of successful software ventures in the US during the 1990s. For example, over 40 per cent of US firms in the Software 500[35] in 2001 were founded after 1990. Despite the decline in custom software for large systems, US firms IBM and Compaq maintained their international positions in software by building on segments in which they traditionally had strengths. For instance, IBM's leading middleware products including Websphere (web application server software), MQSeries (business integration software) and DB2 (data management) have generated greater software revenues. Its Lotus and Tivoli divisions have also achieved substantial sales revenues for the firm.

Though Japanese firms have also engaged in software production, their overall growth in software portfolio is behind the growth of the market. Fujitsu suffered a sharp decline in software revenues from US$6,432 million in 1995 to US$2,690 million in 2000. Despite its efforts to globalise, Fujitsu's software revenues still depended heavily on sales in Japan (which accounted for about 70 per cent of total software sales in 2000). NEC 's software revenues had also increased from US$2,322 million from 1995 to US$3,184 million in 2000 (i.e. an increase of 37 per cent), the increase was based, however, primarily on the growth of its service revenues in Japan.

Table 8.7: Software Revenues among Microcomputer Firms

	Software Revenues (US$ million)	
	1995	2000
IBM	12,949.2	12,598.0
HP	782.2	1,412.0
Sun	325.0	1,367.3
Compaq	1,299.6	1,174.0
Fujitsu	6,431.5	2,690.3
NEC	2,322.0	3,183.5

Note: Compaq's 1995 revenue included that of Digital.
Source: Software revenues for 1995 were based on Datamation 15 June 1996 and do not include software embedded in electronics products. Software revenues for 2000 were based on various 2001 Reports and included computer services. However, software revenues for HP, Sun and Compaq were based on 1998 revenue as quoted in Software Magazine June 1999.

The exhibited pattern of US and Asia Pacific microcomputer firms' competitiveness in software should be examined in the context of the wider discussion concerning US firms' overall strength as well as the persistent weakness among Asia Pacific firms (especially Japanese firms). The case of Japan deserved special attention as it had consciously attempted to strengthen its position internationally.[36] During the 1980s, there had been considerable optimism in Japan on catching up with the product design capability of US software firms, which was reflected in an article in the Business Week:

> The boom in software packages in Japan has been fuelled largely by the nations' growing market for personal computers. About 2,000 applications software packages are now available for Japanese personal computer owners. But by 1985, predicts Kunio Goto, chief researcher at the Japan Research Institute, this will soar to 10,000 to 15,000 microcomputer programs, most of them written by companies with just three to five people and annual revenues of $10,000 to $40,000.[37]

There had been a debate prior to the early 1990s concerning the relative performance of the US and Japan in the software industry. On the one hand, some stated that there had been a continual weakness in the Japanese software industry (e.g. Sakai 1984; Rifkin and Savage 1989; Lewis 1989...); on the other hand, it was claimed that Japanese firms had caught up with US firms in the process of software development or the final software product (e.g.Tajima and Matsubara 1981; Cusumano 1991). Cusumano (ibid. p.5) put it as follows:

> Japanese firms have competed successfully in industries ranging from automobiles and video recorders to machine tools, semiconductor chips, and computer hardware... If Japanese firms were to transfer the same type of skills they have cultivated in other industries to software, which seemed likely only to grow in importance as a technology because of its critical role in so many industries and organisations, users would become better off, with improved products at lower prices.

The second proposition inevitably led to the conclusion that in the long run Japanese software firms (like their electronics counterparts) would threaten the dominant market position of US industry. Managers who embraced such views pointed out that Japanese firms were able to design successful consumer electronics and cars to launch in the US market, hence there was no reason why they could not produce software products for the US market. A software manager in Japan commented in 1981: 'people say that the Japanese have problems developing software, but that is wishful thinking'.[38] Overall, the thinking behind the scepticism of Japan's software development is based on the premise that Japanese firms are imitators rather than inventors. However, writers such as Abegglen and Stalk (1985 p.146) argued that 'successful imitation, far from being symptomatic of lack of originality as used to be thought, is the first step of learning to be creative. This is probably true of nations, as it seems to be of individuals, something which Americans may have forgotten in our almost obsessive belief in originality and individual creativity'.

Unable to establish the software industry internationally, a more subdued view among Japanese firms had gradually emerged by the mid-1990s. Japanese managers switched from the idea of building an indigenous microcomputer software to a conciliatory position of external procurement as suggested in the comment that 'our educational system does not allow for the creativity that is necessary to develop software. However, software is tradeable and can easily be sent across borders so we don't need to develop it in Japan'.[39]

Some US managers in the computer industry already mentioned as early as 1980 that writing software was more akin to producing a work of art than to building a machine and they predicted difficulties for Japanese firms who attempted to overtake US firms.[40] The following quotes highlight that the collective core value in Japan constitutes the basic weakness for competing in the software industry:

Bro Uttal, a technology reporter, summarised one of the often cited reasons for Japanese firms' lack of innovative software as: 'A nation that lives by consensus, imposes strict social conformity' would seem to discourage creativity in software.[41]

Rieko Mashima, an attorney who was interested in the interaction of technology and law commented that: 'Innovative individualism, necessary for developing high-quality software, conflicts with the group-oriented corporate culture in Japan. The history of software development, especially that of the leading software companies, has shown that technological innovation can be achieved by a capable individual or a small group as long as they are willing to be creative and innovative. In Japan, however, such individualism is not encouraged'. She further reported that Kazuhiko Nishi, the president of Japan's software firm ASCII, 'feels that Japanese scientists and engineers do not respect things that are different and tend to avoid them, while familiarising themselves with those things that are familiar.'[42]

Professor Nicholas Negroponte, the director of MIT Media Lab[43] (which is known for its visionary approach to the digital age) commented that: 'Japan's inability to produce software is deeply rooted in their culture... A transition won't happen without a major culture change. What makes a good hacker is not education but a series of things that are all very un-Japanese'.[44]

The general lack of original creation in Asia Pacific firms has been commented on by various writers. Ronsenberg and Steinmueller (1986 p. 230) stated that 'the Japanese have been very successful in borrowing and developing technologies initially created by American firms. These technologies have been largely of a hardware nature, in particular, a stream of highly visible product innovations'. Similarly, Korean firms and Taiwanese firms have also been regarded as lacking creativity. One reporter stated that 'rarely have Korean firms come up with truly innovative products; many times they have pinched a good idea – whether a logo, a semiconductor design or a manufacturing process – from foreigners'; Samsung's chairman echoed this view and considered the firm urgently needed 'a revolution of minds' and to incorporate 'a more creative culture' in 1994.[45] The growth of the Taiwanese computer industry is also based on imitation, i.e. reverse engineering of American products rather than product innovation.

The cultural implication for software development is reviewed further in a study of a Japanese firm's US subsidiary undertaken by Matheson and Tarjan (1998). They found that various cultural differences adversely affected the information flows between the parent and the subsidiary; specifically, they suggested that a clash of values between the individualistic US design team and the collective outlook of the Japanese parent is detrimental towards the understanding of the parent and the subsidiary. They remarked that 'US high-tech employees taking risks expect to be compensated well and to retain some decision rights. Japanese employees expect to sacrifice for the company now to obtain rewards based on seniority later' (ibid. p. 33).

SOFTWARE FACTORIES AND *KAIZEN*

Another interesting theme that arises from the distinctive approach among Japanese software firms is software development, which adheres to a mass production factory system. This contrasts with the notion of individual craftsmanship in US firms. Japanese firms concentrate on formal procedures, which advocate systematic refinements and innovations that draw from task division and standard practices, tools and techniques; US firms place greater emphasis on individual workmanship and rely on talented programmers working in small teams with flexible structure and processes. Richards and Reid (1990) elaborated on the differences between Japanese and US firms' approaches to tools[46] in terms of the former focus on expertise through a continuous process of refinement while the latter leaped quickly from one tool to another, using different tool in different projects.

Japanese firms' formal procedures have been implemented in the software factories of Fujitsu and NEC as listed in Table 8.8. The imagery of the software factory was vividly captured by an industry correspondent:

> Closed-packed rows of workers type lines of code onto standardised forms displayed on computer terminals hooked up to a massive mainframe. The forms make up modules of the program, which begin and end with standard codes used for linking the modules to make a full-blown program. Some factories use 'applications generators', software that automatically turns a description of what a program should do into a rough draft of the program itself. The more advanced shops boast production tools such as Hitachi's software for converting flow charts — diagrams of how a program manipulates data — into lines of computer instructions and for analysing improved versions of those instructions to make sure they conform to the original flow chart.[47]

Table 8.8: Software Factories of NEC and Fujitsu

Firm	Facilities	Year of Establishment	No. of Employees 1988–89
NEC	Fuchu Works	1976	2,500
	Mita Works	1976	4,000
	Abiko Works	1976	1,500
	Tamagawa Works	1976	1,500
Fujitsu	Numazu Works	1974	3,000
	Kamata Software Factory	1979	5,500

Source: Cusumano (1991 p.7)

Paradoxically, the original concept of the software factory could be traced to the experiments in American firms such as AT&T and IBM. IBM implemented the factory system with the design of its operating systems for the System 360 mainframes in the mid 1960s. However, it soon terminated the experiment. The lack of support for the software factory eventually lead to the fading out of this approach in the US. The Japanese experience of software factories, on the other hand, was rather different. Japan's first software factory was the Hitachi Software Works, a five-story structure established in 1969. This project employed 3,000 programmers and had two main goals: improved productivity and reliability through process standardisation and control as well as transformed software from an unstructured service to a product with a guaranteed level of quality. Though the Hitachi Software Works did not achieve tremendous success, other Japanese firms such as Fujitsu and NEC were keen to experiment with the factory system.

The popularity of the software factory system in Japan supports the notion that practices which correspond with a nation's core value would be more easily received by its firms. The factory approach is reinforced by Japan's core value of *kaizen*, where managers believe that continuous improvement is applicable to software development. Such strong conviction has in fact been observed by some writers. Cusumano (1991 p. 428) wrote that: 'Japanese firms that launched factory efforts in the 1960s and 1970s demonstrated a stubborn commitment, not always reinforced by initial results, to analysing, standardising, and then improving the process of software development'. Commenting on this mass production trend in the Japanese software industry, Maital (1990 p. 6) also wrote: 'Japanese executives have an almost heretical conviction that software is not an unmanageable technology'.

CONCLUSION

The pattern of integration among US and Asia Pacific firms which emerged from the discussion in this chapter supports the cultural thesis. It asserts that the pattern of integration contains a cultural element that is operationalised in terms of core cultural values; individualism which impedes microcomputer firms' product design capabilities will lead to different patterns of integrated linkage. In particular, product design capabilities required for software design are derived from the core value of individualism embodied in US firms. On the other hand, the core value of collectivism is not conducive to Asia Pacific firms' integration into software. It therefore provides an explanation as to the reason why Japanese firms' substantial investment in software did not yield highly successful results as compared to under-resourced firms from the individualist nations. The discussion in this chapter further reveals the interwoven pattern of cultural value and firm capability in Europe and Japan. Interestingly enough, recently emerged European firms such as SAP, IONA and Datalex also originate from cultures endowed with the core value of individualism while Japanese firms software development that utilise the factory approach correspond with their core value of *kaizen.*

NOTES

---

[1] Philippe Kahn resigned as Chairman of the firm in 1996.

[2] See R. Brandt 'Can the US stay ahead in software?', *Business Week,* 11 March 1991 p. 62.

[3] Quoted from Dan Bricklin 'The twenty most important people', *BYTE,* September 1995 p. 138.

[4] 'IDC puts the worldwide packaged software market at 154 billion in 1999', *IDC Press Release,* 25 January 2000.

[5] Software 500 as complied by *Software Magazine,* see June–July issue 2000.

[6] Siobhan Almond, 'Irish software startups ready to grow', *Headway Software Press Release,* 9 May 2001.

[7] Steve Mills, 'IBM's Software Strategy', *IBM.com site,* 31 January 2002. IBM also classified Middleware (software that functions in client/server systems) as another major software category; the total revenue for the Middleware segment was estimated at about US$127,000 million in 2000.

[8] Though entertainment software has played a secondary role in the past decade, it should be noted that its importance has been increasingly addressed by software firms. Most notably, the leading software firm Microsoft has expanded from business applications to games software and simulations in recent years.

[9] Spencer E. Ante, Jim Kerstetter and Jay Greene 'The New Software Whizzes', *Business Week,* 11 December 2000 pp. EB30–40.

[10] AMR is based in Boston.

[11] See Software 500, *Software Magazine,* June–July 2000.

[12] The market estimation is provided by AMR Research as quoted *in Modern Materials Handling* February 2001 Volume 56 Issue 2.

[13] E-business software incorporate areas such as E-procurement, E-marketing and E-marketplaces. Spencer E. Ante, Jim Kerstetter and Jay Greene 'The New Software Whizzes', *Business Week,* 11 December 2000 p. EB30–40.

[14] Estimation of E-commerce software was reported in Spencer E. Ante, Jim Kerstetter and Jay Greene (op. cit.) and Jim Kerstetter 'Software', *Business Week,* 8 January 2001 p. 96.

[15] *Datalet.com site* 3 May 2001.

[16] Jim Kerstetter 'Software', *Business Week,* 8 January 2001.

[17] Jim Kerstetter 'The hottest of the hot spots', *Business Week,* 8 January 2001 p. 96.

[18] Reported in an interview with Panasonic's President Michael Aguilar, 'Software Highfliers', *Business Week,* 18 June 2001 p. 108.

[19] Cecily Barnes 'More programmers going Extreme', *CNET News.com site,* 3 April 2001.

[20] Dan Bricklin 'The twenty most important people', *BYTE,* September 1995 p. 138.

[21] Jager and Oritz (1997 p. 106).

[22] See Karlin Lillington, 'Iona thinks radical in recasting of core business', *The Irish Times,* 23 March 2001.

[23] See 'Strength through Joy', *The Economist,* 7 August 1999 p. 70.

[24] Interview with James Gosling by Paul Taylor, 'The man who invented Java', *The Financial Times,* Review of Information Technology 4 February 1998 p.III.

[25] Quoted in OECD's 1991 Publication, *Software Engineering: The Policy Challenge,* OECD Information Computer Communications Policy.

[26] Quoted from *Microsoft.com site,* 21 April 2001.

[27] Quoted from *Sun.com site,* 21 February 2001.

[28] Interview by Dana Rubin, 'Bill's boffin bares (nearly) all', *The Independent on Sunday,* 22 February Business Section p. III.

[29] See Randall E. Stross (1998) *The Microsoft Way,* London, UK: Warner Books.

[30] This comment was made by Doug Jerger of ADAPSO, the predecessor of the Information Technology Assoication of America (ITAA), in Teresa Wantanabe, 'Software: Japan trying to catch up with US', *Los Angeles Times,* 8 July 1990 D17.

[31] Lisa DiCarlo, 'HP is no IBM', *Forbes.com site,* 5 September 2001.

[32] Glovia International LLC, formerly a joint venture with McDonnell Information Systems' Chess business unit, is currently a 100 per cent Fujitsu subsidiary.

[33] TeamWARE was previously a joint venture between Fujitsu and ICL. It is a supplier of collaborative PC software.

[34] Toru Takahashi's comment was reported in 'Management: Time to pull back the screen', *The Financial Times,* 18 November 1996, p. 14. Canon's main business activities are cameras and business machines (i.e. printers and photocopiers); however, it is also involved in activities such as semiconductor production equipment. Canon attempted to enter the microcomputer market during the 1980s, but without much success.

[35] Software 500 is an annual ranking of the largest software firms worldwide by sales revenue. It is published in *Software Magazine.*

[36] Writers such as Anchordoguy (2000) as well as Kim and Choi (1997) argued that the weakness of Japan' software industry lay in institutional arrangements such as a weak intellectual property regime, a centralised, bank-centred financial system that discouraged innovation, entrepreneurship and

individuality, the state targeting policies and the dominance of industrial groups.

[37] See 'Attempting to overcome the US lead in software' in Japan's Strategy for the '80s (Special Report), *Business Week*, 14 December 1981 pp. 57–8.

[38] The comment was made by William Totten, a manager of packaged application software distributor K.K.Ashisuto in *Business Week* Report (op. cit.) 14 December 1981 p. 14.

[39] Dr Mori, Manager, R & D Planning Department, Technical Development Group, Kobe Steel as quoted in Sigvald Harryson (1994) *Japanese Technology and Innovation Management*, Cheltenham, UK: Edward Elgar p. 17.

[40] See *Business Week* Report (op. cit.) 14 December 1981 p. 55

[41] Bro Uttal 'Japan's persistent software gap' *Fortune*, 15 October 1984 p. 115.

[42] See R. Mashima (1996) 'The turning point for Japanese software companies: can they compete in the prepackaged software market?' *Berkeley Technology Law Journal* p. 457.

[43] Massachusetts Institute of Technology's Media Laboratory was established in 1985, it specialised in research concerning the invention and creative use of digital technologies.

[44] Interview by Glenn Rifkin and J.A. Savage 'Is the U.S. ready for Japan software push?', *Computerworld*, 8 May 1989 p. 114.

[45] *London Times*, 18 October 1994.

[46] Examples of tools include programs that enable firms to predict how long their projects will take or how many errors programmers were likely to made.

[47] See Bro Uttal (op.cit.).

9. Continuous Improvement and Manufacturing Process

A recent study by Iansiti and West (1997) which compared the research and development projects of US, Japanese and Korean integrated circuit manufacturers between 1990 and 1995 highlighted differences among the three nations' approach. They found that US projects concentrated on novelty and were substantially ahead of the long-term industry technology trajectory. Japanese projects were concerned with the improvement of actual product performance within existing technologies. Korean projects, on the other hand, combined both technological orientations.

The analysis of the total value of microcomputer components in the earlier Table 3.2 has highlighted that integrated circuits are significant in terms of their contribution towards the total cost of production in microcomputers. Integrated circuits are a great number of transistors, resistors, capacitors and pathways etched onto the silicon substrate at microscopic dimensions. For example, Intel's Pentium 6 incorporates over five million transistors. The basis of integrated circuits is the semiconductor, made of a material such as silicon whose conductivity lies between that of most metals and that of insulators. The semiconductor is then transferred to integrated circuits through an extremely sophisticated technological manufacturing process.

Integrated circuits incorporate product segments such as memory, microprocessors and application-specific integrated circuits. The leading products within the memory integrated circuit segments, the dynamic random access memory (DRAM), the static random access memory (SRAM) and the read only memory (ROM) are all important components for the configuration of microcomputers.

The dynamic random access memory is a type of random access memory (RAM). It holds data or programs which are read in, processed, modified and written out to storage, printer or screen. When the microcomputer is switched on, its RAM acts as the workspace of the processor. In other words, a working version of the software program is copied from the hard disk drive into the RAM for quick access. The program will later be saved to the hard disk for permanent storage before the system is switched off. The size of DRAM module specified in a microcomputer is represented by the number of bytes; the standard prefix for describing them are kilo (K) for thousand, mega (M) for million, giga (G) for billion and tera (T) for trillion.[1] One of Dell's Dimension model desktop computer was designed with, for instance, a minimum of 128M byte Synchronous DRAM.[2] The 128M byte module can be made up by eight 128M bit[3] parts. Alternatively, one can use four 256M bit parts to add up to 128M bytes.

This chapter seeks to demonstrate how the Japanese and Korean core values of continuous improvement or *kaizen* create a predisposition supportive of their national firms' process manufacturing capabilities in capital-intensive components such as DRAM, which contribute to their pursuit of integration. The following sections contain firstly a brief review of the market development in DRAM and an explanation of the process improvement that is essential for DRAM production. Afterwards, I will discuss the relationship between the core value of *kaizen* and microcomputer firms' integration in DRAM. The final two sections will deal with the competitive dynamics of firms that are not equipped with the core value of *kaizen*.

MARKET DEVELOPMENT IN DRAM

Dynamic random access memory includes architectures such as the Fast Page Mode DRAM, Extended Data Output DRAM, the Synchronous DRAM, the Rambus DRAM and the Double Data Rate DRAM. The first two architectures were widely adopted in microcomputers prior to the late 1990s whereas Synchronous DRAM, Rambus DRAM and Double Data Rate DRAM are currently utilised as memory for microcomputers. For example, the clienteles of Nanya Technology's Double Data Rate DRAMs and Synchronous DRAMs in 2001 included Compaq, Acer, IBM, Dell, HP, Toshiba, NEC and Fujitsu-Siemens.[4] Nanya Technology was founded as an own-brand DRAM producer in Taiwan in 1995; however, it had diversified into contract manufacturing service in 1999.

DRAM stores data in millions of minute cells and is dynamic because each of these cells consists of a capacitor that needs to be constantly recharged with minute electrical pulses. Hence, data that is stored in DRAM will be lost when the system is switched off. The key issue connected with insufficient DRAM in a microcomputer is the possible restriction of the range of available software that can be run on the system as well as a decrease in the speed of execution of certain programs, such as databases or statistics. In fact, each new generation of software tends to require more memory; Microsoft's Windows XP operation system, for instance, runs on a minimum of 128M bytes (128MB).

The DRAM segment of integrated circuits achieved a total revenue of approximately US$21,000 million in 1999 and shared 12 per cent of the worldwide semiconductor market.[5] As a result of the recent collapse in the prices of DRAM, this estimated value was paradoxically lower than its total value attained during the mid-1990s, where the DRAM market was nearly US$40,000 million and constituted approximately 25 per cent of total semiconductor revenue.[6]

Table 9.1: Leading Memory Integrated Circuit Segments in 1999

	Global Market Value
Dynamic Random Access Memory	US$20.7 billion
Static Random Access Memory	US$4.7 billion
Very fast Synchronous SRAM	US$2.4 billion
Flash Memory	US$4.6 billion
Total Semiconductor Revenue	US$169 billion

Note: A billion is a thousand million.
Source: Semiconductor Research Corporation as quoted in micron.com site (2001).

Intel launched the world's first dynamic random access memory in 1971. The innovation, which was a 1K DRAM named Intel 1103, dominated the US memory market by 1972. The evolution of DRAM since then have progressed rapidly from 4K, 16K, 64K, 256K, 4MB, 16MB, 64MB, 256MB and 1GB in the following decades. It should be noted that parallel with the advance in the capacity of the standard DRAM chip, the cost per megabyte of DRAM has paradoxically declined from US$16,500 in 1976 to US$1 in 1999.[7] The current technological trend in DRAM is reflected in Korea's approximately US$4,400 million DRAM exports in 2001, which were composed of 48 per cent 128MB DRAM, 28 per cent 64MB DRAM and 13 per cent 256MB DRAM.

Table 9.2 shows the specifications of recent DRAM technology, it can be seen that they all involve building chips with silicon structures of, or smaller than, 0.5 microns. For instance, DRAM chips with configuration of 1G bits (1Gb) have to squeeze more than 1,000 million circuit elements onto a 500 square millimetres of silicon; this will require reducing the size of the features to 0.18 microns and less than 0.01 defects per square millimetre. Furthermore, the technology for the next generation 4Gb DRAM announced by Samsung in 2001 will apply 0.10 micron design rule to achieve a capacity to store data that is equivalent of 32,000 standard newspaper pages, 1,600 still photographs or 64 hours of recorded audio.[8]

Table 9.2: Technology for the Generations of DRAMs during the 1990s

	16Mb	64Mb	256Mb	1Gb
Chip Size (square millimetres)	132	200	320	500
Feature Size (microns*)	0.5	0.35	0.25	0.18
Gates per chip (million)	0.3	0.8	2	5
Number of input/output pins	500	750	1,500	2,000

Note: *A micron or a micrometre (μm) is 0.5 thousandths of a millimetre (mm); a human hair is about 100 microns in diameter and cigarette paper is about 25 microns thick.
Source: Semiconductor Industry Association (2000).

The advance in production technology affects the profitability of DRAM; for instance, researchers in Samsung estimated that the firm can reduce production costs by at least 60 per cent by applying the 0.10-micron design rule of 4Gb DRAM to the 128Mb and the 256Mb DRAM chips that were under production in the early 2001.[9] The most influential determinant in the DRAM business, however, is pricing. Prices of commodity integrated circuits such as DRAM are tied to the fluctuations of the business cycle, which has been driven mainly by the demand for desktop personal computers and the manufacturing capacities invested by semiconductor firms in advance. For example, the collapse of prices in DRAM after the mid-1990s was created by the under utilisation of production capacities as well as the sluggish demand in major microcomputer markets such as the US and Germany.[10]

McClean (2000) identified six cycles within the history of integrated circuits such as DRAMs. Within each cycle, an increase in demand reaches a peak, and then declines. Figure 9.3 shows that in the three year cycle during 1983–85, the demand for DRAM increased at the record level of 50 per cent per year and then declined by 16 per cent. The table, in addition, highlights the end of another dramatic business cycle and the gradual recovery of the DRAM market in 2002. Indeed, the January spot market price of DRAM substantiated the recovery; the average price for a 256MB Synchronous DRAM module in the Asian spot market was US$54 on the 14th January 2002 as compared to US$30 on the 21st December 2001. In addition, the average price for a 256MB Double Data Rate DRAM module was US$12 higher during this period; however, the average price of a 256MB Rambus DRAM remained the same.[11]

Table 9.3: Business Cycles in DRAMs, 1971–2001

Cycle	Key Influence	Demand Pattern		
		Increase	Peak	Stagnant/ Decrease
One (1971–77)	First Oil Shock	1971–73	1973	1974–77
Two (1978–82)	Second Oil Shock	1978–80	1980	1981–82
Three (1983–85)	Surge in Demand	1983–84	1984	1985
Four (1986–92)	The Gulf War and Over Capacity	1986–89	1989	1989–92
Five (1993–98)	The Asian Crisis	1993–95	1995	1996–98
Six (1999–01)	Over Capacity	1999–00	2000*	2000–01

Note: The peak in 2000 was based on IDC forecasts of 18% decrease of total revenue in 2001, and represented a decline of the total revenue of DRAM from about US$29,000 million in 2000 to US$24,000 million in 2001.[12]

Source: McClean (2000), IDC (March 2001) and Benoit and Dickie (2002).

Though it has been mentioned that the demand of microcomputers is the major market driver in DRAMs. Industry analysts, however, have been discussing a new era for DRAM, where microelectronic products such as mobile phones, set-top boxes, high definition televisions, routers and switches will increase their DRAM content. This trend will subsequently erode the dominant share of microcomputers as a percentage of global DRAM revenues.[13] It should also be recognised that the new consumer, communication and network applications are the driving forces for changes in the overall business model for DRAM manufacturing across the next few years. DRAM manufacturers are gradually transiting from commodity models to dedicated models in product design, where they place greater emphasis on product differentiation. However, as the demand for the aforementioned emerging product segments has not yet reached sustainable size, manufacturers tend to alter their existing DRAM architectures to different users with minimal modification in design.

PROCESS IMPROVEMENT AND DRAM

The manufacturing process of integrated circuits such as dynamic random access memory can be divided into three stages. The first stage is wafer fabrication. Wafer fabrication is an intricate series of steps in which the circuit layout of the DRAM is etched onto ultra-pure silicon wafers using photolithographic techniques and a variety of chemical dopants. After this process, grids with identical circuits are created on each wafer. During the next stage of chip assembly, the grids are then scribed and broken into chips. Individual chips are then connected to external wire leads and bonded to the final package. During the final testing stage, packaged devices are subjected to an extensive series of electrical tests and burn-in operations.

Process improvements for Japanese and Korean firms are important as regards gaining a competitive advantage in DRAM integrated circuits as the building of complex circuits onto small silicon chips requires an unprecedented level of perfection. One of IBM's scientists acknowledged that Japan's 'greatest technological strength' vis-à-vis the US was 'the speed with which developments are translated into improved products and processes'.[14] This view was echoed by Tatsuya Terazawa from Japan's Ministry of Economics, Trade and Industry who recently commented that the core strengths of Japanese firms were in the manufacturing process.[15] The capability for process improvement is important towards the cost structure of memory integrated circuits as it impinges on the overall yield. Overall yield is the ratio of non-defective devices to every 100 processed devices, and could be rather low in the early stage of a new manufacturing process. Finan and LaMond (1985 p. 150) commented on the distinctive low yield in the industry:

> Because of the complexity of the process, yields tend to be well below 100 per cent. The industry operates with yields that would be unimaginably low for almost any other mass production process. For example, on complex new parts, yields initially may be as low as 10 per cent. On simpler, mature products, the yields may be as high as 90 per cent. By contrast, it would be unthinkable for a competitive automobile producer to simply discard one out of every ten cars produced.

The overall yield in fact can be broken down and measured at all three stages of the manufacturing process of integrated circuits; measurements at the wafer fabrication stage are referred as die yields or probe yields, those at the chip assembly stage are assembly yields while measurements taken at the final testing stage are test yields. Nevertheless, the scientific understanding of problems inherent in the DRAM manufacturing process is limited, as Khera et al. (1994 p. 143) pointed out:

> When integrated circuits are manufactured, they do not always function as they were initially designed or do not function at all. If the problem lies with the design of the circuit, the engineer must re-evaluate the design. If, however, the circuit does not function because of the manufacturing process, the process engineer can gain relatively little information form the functional test to identify the process that caused the problem.

Improvement of die yields is a complex issue. Due to the minute details involved in the wafer fabrication stage, defective devices are bound to appear even though great attention has been taken during the process. For instance, particle contamination, generated by either the manufacturing equipment or the fabrication process itself, could affect the yield. In addition, DRAM manufacturers have to repetitively etch very fine circuit patterns (as measured in less than one micron) onto silicon wafers using photolithographic techniques; defects arise when subsequent patterns on the photomask do not align with the preceding ones on the wafer.

Langlois et al. (1988 p. 16) also stated that the die yields depended on a number of factors which included die size, number of mask steps, wafer size, purity of materials and clean air control, but he reckoned that 'experience in production is perhaps the single most important factor'. In addition, he pointed out 'yields are improved by engineers and technicians experimenting with such aspects of fabrication as temperatures, time, dopant concentrations, equipment, and scheduling. Yield improvements also result from modifications of devices by circuit designers' (ibid.). In a study of die yield, where die yield is measured as the ratio of non-defective chips per square centimetre of the total wafer area fabricated, Bohn (1995) highlighted the importance of continuous learning and improvement towards higher yield in new manufacturing processes:

> Early in the life of a new process, die yields are usually very low due to a number of problems. They improve as engineers systematically discover these problems, then change the process to reduce or eliminate them. Changes are made to method (such as changing maintenance procedures on a piece of equipment; changing a fixture) or to the process recipe, (such as dose, temperature, and time for a particular step, material supplier or specifications)...

Another study by Hatch and Mowery (1998 p. 1462) reiterated the importance of process improvement for advanced DRAM such as 256Mb DRAM as:

> The fabrication of an integrated circuit with feature sizes and linewidths of less than 0.25 micrometres (μm) requires more than one hundred steps (patterning, coating, baking, etching, cleaning, etc.) The development of many of these steps is based on art and know-how rather than science; they are not well understood or easily replicated on different equipment or in different facilities; and they impose demanding requirements for a particle-free manufacturing environment.

In addition to the significance of continuous improvement in the manufacturing process, existing literature has pointed to inter-firm variation in overall yields. Hatch and Mowery observed inter-firm differentials in process manufacturing capability in commodity devices, and wrote about the differences in yields for both the micron class and sub-micron class of integrated circuits: 'firm-specific capabilities differ most substantially for the most advanced forms of this complex manufacturing technology, much of which is not well-codified or easily transferred among or within firms' (ibid.).

The higher yield among Japanese firms has been observed at different stages of the manufacturing process. Finan and LaMond (op. cit.) observed that the die yield and assembly yield of Japanese firms in relation to 64K DRAM were much higher than their US counterparts during the early 1980s. Table 9.4 shows, for instance, that the die yield of Japanese firms was 52 per cent while that of US firms was 40 per cent.

Table 9.4: Yields among US and Japanese Firms during the early 1980s

	Japan	USA
Die Yield	52%	40%
Assembly Yield	95%	90%
Final Test Yield	80%	80%

Source: Finan and LaMond (1985 p. 156).

Comparative data by Macher and Mowery (1998) also reported the higher average die yields of Japanese firms between 1986 and 1991 in semiconductors as follows:

Table 9.5: Yields among US and Japanese Firms during the late 1980s

	1986	1987	1988	1989	1990	1991
Japan	75	79	81	85	89	93
US	60	60	67	74	80	84

Source: Macher and Mowery (1998 p. 116).

The low defect rate of DRAM products among Japanese firms has been documented in the US since the late 1970s. Early US buyers of Japan's 16K DRAMs, notably Hewlett-Packard, found that Japanese products had a lower frequency of defects than American ones over a period of years. Weinstein et al. (1984) reported the findings concerning Hewlett-Packard in March 1980 that drew attention to Japanese firms' manufacturing process capabilities. Hewlett-Packard's component monitoring showed that Japanese memory integrated circuits were consistently of a higher quality than US products in tests of approximately 300,000 memory chips, which consisted of an equal number of chips from three American suppliers and three Japanese suppliers. Weinstein et al. (ibid. p. 53) quoted: 'None of the Japanese lots was rejected because of failures, whereas failure rates for lots from the US companies ranged from 0.11 to 0.19 per cent'. Further tests on the stimulated field failure rate of the best Japanese supplier was 0.01 per cent failures per thousand hours while that for the worst Japanese supplier was 0.019 per cent per thousand hours. In comparison, the range for US suppliers was 0.059 per cent to 1.593 per cent. Weinstein also stated that the historic data of Xerox's field simulations in the late 1980s illustrated higher quality among Japanese memory devices; the average failure rates for Japanese firms' were typically in the 0.14 to 0.7 per cent range while those for US firms were 1.3 to 2 per cent.

Though there were defensive arguments among the US firms concerning the claim of Japanese firms' superior product quality, there was a consensus on the differences in quality by the late 1980s. Egelhoff (1993) remarked that though US firms such as Texas Instruments made major progress in quality improvements and cost reductions during the 1980s, 'few would argue that US firms can out-implement their Japanese competitors in DRAMs and other standard products'. Macher and Mowery (op. cit. p. 116) also stated that 'By 1991, US manufacturers had narrowed but had not eliminated the gap between their performance and that of Japanese manufacturers'.

The process improvement capability of Korean firms, though not as widely discussed as their Japanese counterparts, has been registered by Jackson (1997) in the area of the Erasable Programmable Read Only Memory (EPROM). He mentioned that one of Intel's senior managers visited Samsung's Korean plant and were amazed at its superior process manufacturing capability. As Jackson (ibid. p. 300) explained:

> Samsung was actually building EPROMs at barely half Intel's costs. The difference was not because of labour costs, since labour accounts for only a small percentage of total cost in semiconductor manufacturing; nor was it because of experience, since Samsung was new to the game and Intel had been playing it since the beginning. Nor was it to do with the size of wafers, which allowed you to get more good die from each process step; Samsung was using smaller wafers than Intel. It was simply that the Koreans knew how to run the wafer fabs better than Intel did.

KAIZEN AND INTEGRATION IN DRAM

The core value of *kaizen* supports the process improvement capabilities of Japanese and Korean firms as demonstrated in their global market shares positions in Table 9.6. It can be seen that the production volume of DRAMs reached 80 terabytes in 1998; Japanese and Korean firms dominated the market with a combined market share of about 70 per cent; Japanese firms shared 40 per cent while Korean firms had 30 per cent of the total volume.[16] Japanese and Korean firms also shared about 60 per cent of the approximately US$31,500 million worth of the worldwide DRAM market in 2000; the leading firm Samsung had gained about 21 per cent market share.[17]

The position of Samsung as the leading producer of DRAM has been very stable since the mid-1990s. Nevertheless, Micron Technology has grown considerably during the past few years; it was formed in 1978 by two engineers from Mostek Corporation with a mission to design and manufacture semiconductor. Though only shipped its first DRAM in 1981, Micron Technology's sales revenues were about US$2,600 million in 2000 and ranked second in this segment of the integrated circuits industry. With its recent discussion of strategic alliance with the near bankrupted Korean firm Hynix Semiconductor (or previously Hyundai), Micron Technology could pose a challenge to the entrenched position of Samsung.[18]

Table 9.6: Market Shares of Leading DRAM Manufacturers in 1998
(by terabytes)

Firms	Nationality	Global Market Shares
Samsung	Korea	20.1%
Hyundai	Korea	12.4%
Micron Technology	USA	9.2%
NEC	Japan	9.2%
LG Semicon	Korea	8.4%
Toshiba	Japan	7.9%
Siemens	Germany	7.8%
Mitsubishi	Japan	6.9%
Hitachi	Japan	6.5%
Fujitsu	Japan	5.9%

Source: IDC as quoted by Warburg Dillion Read (Asia) 1999.

Table 9.7 shows subsidiaries or divisions of microcomputer firms NEC, Toshiba, Fujitsu and Samsung that are associated with captive production of DRAMs in 2001. For example, Toshiba's DRAM manufacturing bases consisted of the US subsidiary Dominion Semiconductor and the Japanese subsidiary Toshiba Yokkaichi Works. Specifically, it manufactured 18 million 64Mb DRAMs in September

2001 from the two sites, i.e. 6.5 million from Dominion Semiconductor and 11.5 million from Yokkaichi Works. In addition, Taiwan's Winbond also produced 9 million Toshiba-brand 64Mb DRAMs.[19] Toshiba is also involved in a joint venture named Walton Advanced Electronics in Taiwan that specialised in the packaging and testing of DRAMs.

NEC's DRAM production, on the other hand, are located in the UK, China and Japan. NEC Semiconductors (UK) was founded in Scotland in 1981; it has grown during the 1980s and the 1990s and employed over 1,000 staff by the end of 2001. Though it relied heavily on imports from Japan and Singapore, this plant had established nearly 100 suppliers in Scotland in the early 1990s and implemented just-in-time delivery widely.[20]

Table 9.7: Microcomputer Firms and Integration in DRAM, 2001

	Nationality	Division/Associated Firm
NEC	Japanese	Elpida Memory Inc., Japan (a joint venture with Hitachi)
		NEC Semiconductor, Scotland, UK
		NEC Semiconductor Yamagata Plant, Japan
		NEC Semiconductors Shanghai, China.
Toshiba	Japanese	Dominion Semiconductor, US
		Toshiba Yokkaichi Works, Japan
		Walton Advanced Electronics Ltd (a venture with Windbond, Mitsui & Co. and WAE Semiconductor)
Fujitsu	Japanese	Fujitsu Microelectronics, Iwate Plant, Japan
Samsung	Korean	Samsung Electronics, Portugese Plant
		Samsung Electronics Kiheung Plant, Chonan Plant and Hwasung Plant, Korea

Source: Various.

Dynamic random access memory has been and is a volatile business; more than 50 firms worldwide have participated in this segment of the integrated circuit industry since its launch. NEC, Toshiba and Fujitsu entered the DRAM market in the late 1970s with a licensing agreement from Intel. At the time, the emerged product segment was microprocessors and memory. Linvill et al. (1984 p. 47) suggested that the reason Japanese firms chose DRAM was because it was 'a high-volume, standardised product, was an ideal first target for the Japanese'. It allowed them to capitalise on their traditional strength (low-cost manufacturing) and to minimise their weaknesses (innovation and distribution/support service). This view was echoed by Finan and LaMond (op. cit. p. 166) who stated that DRAM was an ideal first target for the Japanese firms.

Japanese firms' successes were actually unexpected by their US counterparts. After the launch of DRAM in 1971; 15 US firms which included Texas Instruments, Mostek, Motorola and Advanced Micro Devices had entered the market. By 1974, US firms had monopolised the global DRAM market. Japanese firms, who participated in the industry in the late 1970s, however, gradually captured market shares in the US on the basis of lower price and higher quality. By 1981, Toshiba, NEC, Mitsubishi, Hitachi, Fujitsu and Oki respectively shared 2.3 per cent, 12.8 per cent, 3.1 per cent, 11.9 per cent, 13.1 per cent and 1.3 per cent of the global DRAM market.[21] As a result, US firms began to exit the DRAM segment of integrated circuits across the 1980s. The most shocking news was that the industry's pioneering DRAM designer Intel announced its decision to withdraw from this segment with the closure of eight plants in 1983. Micron Technology, IBM, Motorola and Texas Instruments were the only US firms competing in DRAM by the 1990s while Micron Technology was the remaining US firm in the industry in 2001.

Global prices of DRAM continuously spiralled downwards after reaching their peak in 1995 during the industry's fifth business cycle. Prices of DRAM in mid-1989 were only one-tenth of those in 1995; more specifically, they declined by 75 per cent in 1996, 65 per cent in 1997 and a further 50 per cent in 1998. Japanese firms who were deeply entwined with the economic downturn at home, as a result, consolidated some DRAM activities to alleviate their financial plight. Fujitsu closed, in 1998, its DRAM production plant in Durham, northern England; a Japanese industry analyst commented on the retrenchment as: 'their losses are so large that they need to do this, to cut their losses'.[22] The Durham plant was sold to Filtronic who converted it into a facility in 2000 for gallium arsenide semiconductor devices. Fujitsu also introduced the production of flash memory incorporated in cellular telephones[23] in its most important DRAM manufacturing site, the Iwate Plant in Japan.

Toshiba also restructured its business and engaged in a DRAM venture with the Taiwanese firms Walsin and Winbond since 1998,[24] and delayed its plan to open a 256Mb DRAM facility in Japan in 2000 for a couple of years. Furthermore, it announced the disposal of the Virginia based Dominion Semiconductor to the US firm Micron Technology in December 2001.[25] Dominion began full-scale wafer production in 1997 as a 50–50 joint venture with IBM; Toshiba acquired full ownership of Dominion only in 2000. Nevertheless, the sales included the land, buildings and DRAM production equipment of Dominion. It should, however, be noted that Ichiro Hirata (the Vice President of Toshiba's memory business unit) announced Toshiba's commitment in developing and producing high-performance DRAM to meet the demand of its customers. Toshiba has opted for co-developing the 1Gb DRAM with Fujitsu so as to lower the R&D cost; this collaboration involves a joint project team of approximately 100 researchers working at Toshiba's Advanced Microelectronics Centre (AMC) in Yokohama and cost in 1999 more than 30,000 million yen.[26] Winbond joined Toshiba and Fujitsu's DRAM project in 2000; as a result, approximately 30 Winbond engineers participated in the research work at AMC. Toshiba stated at the time that: 'the participation of Winbond in the project will bring additional resources to bear on achieving technical advances, and will shorten the development term and enhance the programme through a broader sharing of development costs and resources that reduces the overall burden on each participant'.[27]

Similarly, NEC consolidated its DRAM production and reduced the volume of production. It revised its monthly DRAM output in late 1998 from 11 million to six million. It then took part in a joint venture with Hitachi in DRAM in 2000. In July 2001, NEC announced that it would abandon all its DRAM ventures with the exception of Elpida by 2004 in response to its worsened financial situation. Meanwhile, it restructured its older domestic DRAM facilities in Japan such as its Sagamihara plant, Yamagata plant and Takahata plant in order to reduce monthly output by nearly 50 per cent as well as to eliminate about 40 per cent of its work force in the semiconductor business. In addition, NEC announced a delay in the expansion of its Chinese plant[28] as well as a layoff in its UK plant in 2001. It planned to close down the plant in Scotland temporarily in April 2002 in response to the severe decline in demand of DRAM. It was reported that 'all 1,260 employees at the plant will be laid off and the company will decide whether to reopen the plant based upon future market trends'.[29]

The Korean firm Samsung, which also originates from a culture utilising the core value of *kaizen*, has, since the mid-1970s, engaged in the assembly activity of transistors and large-scale integration (LSI) circuits.[30] Samsung entered the DRAM market in 1984 after being turned down by Texas Instruments, Motorola, NEC, Toshiba and Hitachi for the licensing of the 64K DRAM.[31] In order to tackle the design and wafer fabrication, Samsung assigned two task force teams, one in the Silicon Valley and the other in Korea, to assimilate the knowledge it licensed from Micron Technology and Zytrek. They successfully accomplished the task and produced functionally operating wafers that were ready for the next assembly stage. Kim (1997 p.90) described Samsung's smooth transition to the very large scale integration (VLSI) technology in DRAM as: 'Samsung first imported 3,000 64K DRAM chips from Micron Technology to assemble in Korea. With eight years of experience in the assembly of LSI chips, Samsung assimilated VLSI assembly technology without much problem, but this experience enabled Samsung engineers to gain initial familiarity with the new product'.

Samsung shared 0.1 per cent of the worldwide DRAM market in 1984[32] and continued to gain its market shares throughout the 1980s at the expense of Japanese firms. Samsung surpassed Japanese firms and US firms as the leading DRAM manufacturers in 1995; and by the late 1990s had more than 20 per cent of worldwide market share. Samsung has also managed to shorten the time lag with its competitors; in 1994, it was the first semiconductor firm to successfully develop the first 256Mb DRAM. It stated that it was the first firm to complete the prototype circuit design for the 1Gb Synchoronous DRAM. In addition, it was the first semiconductor firm to operate a 300 millimetre wafer pilot line, and the fully operational line (Line 11 at its Hwasung plant in Korea) is scheduled to be completed in 2001. Samsung was also the first to secure the technology for the 4Gb DRAM chips.

Samsung's DRAM investment in Europe is represented by its Portuguese facility which focuses on chip assembly and final testing facilities. This plant relied on the supply of silicon wafers from NEC's Livingston wafer fabrication plant in Scotland as underlined in a collaborative agreement in 1995. The terms of the agreement included NEC's Scottish plant to supply Samsung's Portuguese plant some 100,000 chips a month in the form of wafers that were ready to be sliced into individual chips.[33] In return, Samsung's Portuguese plant would test the memory integrated circuits for NEC Semiconductors (UK).

Table 9.8 summarises the pattern of integration among US and Asia Pacific firms. It can be seen that IBM, Hewlett-Packard, Compaq, Dell,

Gateway, SGI, Sun, Twinhead, Acer and Mitac that are not equipped with the core value of *kaizen*, did not pursue integration into DRAMs as stated in the cultural selectivity theory. It should, however, be noted that IBM, HP and Acer had in fact previously engaged in the captive production of DRAMs. IBM Microelectronics, in particular, is an early entrant in the memory market. IBM incorporated memory in their model 145 within the highly regarded System 370 mainframe series in September 1970; the emerged memory segment at the time contributed to only one per cent of the total semiconductor market. Though IBM was only engaged in captive production during the 1980s, it was a leading producer of DRAM by sales volume; it had expanded during the 1990s into the merchant market sales of DRAM. Nevertheless, IBM converted its DRAM facility in Essonnes, France into a joint venture with Siemens' Infineon Technologies to specialise in customised logic semiconductors in 1999; besides, it sold its 50 per cent equity stakes in another American DRAM facility, the Dominion Semiconductor, to Toshiba in the same year[34].

Regarding its decision to withdraw from DRAM production, IBM's CEO Louis Gerstner commented that: 'the actions we're taking in our microelectronics are intended to strengthen our technology segment substantially over the long term'.[35] In other words, IBM wanted to focus on the newer semiconductor technology such as magnetic random access memory (MRAM) with greater growth and profit potential. Its Vice President of Technology and Emerging Products stated that 'MRAM has the potential to replace today's memory technologies in electronic products of the future'.[36] For instance, MRAM could expand the battery life of notebook computers and allow them to be left on standby mode for several years compared to the current limit of about 12 hours.[37]

Table 9.8: Continuous Improvement and Integration in DRAM

	Continuous Improvement	Not Continuous Improvement
Integration	4	0
Not integration	0	10

Source: Various.

Acer's participation in DRAM, on the other hand, was through the 50–50 joint venture Texas Instruments-Acer in 1989. It should be noted that Acer entered the semiconductor industry without any previous experience in simple integrated circuit development. The basis of the joint venture was Acer's construction of the DRAM fabrication plant in Taiwan while Texas Instruments provided the technology to the venture. However, Texas Instruments withdrew from the DRAM market in 1999, and sold its 50 per cent stakes to Acer. Acer initially continued with the operation but it quickly merged the operation with TSMC, who eventually bought the majority of Acer's stakes in the firm.

Up to this point, the discussion has focused on the core cultural value of *kaizen* or continuous improvement in firms' competitiveness and integration pattern in DRAM. It has suggested that microcomputer firms that are embodied with the core value of *kaizen* are able to capitalise their process manufacturing capabilities and undertake integration in DRAM; it also highlights the fact that firms without the core value of *kaizen* might only compete in the industry in the short run. In the next section, I will look at an added dimension of competitiveness that is demonstrated by the product strategy of US and Taiwanese firms.

US DESIGN-INTENSIVE PROUDCT STRATGY

While US firms lagged behind Japanese and Korean firms in process manufacturing capabilities, their core cultural value of individualism supported their product design capabilities which can be seen in Micron Technology's strategy as well as other US firms' involvement in design-intensive integrated circuit products. Micron Technology, the remaining US firm competing in the DRAM industry, has, in fact, a history of competing with an innovative product strategy that could be traced back to the early 1980s. As Afuah (1999 p. 105) pointed out:

> To offer the low cost dictated by the nature of the DRAM business, Micron decided to capitalise on its competencies in design rather than try to out-manufacture its deep-pocketed, vertically integrated Japanese competitors. Micron used its design skills to create what has been described as a 'phantom' fabrication plant...
>
> Much of Micron's success has been attributed to its ability to increase the number of chips, or dies, per silicon wafer, while minimising the number of layers required to build the chip's electronic infrastructure. By using this

technique, Micron produced low-cost chips without the first-class manufacturing know-how of its Japanese competitors.

Micron Technology successfully produced 64K DRAM that was about 33 per cent smaller than the industry standard in 1983; such small die size, as a consequence, allowed the firm to produce more usable chips on each wafer and reduce its production cost by 50 per cent. Micron Technology's product design capability is further demonstrated in its ability to reduce the die size of the 4MB generation of DRAM five times compared to the industry average of two times.[38] Micron Technology currently possesses some die sizes that are the smallest in the industry.

Moreover, Micron Technology's innovative launch of the preferred market package for 4MB DRAM module in 1995 allowed it to secure premium price for the devices at a time where personal computer manufacturers were seeking additional supply for systems to run the Windows 95 operating system. At the time, Japanese manufacturers had made the transition to the bigger 16MB DRAMs, which were difficult to wire together in a plug-in DRAM module in the way that manufacturers preferred.[39]

While Micron Technology constitutes the most visible example of product design capability among firms with the core value of individualism, one can expand the theme of individualistic US firms' strength in product design by considering US firms' engagement in devices such as microprocessors and digital signal processors. Intel, who withdrew from the commodity DRAM market in 1985, has focused on the emerging microprocessor market since then; it is the largest semiconductor firm in the world with a sales revenue of US\$26,273 million in 1998. Afuah (ibid.) recognised that:

> After dominant-design status has been attained, a firm can prevent imitation by defending its intellectual property rights in the court. To have the leading market share, a maker of microprocessors does not have to be the best at manufacturing... Replicating DRAM technology is easier, and firms depend on low-cost strategies, such as efficient manufacturing or designs that 'substitute' for manufacturing.

Texas Instruments, who eventually abandoned DRAM, also has a keen interest in the fast growing product segment of digital signal processors, which are components within hard disk drives. Texas Instruments has captured an estimated 45 per cent of this design-intensive device. It has rightly concentrated on digital signal processors since 1997 through a decisive corporate consolidation. It sold its defence business to Raytheon, its portable computer business and DRAM joint venture to Acer, as well as assets of its computer integrated manufacturing business to Gores Technology. Its eventual sales of DRAM business to Micron Technology which totalled US$800 million contained arrangements such as the transfer of ownership of its wafer fabrication plant in Avezzano, Italy.[40]

The strength of US firms' product design capability was further attested to by Motorola's market position in the design-intensive integrated circuit area. Motorola is one of the partners in the development of Power PC processor chips that are used in Apple's microcomputer systems. Motorola which had less then five per cent of the global market share since the mid-1980s phased out its capital-intensive DRAM production in 1997. It shifted its focus gradually from 16MB DRAM towards logic products in the Japanese joint venture plant with Toshiba. It also converted the DRAM joint venture facility with Siemens in the US to other types of memory chips.[41] It wrote off US$170 million associated technology development costs and manufacturing equipment and declared that it aimed to concentrate on microprocessors and other logic chips.

US firms have also demonstrated innovative design to tackle the physical limitations of manufacturing memories, microprocessors or other integrated circuits. The limitation has been described: 'as chips become ever smaller and ever more densely packed with processing power, there comes a point at which the laws of conventional physics break down... within a few years, makers of chips using established technology will hit a wall'.[42] US firms IBM and HP are among those at the forefront of the innovative nano technology that allows the fabrication of circuits with feature sizes below 0.1 micron. It has been demonstrated that: 'scientists at IBM Corp found a way to build structures one atom at a time using atomic-force microscope techniques.... A group at Hewlett-Packard simulated fault tolerant circuit designs suitable for chemically defined electronics'.[43] Nevertheless, observers such as Ben Laurance predicted that 'the winner will be large and it will be American'.[44]

A perplexing point in conjunction with DRAM is that the issue of quality underlying firms' process improvement capabilities actually originated in America. Deming and Juran, who advocated constant improvement in quality that would eventually decrease costs since the 1950s, were important figures in the quality movement. Though the two management gurus' ideas were not taken up in America during the

1950s, their lectures in Japan, as a contrast, were received enthusiastically by managers. Deming's 14 points for firms have been incorporated into continuous improvement in Japanese industry. The points included: '1. Create constancy of purpose toward improvement of product and service... 3. Cease dependence on inspection to achieve quality. Eliminate the need for inspection on a mass basis by building quality into the product in the first place... 13. Institute a vigorous programme of education and self improvement...'.[45]

In addition, the American government's war time innovation 'Training Within Industries' programme also played a role in the promotion of continuous improvement in quality. The actual 'Training Within Industries' programme that were implemented by the Occupation authorities in Japan in 1951, were still widely adopted by Japanese firms in the 1990s. Robinson and Schroeder (1993 p. 38) commented on their popularity: '... they are well-respected in Japanese management circles and are viewed as important enough to the national interest to be overseen by the Ministry of Labour'.

The 'Training Within Industries' programme consisted of three standardised training courses (the famous three 'J' courses): Job Instruction Training, Job Methods Training and Job Relations Training. Individuals that have completed any one of the 'J' courses would receive certificates. The aim of the Job Methods Training course was to teach supervisors 'to make incremental improvements continually to processes and operations, how to generate such improvements, and the importance of putting their improvement suggestions in writing' (Robinson and Schroeder ibid. p. 41). Japanese Human Relations Association (1988 p. 202) recognised the importance of continuous improvement in Job Methods Training. It stated:

> The forerunner of the modern Japanese-style suggestion system undoubtedly originated in the West... TWI (Training Within Industries), introduced to Japanese industry in 1949 by the US occupation forces, had a major effect in expanding the suggestion system to involve all workers rather than just a handful of the elite. Job modification constituted a part of TWI and as foremen and supervisors taught workers how to perform job modification, they learned how to make changes and suggestions...

Though the 'Training Within Industries' did not manage to operate in Korea as a result of the outbreak of the Korean War. It had percolated into Korea through Japanese firms and is vigorously employed today. One should, however, bear in mind that competitive force also serves as an incentive for Korean firms to implement quality. An important point relating to the successful accumulation of manufacturing process capability is that the top management of Japanese and Korean firms are committed to the upgrade of quality as it is consistent with their core value of *kaizen*.

FOUNDRIES AND FLEXIBILITY

The emergence of Taiwanese DRAM manufacturers in the last decade also deserves attention. Though Taiwanese firms are not endowed with the core value of continuous improvement, they accounted for more than ten per cent of the market share of DRAMs incorporated in microcomputers.[46] It should, however, be noted that Taiwanese firms competed with a different strategy from other semiconductor firms in the industry. As mentioned earlier, the manufacturing process of integrated circuits can be classified into the wafer fabrication stage, the assembly stage and the final testing stage. The three distinctive stages of integrated circuit manufacturing can be performed within a single firm or be undertaken separately by different firms. The prominent example of disaggregation in the production process can be seen in the numerous specialist design firms in the Silicon Valley that contract out their production activities to firms (or foundries) that produce devices according to the blueprint provided by the designers.

The activities of Taiwanese DRAM manufacturers are associated with contract manufacturing. The success of Taiwanese firms as DRAM foundries, to a certain extent, reflects their core cultural value of flexibility. DRAM manufacturers such as Vanguard International Semiconductor, Nanya Technology and Powerchip Semiconductor alleviated losses incurred within the cyclical nature of DRAM by serving as foundries for other firms. After transforming itself as a foundry in 1999, about 50 per cent of Nanya Technology's sales in the early 2002, for example, derived from contract manufacturing business.[47] Flexibility is essential to the foundry model; flexibility is the ability to take actions to maximise the benefit from altered conditions and therefore relates to varying production orders, with device-type and lot-size requirements changing constantly. An observer indeed commented on Taiwanese firms' flexibility as regards their success in the foundry business as:

> Their flexibility gives them an advantage over the South Koreans and Japanese. Unlike their Asian competitors, most Taiwanese chip makers are

still doing foundry work for others. Profits in that business, while usually good, offer nothing like the riches collected by firms that make their own memory chips during a shortage; but foundry work is a good way of using spare capacity...[48]

The chairman of Taiwan's United Microelectronics Corporation (UMC), John Hsuan, commented on the logic of utilising Taiwanese foundries by firms such as Motorola and NEC as: 'They have started to realise that the foundries' efficiency and performance are better than their own captive supply'.[49] Indeed, the concept of the foundry was based on the idea that no semiconductor firm (except the industry leader Intel) can be competitive in all stages of the manufacturing process. Taiwanese firms' success, however, is confined mainly to low-end foundries;[50] Fujitsu's President of Electronic Devices, for instance, stated that though Fujitsu utilised Taiwanese foundries for DRAMs, it still possessed advantages in some other advanced products.[51] Indeed, the sales revenues of Taiwan's leading foundry TSMC was predominantly derived from low-end products in mid-2001[52].

The concept of the foundry was pioneered by Morris Chang, who started TSMC in 1986 with capital from the Taiwanese government's Taiwan Development Fund, Philips and local investors of a ratio of 45:25:30. TSMC has achieved a 30 per cent annual growth rate in revenues between 1995–1999, and is the largest dedicated foundry in the industry with sales of approximately US$5,000 million in 2001. It has provided contract manufacturing services to the world's largest information technology and consumer electronics firms such as Broadcom, Qualcomm, Motorola and NEC.

Despite temporary setback in 2001 as a result of the global decline in semiconductor business, the foundry business is expected to grow at a phenomenal compound rate of 25 per cent annually over the next decade. In addition, the industry's share of semiconductor output was expected to increase from 10 per cent to 40 per cent. The accelerating demand reflected the fact that traditional semiconductor firms that used to undertake all manufacturing in their own facilities, such as Motorola, Fujitsu and IBM, have began to use foundries for a certain percentage of their manufacturing capacity on an ongoing basis as a method of channelling their overflow capacities. Nevertheless, the cosy relationship between foundries and established semiconductor firms such as Motorola are relatively recent. Motorola which used to manufacture most of the integrated circuits used in its industrial or consumer products outlined its new strategy in February 1999 of procuring as much as 50 per cent of the integrated circuits consumed externally by 2002.

Taiwanese firms' entry into the foundry business reiterates the theme that they are willing to improvise existing constraints in the industry and capitalise on their flexibility. Similarly, Korean firms have invested substantially into the foundry business recently. For instance, Hynix invested more than US$400 million in foundry production facilities in 2000 and an additional US$600 million in 2001, hence its total foundry capacity had increased to 140,000 wafers per month. Though Korean firms such as Samsung, Hynix and Anam Semiconductors that are embodied with the core value of flexibility have also established themselves in the foundry business; however, they only undertake foundry business when they have spare capacity.

CONCLUSION

Deming (1982 p. 486) recalled that the quality improvement in Japan since the 1950s is a result of the fact that 'top management became convinced that quality was vital for export, and that they could accomplish the switch'. Such conviction was underlied by the core value of *kaizen*. This chapter has shown that the competitiveness of Japanese and Korean firms in the capital-intensive microcomputer component area such as DRAM is consistent with the cultural selectivity theory suggesting that the core cultural value of continuous improvement is related to firms' capabilities.

We have also seen in this chapter that US firms and Taiwanese firms managed to compete in DRAM despite not being endowed with the core value of continuous improvement. Interestingly enough, US firms' product design and the Taiwanese firms' foundry model were built on the basis of their respective core cultural values. This finding corresponds with Japanese firms' approach to software in terms of the software factory. One of the distinctive features of Japanese software factories is their capability to exploit their core value of continuous improvement in code reuse. The idea of code reuse is to recycle software designs or code across more than one project. Aoyama (1996 p. 133) stated that 'the process standardisation and CPI (Continuous Process Improvement) are the basis of Japanese software factories... In practice, hundreds of software QC (Quality-Control) circles were formed in numerous computer and software companies'. The cultural element of code reuse has been identified by Isoda (1996), who wrote 'One of the reasons for the Japanese success with software reuse is that the inherent nature of software reuse is well in accordance with the Japanese tendency of groupism and gradualism. That is, software reuse requires collaboration of individuals who work for the whole and continuous *kaizen* of several years' (p. 170).

The overall pattern of integration in DRAM among US and Asia Pacific firms that I have covered in this chapter follows the pattern in concept-intensive components such as software, in the sense that US firms' competitiveness was built on their product design capabilities derived from the core value of individualism. Micron Technology's ability to compete in the DRAM industry has been and is associated with its innovation; indeed Micron Technology was regarded by the Technology Review Magazine published by the Massachusetts Institute of Technology as the number one firm in the semiconductor industry in terms of its quality and quantity of patents.[53] This chapter demonstrates that Japanese and Korean firms' process manufacturing process was driven by their value of kaizen. Paradoxically, as firms are increasingly adjusted to the use of foundries and the demand for foundries increases, the competitive dynamics in the DRAM industry will favour Taiwanese and Korean firms that are endowed with the core value of flexibility.

NOTES

[1]   The symbol for 1,024 bytes, 1,048,576 bytes and 1,073,741,824 bytes are 1K, 1MB and 1GB respectively (Press 1996 p. 10).

[2]   The Dimension 2200 Model can be upgraded to 512M bytes. See *Dell.com (UK) site*, 22 March 2002.

[3]   A bit is a single character of data (either 1 or 0); it takes eight bits to make a single byte.

[4]   'Nanya Technology OEM contracts to account for 41 per cent of March parent sales', *AFX Asia (Focus)*, 6 March 2002.

[5]   The semiconductor industry is divided into discrete devices and integrated circuits.

[6]   The shrinking value of the market was due to the collapse of prices. For instance, Dataquest and Morgan Stanley Dean Witter Research stated that contract prices for 64Mb DRAM dropped from US$1.60 a piece in mid-1996 to US$0.50 at the end of the year. Also see Laura Tyson, 'A market plagued by over-supply', *The Financial Times*, 4 February 1998 as well as 'Remind me how to make money', *The Economist*, 26 August 1995 pp. 55–6.

[7]   Walters (2001) p. 53.

[8]   'Samsung secures technology for 4Gb DRAM', *Samsung Electronics News*, 9 February 2001.

[9]   Ibid.

[10] Paul Taylor, 'Sharp drop in semiconductor global sales growth predicted', *The Financial Times*, 29 April 1996 and 'DRAM market to shrink by 55 per cent in 2001', *IT word.com site*, 21 June 2001.

[11] ICS-LOR prices as quoted in 'DRAM prices triple within two months', ITworld.com site, 15 January 2002.

[12] 'IDC forecasts worldwide DRAM market will shrink to $24 billion in 2001', IDC Press Release, 2 March 2001.

[13] Farhad Tabrizi   'New forces are changing DRAM market landscape', *Electronic News*, 5 March 2001 p. 28.

[14] Clark, Hayes and Lorenz (1985) p. 139.

[15] The comment by Terazawa can be found in M. Dickie and A. Harney 'Japan Warms to Outsourcing', *The Financial Times*, 22 February 2001.

[16] 'And Then There Were Two', *The Economist*, 23 January 1999 p. 58.

[17] 'Dataquest: DRAM market to get worse', ITworld.com site, 18 October 2001.

[18] 'Hynix and Micron Technology initiate preliminary discussions', *Micron Press Release*, 2 December 2001.

[19] 'Toshiba to close fabrication line no. 1 at its Yokkaichi Operations', *Toshiba Press Release*, 8 August 2001.

[20] The UK plant had about 700 suppliers in total in the mid-1990s.

[21] Terry Dodsworth, Louis Kehoe and Stefan Wagstyl, 'The chase to catch the Japanese', *The Financial Times*, 23 July 1988 p. 18.

[22] Paul Taylor, 'The semiconductor revolution: an industry unique in history', *The Financial Times*, 4 February 1998 Information Technology Survey p. iv.

[23] Fujitsu has contracted with Taiwan's TSMC for the supply of DRAM.

[24] Alexandra Harney and Ken Hijno, 'Toshiba forecasts loss and cuts 10% of workforce', *FT.com site*, 27 August 2001.

[25] 'Toshiba announces reorganisation of memory business', *Toshiba Press Release*, 18 December 2001.

[26] 'Winbond to join in Fujitsu Toshiba DRAM Development Programme', *Toshiba Press Release*, 8 May 2000.

[27] Ibid.

[28] 'NEC announces mid-term strategies', *NEC Press Release*, 31 July 2001.

[29] 'NEC to suspend chip production in UK', *ITworld.com site*, 19 December 2001.

[30] Integrated circuits can be distinguished by their component density per square inch of the silicon wafer. The small scale integration (MSI) circuits of the early 1960s contained the maximum of 99 active elements; the medium scale integration (MSI) circuits constructed in the late 1960s were composed of 100-999 active elements. The large scale integration (LSI), the very large integration (VLSI) and the ultra large scale integration (ULSI) referred to the extension of microcircuitry beyond a component density of 1,000 active elements.

[31] To a certain extent, Samsung's launch of 64K DRAM, which utilised the very-large-scale integration could be considered as a major technological advancement.

[32] Terry Dodsworth, Louis Kehoe and Stefan Wagstyl (op. cit.).

[33] Michiyo Nakamoto and Alan Cane 'NEC and Samsung to link the European chips deal', *The Financial Times*, 7 February 1995 p. 20.

[34] To secure the sourcing of DRAM, IBM extended its technology licensing with firms such as Nanya Technology in Taiwan. In addition to its 0.25-, 0.20- and 0.175-micron process technology, IBM signed new agreement to transfer the 0.14- and 0.11-micron DRAM technology to Nanya.

[35] 'IBM announces second-quarter 1999 results', *IBM Press Release,* 19 July 1999.

[36] Martin Arnold, 'IBM joins Infineon in magnetic race', *FT.com site*, 7 December 2000.

[37] IBM and Infineon have announced their joint-development of MRAM in December 2000; the two firms expect to launch a commercially viable product by 2004.

[38] Norm Alster, 'Drowning in DRAMs' *Forbes*, 11 January 1991 p. 41.

[39] 'Remind me how to make money', *The Economist*, 26 August 1995 pp. 55–6.

[40] Dylan McGrath, 'Micron buys TI DRAM operations in $800m deal', *Electronics News*, 22 June 1998.

[41] Louise Kehoe, 'Motorola plans to stop making DRAM chips', *The Financial Times*, 2 July 1997.

[42] Paul Taylor, 'Race is on to find chips of the future', *The Financial Times: Information Technology Survey*, 1 December 1999.

[43] Chappell Brown 'Big Push on A Nano Scale', *Electronic Engineering Times*, 22 January 2001 p. 1.

[44] Ben Laurance is a former editor in The Observer. His view is presented in Ben Laurance 'Quantum leap in memory lane' *Shares*, 9 December 1999 p. 39.

[45] The 14 points can be found in Deming (1982 pp. 23–4).

[46] The market share of Taiwanese firms included contract manufacturing of DRAMs. Mure Dickie and Paul Taylor, 'Computer groups may face trouble meeting demand', *The Financial Times*, 4 November 1999.

[47] 'Nanya Technology OEM contracts to account for 41 per cent of March Parent Sales', *AFX Asia (Focus)*, 6 March 2002.

[48] 'Nice market, we'll take it', *The Economist,* 4 July 1998 p. 64.

[49] Andrew Tanzer, 'Made in Taiwan', *Forbes,* 29 May 2000 p. 186.

[50] The indigenous Singaporean firm Chartered Semiconductor Manufacturing, as a contrast, is regarded in high-quality contract manufacturing service.

[51] Dickie and Harney (op. cit.).

[52] See Philip Liu, 'Contract IC makers see brighter times, but DRAM prospects remain dim', *Taiwan Economic News,* 12 November 2001 p. 34.

[53] See *Micron.com site*, March 2002.

10. People and Culture

The preceding chapters have established a culturally induced pattern of integration in concept-intensive and capital-intensive microcomputer components. This chapter confronts the labour-intensive issue with reference to cathode ray tube-based (CRT) display monitors. CRT monitors are important microcomputer components in terms of monetary value. In addition, a recent study by the Microelectronics and Computer Technology Corporation estimated that as many as 100 million CRT monitors would be sold worldwide in 2002.[1]

It was suggested in chapter six that the core cultural value of flexibility will enhance the competitiveness of microcomputer multinational firms in the people-driven labour-intensive component area, which will subsequently determine their pattern of integration in CRT monitors. In order to delineate the relationships among national culture, firm capability and microcomputer firms' integration pattern, I will first review the marketing and technological dynamics of CRT monitors, which will be followed by a discussion of the core value of flexibility and people management capability among Taiwanese and Korean firms. Finally, US and Asia Pacific firms' overall pattern of integration and the implications will be examined.

MARKET AND TECHNOLOGY IN DISPLAY MONITORS

Table 10.1 illustrates the specifications of Hitachi's CM2110MU SuperScan 21-inch CRT monitor which serve as criteria for buyers to make purchasing decisions. The screen resolution is generally considered to be an important attribute of display monitors. It can be seen that the screen resolution of this model as measured by the number of pixels (1600x1280) is high, and will therefore provide very detailed images for the 21-inch monitor. However, it should be noted that the actual display area of this 21-inch monitor measures only 19 inches. In addition, the resolution can be determined by the screen technology employed. Current technology embodies aperture-grille and shadow mask colour display tubes[2], which were derived from the braun tubes invented in

1897. Nevertheless, the actual shadow-mask tube used nowadays was first introduced by RCA in the 1950s while the most popular aperture-grille tube was developed by Sony in the 1960s. It is generally considered that aperture-grille tubes provide sharper pictures. As this Hitachi model is based on the shadow-mask tube, its image is not as sharp as one based on the Trinitron tube. Moreover, this display monitor's frame rate at the highest resolution of 1600-by-1280 is 68 Hz, hence it will probably not be suitable for users particularly sensitive to flickers. As for the dot pitch, this model is measured at 0.26 millimetres (vertical) and 0.21 millimetres (horizontal), and can be regarded as reasonable. In particular, the 0.21 millimetres dot pitch will provider finer detail.

Table 10.1: Hitachi's SuperScan Pro 21 CRT Based Display Monitor

	Specification
Screen Size	15.55 inches (horizontal)
	11.61 inches (vertical)
	19.41 inches (diagonal)
Dot Pitch	0.26 millimetres (vertical)
	0.21 millimetres (horizontal)
Frequencies	31 to 85 kHz (horizontal)
	50 to 160 Hz (vertical)
Resolution	1600 by 1280
Maximum Video Bandwidth	160 MHz
Colour Temperature	9,300 K, 6,500 K, 5,000 K
	(settable)
Dimensions	19.21 inches (width)
	18.66 inches (height)
	21.02 inches (depth)
Weight	33 kilograms

Source: Press (1996 p. 457).

Display tubes are considered to be core components of CRT monitors and account for some 30 per cent of the total costs. Leading display tube manufacturers include Sony, Samsung, Mitsubishi, Matsushita, Chung Hwa, Philips and Toshiba. The Taiwanese firm Chung Hwa is the largest manufacturer in terms of market share, its operations are located in

Taiwan, Malaysia, China and Scotland. Chung Hwa's UK plant supplied to Tatung[3] in Telford, whose capacity was approximately 250,000 CRT monitors and 100,000 PC/TVs in 1998. Chung Hwa's £260 million investment in Eurocentral in 1995 (a business park at Mossend, Lanarkshire) is significant for the European microcomputer industry; it has not only provided a major source of supply to existing display monitor manufacturers in the UK, but has also strengthened the supply base for CRT monitors. The investment, for example, has attracted other firms such as Shinho Tech, Lite On and ADI to the UK. The leading Taiwanese monitor manufacturer ADI invested a £25 million manufacturing facility in Newcastle in 1997. ADI was the sixth largest monitor producer worldwide in 1996, with annual sales of nearly £600 million and a 3,000 workforce in Taiwan, China and Thailand. ADI's UK plant contributed to nearly half its total sales revenue by the late 1990s.[4]

FLEXIBILITY AND PEOPLE MANAGEMENT

The core national cultural value of flexibility is essential for display monitors as it enhances people management capability which in turn addresses the productivity issue during the monotonous assembly work. Labour-intensive assembly involves workers using hand tools to assemble various components into sub-systems during the process; the sub-systems are then transported to locations where the next assembly tasks proceed. In addition, the tedious labour-intensive work procedures tend to be undertaken within peculiar constraints of low cost locations such as lack of awareness of health and safety, ambiguous or constant changes of law and regulations and unfamiliarity with the factory system.

In a recent article on overseas Chinese entrepreneurship, Yu (2000 p.183) wrote that Hong Kong entrepreneurs were highly flexible in the early stages of the industrialisation and 'could adapt their production lines from making transistor radios to making electronic watches within three months, or from electronic calculators to black and white TVs within six months, or from black and white TVs to colour TVs within nine months'. Taiwanese firms, which lead CRT monitor production, have successfully set up diverse manufacturing bases over low-cost locations in South East Asia. It is estimated that 45 per cent of Taiwanese firms were in Malaysia during the mid-1990s, 25 per cent in Thailand and 22 per cent in Indonesia. It can be said that capabilities concerning people management enable them to operate successfully in these low cost production sites as well as conduct manufacturing activities at lower costs.

Taiwanese and Korean firms' people management capabilities, though not well documented, are indicated in the proportion of management expenses as a percentage of total sales revenue generated. Management expenses are the marketing, general and administrative expenses of running an operation; a consistent low ratio of management expenses to total sales reflects the managerial expertise to extract the maximum productivity of the workforce during the process of revenue generation.

Management expenses tend to be remarkably stable over time. For instance, Sun and Toshiba's management expenses were around 25 per cent throughout the 1990s. However, strategic changes such as restructuring or expansion can alter the ratios substantially on a year-to-year basis. For instance, Fujitsu's management expenses declined from over 30 per cent in the early 1990s to the recent ratio of about 25 per cent as a result of its lower extent of involvement in the mainframe computer manufacturing and software programming and the increased commitment to microcomputer manufacturing, telecommunication and computer services. On the other hand, Gateway's management expenses have increased from seven per cent to ten per cent between 1993–95 as a result of factors such as the overhead expenses incurred in its new Japanese and Australian operations, expenses associated with the design and implementation of new management information systems as well as concerted marketing efforts directed at family and major accounts such as nationwide consumer-oriented television advertising campaigns in the US.[5]

The management expenses of US and Asia Pacific microcomputer firms in 2000 are used as indicators for their people management capabilities. In fact, the figure for 2000 is comparable to the averages between 1998 and 2000. For example, there is 0.6 point difference between IBM's three year average management expenses and that of 2000 (i.e. 18.3% minus 17.7% = 0.6%) whereas there is a 1.4 points difference in Compaq's (i.e. 18.3% minus 1.4% = 16.9%). In addition, SGI's three year average of 33.7 per cent is, as a coincidence, the same as its people management expenses in 2000. However, it should be noted that Gateway's management expenses have increased from 11.9 per cent in 1998, to 13.8 per cent in 1999 and 16.1 per cent in 2000.

When comparing management expenses across firms, one should bear in mind the impact of business profile. A higher level of management expenses is not uncommon in business segments such as computer software and computer services as a result of higher marketing expenditure; for example, the management expenses of Microsoft are 22 per cent in 2000, which consist of 18 per cent selling and marketing and four per cent general and administrative expenses.

In order to facilitate the comparison of US and Asia Pacific firms' people management capabilities, their business portfolios have been classified into three areas as shown in Table 10.2. It can be seen that US and Asia Pacific microcomputer firms are grouped into those who derived their sales revenues from microcomputer and component assembly, those that derived their sales revenues from engaging in microcomputer software and IT services as well as those that participate in microcomputer and component assembly as well as in other areas of manufacturing. Dell, Gateway, Mitac and Acer Inc. represents firms that focus on microcomputer hardware. Seven firms which include IBM, Compaq, Hewlett-Packard, Sun, SGI, NEC and Fujitsu engaged in microcomputer hardware and related areas such as software, IT services, IT financing and microcomputer components. IBM is an example of a firm focusing on microcomputer hardware and software; its profile in 2000 was 43 per cent in computer and related component manufacturing and 57 per cent in software, IT services and finance.[6] The last category of firms such as Samsung and Toshiba are engaged in a wide variety of businesses such as consumer electronics and industrial equipment.

Table 10.3 illustrates the calculations of people management capabilities of US and Asia Pacific microcomputer firms. Overall, the ratios of management expenses to total sales among firms that concentrate on the microcomputer hardware system business are the lowest. The ratios for Taiwanese microcomputer manufacturers Acer Inc. and Mitac are as low as 5 per cent while those for US firms Dell and Gateway are at least 4 points higher; Taiwanese firms' low ratios are particularly impressive since they are smaller than their US counterparts and are subject to a lower extent of economies of scale. The table also shows that the ratio for the Acer Group (which represents the consolidated business and is involved in capital-intensive areas such as integrated circuits packaging and testing, CD-ROM drives and logic chips) is lower than other firms in the category. The management expenses of Acer Group is, for instance, 50 per cent lower than that of Hewlett-Packard, which is the second best performer in this category. Finally, the Korean firm Samsung which originated from a culture with the core value of flexibility has obtained a ratio 14 per cent, which is some ten points lower than that of Toshiba. This difference is still substantial even when one takes into account the more diversified business portfolios of Toshiba.

Table 10.2: Profile of Microcomputer Firms by Sales Revenue

Firms	Business Segments
	Profile 1: Microcomputer hardware
Mitac	Microcomputer and related manufacturing (100%)
Acer Inc.	Microcomputer and related manufacturing (100%)
Dell	Microcomputer manufacturing (100%)
Gateway	Microcomputer manufacturing (100%)
	Profile 2: Computer hardware and others
Compaq	Microcomputer and related manufacturing (84%) Software, IT Services (16%)
Sun	Microcomputer manufacturing (85%) Software (15%)
HP	Microcomputer and related manufacturing (85%) Software and IT services (15%)
Acer Group	Microcomputer and related manufacturing (82%) IT services, software and publishing (18%)
IBM	Computer and related manufacturing (43%) Software, IT services and finance (57%)
Fujitsu	Computer and related manufacturing (59%) Software, IT services and finance (41%)
NEC	Computer and related manufacturing Software and IT services
	Profile 3: Diversified
Samsung Electronics	Microcomputer and related manufacturing (89%) Other manufacturing (11%)
Toshiba	Microcomputer and related manufacturing (74%) Other manufacturing (26%)

Notes: Microcomputer related manufacturing incorporates the assembly of component items such as add on cards, hard disk drives as well as telecommunication products such as mobile phones. Other manufacturing refers to consumer products such as refrigerators and vacuum cleaners. The data for Samsung Electronics relates to the 4th quarter of 2000.

Source: Annual Reports (2000).

Table 10.3: People Management and Microcomputer Firms

(US$ million)

Firms	Nationality	Total Sales US$ million	Management Expenses	Management Expenses
Profile 1				
Mitac	Taiwanese	US$1,430	US$77	5.4%
Acer Inc.	Taiwanese	US$3,106	US$134	4.3%
Dell	US	US$25,265	US$2,387	9.4%
Gateway	US	US$9,600	US$1,548	16.1%
Profile 2				
Sun	US	US$15,721	US$4,137	26.3%
SGI	US	US$2,331	US$785	33.7%
IBM	US	US$88,396	US$15,639	17.7%
Compaq	US	US$42,383	US$6,044	16.9%
HP	US	US$48,782	US$7,383	15.1%
Acer Group	Taiwanese	US$4,761	US$505	10.6%
Fujitsu	Japanese	US$49,576	US$12,342	25.0%
NEC	Japanese	US$48,461	US$11,811	24.4%
Profile 3				
Toshiba	Japanese	US$54,239	US$13,151	24.2%
Samsung	Korean	US$27,230	US$3,856	14.0%

Source: Various Annual Reports (2000).

Taiwanese and Korean firms' people management capabilities are reflected in some documented incidents concerning their management. When Acer's CEO Stan Shih offered his resignation as a result of consecutive financial losses in 1992, the board refused it and announced publicly that they admired and confirmed his outstanding leadership ability.[7] Acer turned around and has become one of the leading microcomputer manufacturers worldwide. This was parallel with the gesture of Samsung's CEO Kun-Hee Lee, who promised to donate up to 80 per cent of his personal fortune to a fund as a reward for Samsung employees if his programme on quality improvement was successful. He also stated that if the quality programme resulted in financial loss in any part of the group, he would be personally responsible. He further demonstrated his belief in his own vision by announcing: 'I have staked my honour, my life and my assets on these changes'.[8]

Person-to-person interviews with two microcomputer firms engaged in a labour-intensive component business (Firm G and Firm H) originating from a culture endowed with the core value of flexibility demonstrated traces of flexibility in firms' practices. Both firms can be described as embracing flexible attitudes in their management operations within Europe. Firm G had always stressed that one of its strengths was human resources, and it believed that the utilisation of local management was indispensable for its expansion into Europe. It appointed local nationals as General Managers in its subsidiaries and granted them full autonomy in decision making. Firm G had also allowed the use of a trilingual communication mode in its manufacturing plant situated in a predominantly English speaking country to lower the communication costs. This contrasted with US firms' tendency to persist in the use of English to the extent that it encouraged its European staff to adapt to anglicised names. Another area of flexibility can be seen in Firm G's transforming of one of its warehouse facilities for manufacturing purposes prior to the completion of its relocation to the purpose-built facility.

Firm H had expanded rapidly in the 1990s, and grew from a 40 person operation to approximately 1,000 employees worldwide during the 1990s. Firm H emphasised the importance of trust towards its staff and as a result elicited good faith from them. Its UK personnel, on one occasion, worked overtime to undertake repair work on a notebook computer sold by its US subsidiary under an original equipment manufacturing contract. Firm H also incorporated flexibility in its European operations, and expected its employees to combine flexibility with self-discipline in handling all issues. For example, it did not perceive a need to provide clear definitions concerning the job responsibilities of its senior managers, and it did not have precise rulings on the replacement of cars for its sales staff. When asked about the scope of authority with its UK sales manager, Firm H's General Manager replied; 'he can have all the authority he wants if what he does is good for the firm'. He also explained that there were various factors affecting the replacement of cars for its UK sales team such as total mileage, model and financial position at the time, hence there would not be rigid guidelines for the replacement of cars. This to a great extent contrasted with its US counterparts that tended to adhere to a set of standardised corporate policies. The flexibility with Firm G and Firm H, therefore contributes to their people management capabilities.

COMPARATIVE BACKWARD LINKAGE STRATEGY

In this section, I will examine US and Asia Pacific firms' pattern of integration in CRT monitors. Table 10.4 and Table 10.5 summarise microcomputer firms' pattern of integration. It can be seen from Table 10.4 that Taiwanese and Korean firms Acer, Mitac and Samsung that are endowed with the core value of flexibility have successfully exploited the optimum manufacturing locations and integrated into display monitors that serve as components for their own brand microcomputer systems in 2001. It should also be noted that these firms are engaged in contract manufacturing and produce CRT monitors for other firms. Samsung and Acer are in fact leading producers of CRT monitors worldwide by volume.

Among firms originating from a culture which is not associated with the value of flexibility, the Japanese firm NEC is involved in a CRT monitor joint venture with Mitsubishi while the remaining nine microcomputer firms refrain from integration into CRT monitors. The Japanese firms Toshiba, however, is a leading producer of cathode ray tubes. Toshiba's microfilter tubes are mass produced in its Thai facility in Bangkok. Nevertheless, Toshiba and Matsushita formed a 60–40 joint venture named Toshiba Matsushita Display Technology in April 2002; the new firm will standardise their CRT tube components and centralise the relevant procurement as to lower production cost. The evidence presented here, therefore, overwhelmingly substantiates the final part of the cultural selectivity theory in relation to the importance of people management capabilities towards microcomputer firms' competitiveness in labour-intensive components.

Table 10.4: US and Asia Pacific Firms and CRT Monitors, 2001

	Taiwanese firms	Korean firm	Japanese firms	US firms
Integration	Acer, Mitac	Samsung	NEC	
No Integration			Toshiba, Fujitsu	Compaq, Dell, Gateway, Sun, IBM, SGI, HP

Source: Various reports.

Table 10.5: Flexibility and Integration in Display Monitors

| | Core Cultural Value | |
	Flexibility	Not Flexibility
Integration	3	1
No integration	0	9

Source: Table 10.4.

The aggregate data of global market shares on CRT monitors further reinforces the cultural theme. Taiwanese and Korean firms had about about 70 per cent since the late-1990s, which comprised 50 per cent from Taiwanese firms such as Acer, Tatung, ADI and Delta and Compal and the remaining 20 per cent from Korea's Samsung and LG Electronics (formerly Goldstar).[9] Their people management capabilities enabled them to transplant labour-intensive component assembly to low cost localities in Asia such as China where wages are only one-fifteenth of those in the more developed economies such as Taiwan[10]. Indeed, Acer, Mitac and Samsung all have established monitor production facilities in China. In addition, Samsung and Acer have facilities in Mexico.

The Korean firm Samsung is not only a leading producer of display monitors in the world, it is also the largest producer in Europe by total sales volume. Its UK manufacturing complex in the Wynard Park, Cleveland, employed more than 1,200 workers in 1997.[11] One notable feature of Samsung's CRT monitor operation is that it has extensively engaged in the manufacturing of core components. For instance, it engaged in the production of colour display tubes, deflection yokes and electron guns as well as glass bulbs. This contrasts sharply with Taiwanese firms Acer and Mitac who rely extensively on independent suppliers for core components, and manage to achieve competitive positions internationally by leveraging the capabilities of suppliers.

The remaining firms that are not endowed with the core value of flexibility have abstained from integration and relied on external suppliers. In terms of display monitor procurement from the Far East, Dell, Compaq and Fujitsu fulfilled some of their requirements from the Taiwanese firm Delta Electronics in 1999.[12] Delta increased its sales by 75 per cent between 1999 and 2000, and has rapidly expanded into

Thailand and China. Delta's Thai facility is the largest display monitor manufacturer in the country. Hewlett-Packard also has a long established buyer-supplier relationship with Taiwan's Compal.[13] Compal, which was established in 1984, achieved a sales revenue of US$2,252 million in 2000. It produced about four million CRT monitors in Taiwan and China in that year. Similarly, Toshiba procured 15-inch and 17-inch CRT monitors that were estimated at US$50 million with Korea's Orion Electric in 1999.[14]

As for European procurement, Sony, Samsung, Tatung and ADI provide CRT monitors to microcomputer firms that utilise disintegrated backward linkage strategy. Samsung served as a supplier to Compaq in 1999 and won Compaq's Best Supplier Award of the year out of some 2,000 suppliers. Samsung also supported other microcomputer firms locating in Scotland and Ireland. The Japanese firm Sony, on the other hand, specialised in very high quality display monitors. Its colour display tubes and display monitor assembly facilities are located in Wales. Finally, Taiwanese firms Tatung and ADI's investment in Mossend and NewCastle, though only a few years old, have achieved steady growth.

Up to this point, I have shown the association between flexibility and firms' integration in CRT monitors as in 2001. A historical review, however, reveals that IBM and NEC (that do not originate from a culture with the core value of flexibility) were actively engaged in captive production of CRT monitors. Nevertheless, they either withdrew or consolidated their activities during the 1990s. For example, IBM which undertook monitor development and production in its Greenock plant in Scotland since the late 1980s switched to external procurement in 1996 amidst the concern of the Scottish Electronics Forum on the insufficient product design and development activities among foreign firms in Scotland.[15] Furthermore, NEC has officially withdrawn from the production of CRT display tubes as well as CRT monitor production with the creation of NEC-Mitsubishi Visual Systems in January 2000.[16] NEC-Mitsubishi Visual Systems is a US$1,900 million 50–50 joint venture between the two firms. The aim of the joint venture is to develop, design, manufacture and market display monitors. The joint venture's assembly operations are in China, Japan, Malaysia and Mexico. Other than the high research and development expenditure and the need to reinvest, it has been reported that the consolidation was triggered off by their inability to match prices offered by Taiwanese and Korean firms.[17]

In addition, it should not be ignored that a key feature of NEC and other Japanese firms such as Sony's involvement in display monitors are driven by their screen technology rather than their people management capabilities. Sony and NEC lead in the technology of colour display tubes. Sony's Trinitron tubes are well regarded for the quality of their pictures. The Trinitron tubes have been licensed widely to other firms; for example, Mitsubishi manufactures a series of monitors under the trade name of Diamondtron. Moreover, NEC's shadow-mask tubes, which trade under CromaClear tubes, have also been highly regarded for their clarity and focus. They are brighter than the standard shadow-mask tubes, are mechanically more stable than the Trinitron tubes and allow the design of display monitors with a balance of focus, brightness and contrast without image distortion.[18]

Moreover, Japanese firms' leadership in screen technology[19] extends to the new generation of liquid crystal display (LCD) monitors[20] that utilise thin film transistor-liquid crystal displays (TFT-LCD). TFT-LCDs were originally used in notebook computers; they were extended to the design of desktop display monitors in 1997. TFT-LCDs were first mass produced at 8.4-inch by the Japanese firm Sharp in 1991; Japanese firms became early leaders and shared about 56 per cent of the global market by early 2000.[21] A number of Taiwanese and Korean firms entered TFT-LCD production through technology licensing from the mid 1990s onwards, despite their late entry into the market; indeed, Samsung is currently a leading producer in terms of total volume.

LCD monitors represent a niche market and shared 5 per cent of the total volume in the worldwide desktop monitor market in 1999. The European demand for LCD monitors, which mirrored this trend, was 375,000 units in the fourth quarter of 1999. Hence, it represented 4.2 per cent of the demand for display monitors. The European LCD monitor users were businesses that require high specification display monitors. It has been reported that there were 17.3 per cent in the finance sector, 18 per cent were in small businesses and 13 per cent in the medical sector.[22] However, there has been an increasing popularity of LCD monitors in the leading economies; the UK computer reseller Computacenter reported that over 50 per cent of its monitor sales during the second quarter of 2001 was 15-inch or above TFT-LCD monitors. The analysts from IDC had also predicted that one in three monitors sold by 2005 would be of the thin film transistor (TFT) flat screen technology.[23]

LCD monitors are more superior than their CRT counterparts in some aspects. Firstly, the viewing area of LCD monitors is larger. The screen size of a 15-inch LCD monitor, for instance, is equivalent to a 17-inch CRT monitor. Secondly, LCD monitors consume 25 watts of electricity as compared to 130 watts in the CRT model; they also take up much less desk space than CRT monitors. Finally, they substantially reduce or eliminate the rate of magnetic emissions and x-rays. However, the costs for manufacturing TFT-LCD are far greater than the conventional cathode ray tubes. As a result, there is a substantial price difference between display monitors utilising the traditional CRT technology and the LDC technology. For example, the high-end Sony 17-inch Silver Flatscreen CRT monitor was priced at £299 in the UK in 2000 whereas the Samsung Angle 15-inch LCD monitor was £749.[24]

Japanese firms had a considerable market share in LCD monitors by the late 1990s. Table 10.6 shows that NEC, Fujitsu and Mitsubishi shared more than one-third of the global branded LCD monitor market in late 1999. Nevertheless, NEC has recently announced a joint development of TFT LCD with Chi Mei Optolelectronics that would lead to its purchase of LCD monitors from Chi Mei on an original equipment manufacturing basis. Chi Mei was founded in Taiwan in 1997; it had a total output of 850,000 LCD panels and monitors in 2000. The logic of the collaboration for both parties can be seen. It allows NEC to concentrate on liquid crystal display production for mobile phones and personal digital assistants as well as large screen display monitors. Most importantly, NEC can capitalise on people management capability that is essential for a labour-intensive assembly process. As for Chi Mei, the collaboration not only allows it to increase production volume but also allows it to acquire display monitor technology from NEC[25].

Table 10.6: Branded LCD Monitors Manufacturers, 4th Quarter 1999

Market Shares by Sales Volume

NEC	19.3%
Fujitsu	11.5%
Mitsubishi	5.5%
Samsung	4.8%
Viewsonic	3.7%

Source: DisplaySearch (1999).

CONTRACT MANUFACTURING IN MICROCOMPUTERS

The assembly of a standard personal computer is labour-intensive and requires approximately 130 manual steps which suggests that the people management capabilities of Taiwanese and Korean microcomputer firms will enable them to compete in the contract manufacturing of microcomputers. Indeed, there is a prosperous sector of electronics contract manufacturing businesses in Taiwan and Korea. Taiwanese electronics contract manufacturing, which is dominated by personal computer firms, has grown from approximately US$12,900 million in 1995 to US$23,700 million in 1998.

Figure 10.1: Electronics Contract Manufacturing in Taiwan

US$ billion

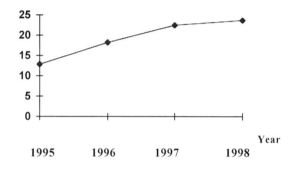

Source: Market Intelligence Centre, Taiwan as quoted in Electronic Business News 11 May 1998 p. 42.

Taiwanese firms have entrenched positions in notebook and desktop personal computer contract manufacturing. It was estimated that its contract manufacturers shared approximately 50 per cent of notebook computers worldwide in late 1999 as well as 20 per cent of the global desktop personal computer market.[26] Other than delivering microcomputer systems as specified in contracts, Taiwanese firms have further developed design services. In other words, they can design and build personal computers according to customers' general concepts. Alternatively, they can provide the basic systems lacking key components such as microprocessors and hard disk drives (i.e. bare-bones systems) which allow microcomputer firms to undertake final assembly. Korean firms have also actively engaged in the contract manufacturing of desktop microcomputers. Indeed the emergence of low price but high specification systems such as the US$499.99 personal computer that 'featured a 266 megahertz processor, 32 megabytes of fast memory and a 56K fax modem' in 1998 was due to the people management capabilities of contract manufacturers such as Trigem

Computer.[27] The founder and chairman of Trigem commented on the impact of the firm's provision of low price but high specification microcomputers as widening the availability of personal computers to that of high end televisions or video recorders.[28] Korean firms have also made progress in the contract manufacturing of notebook computers in recent years; it is reported that Korean firms' output for contract manufactured notebook computers is approximately one million units in 2001.[29]

US microcomputer firms have been utilising the services of Taiwanese and Korean contract manufacturers since the end of the 1980s while Japanese firms have increasingly followed suit from the early 1990s onwards. It was estimated that, for instance, the use of contract manufacturing as a percentage of total notebook computer shipments among the five leading Japanese and US firms was about 8 per cent and 70 per cent respectively in 1998. The percentage for Japanese firms employing contract manufacturers, however, is on the increase as firms such as Sony and Toshiba (who used to insist on 100 per cent of their own manufacturing capacities) have resorted to the use of Taiwanese contracting firms such as Acer, Quanta, Inventc, Arima and Compal[30].

Individual examples of US and Japanese microcomputer firms' use of contract manufacturing are abundant. Hewlett-Packard, for instance, spent about US$1,000 million on product procurement and contract manufacturing with twenty Taiwanese firms in 1997; it had also signed a manufacturing contract with the Korean firm Trigem for the supply of 1.2 million personal computers in 2000.[31] In addition, it was estimated that approximately 50 per cent of NEC's personal computers in 1999 were partially assembled by Taiwanese contract manufacturers such as First International, Arima and Compal.[32] Moreover, Sharp signed a five-year contract which incorporated the annual purchase of 70,000 notebook computers from Twinhead in 1999[33] whereas Acer contracted with IBM to provide fully assembled IBM branded personal computers in 1997.[34] It was further reported that IBM's PC division, which suffered a pre-tax loss of US$992 million on US$12,800 million sales in 1998, attempted to cut its costs by 'stepping up its procurement activities in Taiwan' to US$3,000 million in 1999.[35] Korea's LG Electronics have recently obtained contracts from IBM in relation to notebook computers.[36]

Nevertheless, it should not be ignored that US firms such as SCI and Solectron are also leaders in the provision of manufacturing services to microcomputer firms. SCI was formed as a defence electronics subcontractor, the Space Craft Inc., in Alabama 1961. It diversified into the microcomputer industry with the assembly contract for the printed circuit boards of IBM PCs in 1981. It then expanded from printed circuit board manufacturing to build-to-order as well as configure-to-order services of microcomputers since the early 1990s. It was responsible for IBM's Aptiva line of personal computers.[37]

SCI obtained more than 50 per cent of its revenue from microcomputer businesses in 2000. Table 10.7 shows the breakdown of its microcomputer business segment. SCI expanded in Europe in late 1997 by establishing a green-field site in Heerenveen, the Netherlands, to service its clients such as Hewlett-Packard. After receiving orders via the internet, it aims to assemble and ship the products within 24–48 hours. SCI has, however, acquired Taiwan's notebook computer manufacturer Uniwill in 2000. To a certain extent, the acquisition can be considered as SCI's effort to internalise Uniwill's people management capability that is critical for the labour-intensive personal computer assembly process.

Table 10.7: SCI's Microcomputer Business in mid-2000

	As a % of Total Revenue
Workstations and Servers	5.6%
Personal Computer Systems	34.2%
Personal Computer Subassemblies	21.2%
Peripherals	10.1%
Multimedia	8.0%
Others	20.9%

Note: Personal computer subassemblies refer to items such as motherboards.
Source: SCI Systems (2001).

CONCLUSION

The evidence in this chapter supported the impact of the core value flexibility on Taiwanese and Korean microcomputer firms' integration into labour-intensive CRT monitors. Though US and Japanese microcomputer firms had assembly facilities in low-cost localities that can be easily converted into display monitor facilities, they relied heavily on Taiwanese and Korean firms for these components. In addition, the overall strength of Taiwanese and Korean microcomputer firms (characterised by the core value of flexibility) in this segment and the retreat of US and Japanese microcomputer firms (not endowed with the core value of flexibility) also suggests that only firms with culturally supported capabilities will be able to compete efficiently in the long run. The result therefore support the recurring theme that each culture features a set of core values which affect the capabilities of their firms and subsequently determine their pattern of integration within integrated linkage.

NOTES

[1] Microelectronics and Computer Technology Corporation is a semiconductor and electronics trade group in the US. The data was reported in Andrew T. Angelopoulos 'Choosing and Tweaking Monitors', *Popular Electronics,* October 1999 p. 3.

[2] Colour display tubes are based on three electron guns to blend red, blue and green light to create different colours. These electron guns fire a stream of focused electricity at dots or stripes of red, green or blue light-emitting phosphors coated on the back of the display monitor screens to display images.

[3] Chung Hwa is a subsidiary of Tatung in Taiwan.

[4] The sheer weight of CRT monitors means that suppliers with an overseas facility will face a dilemma in terms of sudden surge of demand. They can either deliver the monitors from the overseas plants by air to their customers (which is very expensive); alternatively they will have to deliver the monitors with a long time lag if it is acceptable to the buyers. See 'Dollars 3m state aid may have sealed factory deal', *The Financial Times,* 8 December 1997 as well as 'Reporting Britain 98 Survey', *The Financial Times,* 15 July 1998.

[5] Gateway mentioned in its Management's Discussion section of 1995 Annual Report that the annual increase in personnel related costs and marketing expenses was over 75 per cent in 1995 compared to 1994.

[6] IBM made a conscious attempt to transform its business profile from computer hardware manufacturing to software and services in the early 1990s after suffering historic losses.

[7] Louis Kraar 'Acer's edge PCS to go', *Fortune,* 30 October 1995 p. 74.

[8] Louis Kraar 'Korea goes for quality', *Fortune,* 18 April 1994 p. 37.

[9] Market Intelligence Centre Taiwan.

[10] 'Taiwan' Country Survey, *The Financial Times,* 24 November 1999 p. 4.

[11] Quoted in *Key British Enterprises,* Dun and Bradstreet 1999.

[12] 'Delta Electronics Projects 25% Sales Growth', *Business Day Thailand,* 2 August 1999.

[13] *Electronic Business News,* 24 July 2000.

[14] *Korea Electronic Weekly,* 17 August 1999.

[15] See *The Financial Times,* 4 June 1996. In addition, IBM switched to supplies from independent firms such as Sony, Samsung, Lite On and Philips in the late 1990s; IBM has also recently announced the purchase of US$1,000 million worth of display monitors from Acer.

[16] NEC and Mitsubishi produced approximately 30 million units of display monitors in 1998. See Paul Abrahams, 'Electronics competition in computer monitor market forces Japanese groups to rationalise', *The Financial Times*, 27 September 1999 p.32. The new venture has however led to some rationalisation of production, which can be seen in NEC's closure of its colour display tube operations.

[17] *The Financial Times*, 27 September 2000 p. 32.

[18] See nectech.com/monitors/home/cromclear.htm. 12 February 1998.

[19] Japanese firms have also researched into areas such as plasma displays and organic light emitting diodes. Nevertheless, these display types still incur significant manufacturing costs and are available in only smaller screen sizes.

[20] The different types of LCD are STN, DSTN and TFT.

[21] IDC Japan as quoted in 'Samsung Electronics Dominates World TFT-LCD Market', *Samsung News*, 4 July 2000.

[22] *Display Search*, 1 March 2000.

[23] Gordon Kelly, 'Analysis – flat out for low-cost style in the monitor market', *Global News Wire*, 10 June 2001.

[24] *Dixons Computing Buyer*, August 2000.

[25] See 'NEC and Chi Mei Optoelectronics agree to collaborate in the area of TFT LCD', *NEC Press Release*, 26 April 2001.

[26] Murie Dickie 'Japanese pay price of pride: Taiwan set for growth in PC outsourcing', *The Financial Times*, 25 November 1999 p. 33.

[27] 'Trigem plans sub-Dollars 500 PC', *The Financial Times*, 10 September 1998.

[28] ETRE computer conference was held in Estoril Portugal (September 1998).

[29] Mark Fihn, 'Notebook PC OEM Manufacturing News', *Display Research Monitor*, May 2001 p. 61.

[30] Joe Leahy, 'Outsourcing to boost Asia tech stocks' *FT.com site*, 14 February 2001.

[31] 'Trigem Expanding Continues PC Exporting by Signing Supply Contract', *The Korean Economic Weekly*, 16 August 1999 and 'HP's Outsourcing Vision', *Electronic Buyers News*, 11 May 1998.

[32] Mure Dickie (op. cit.).

[33] *Asia Technology Weekly*, 4 June 1999.

[34] This contract constituted IBM's first attempt to procure fully assembled systems externally.

[35] *Electronic Buyer News*, 2 April 1999.

[36] Mark Fihn (op. cit.).

[37] Morgan Stanley 14 November 2000.

11. Conclusion

One of the great things about this industry is that every decade or so, you get a chance to redefine the playing field. We're in that phase of redefinition right now. — Louis Gerstner, IBM (1995).

The European microcomputer industry is fast-paced and highly competitive. Indigenous and foreign firms that exited involuntarily in the past two decades have included ICL, Digital, Olivetti, Commodore, Texas Instruments, Sanyo..., business strategy is therefore critical in the rapidly changing market and technological landscape. Though this book has involved the microcomputer industry and is, to a great extent, limited in the generalisation of its findings to other industries, it can, however, be counter-argued that as the assembly process of microelectronic products is standardised, it is reasonable to utilise the results in similar or related product areas.

Managers have traditionally pursued either a market-based or a resource- based orientation in business strategy. The market-based strategy embraces the environment completely; accordingly, managers will select an advantageous strategic option and then acquire the resources needed to implement the strategy. The resource-based strategy advocates an internally-driven strategy, in which the firm adapts to the environment to align with its tangible and intangible resources. The preceding chapters have presented a cultural theory of backward linkage that built on the dichotomous philosophical basis of strategy. The major tenet of this theory can be summarised by the concept of core cultural values, industry recipe and firm capability.

In this concluding chapter, I will not only draw attention to the lessons that can be learned from the earlier findings, but also try to glimpse the future competitive dynamics regarding backward linkage strategy in the European microcomputer industry. The paradox running through this book is that within the context of technological and marketing convergence some profit maximising microcomputer firms pursue disintegrated linkage strategy while others adopt integrated linkage strategy. It has been pointed out that, though the adoption of disintegrated backward linkage strategy is economically rational and proponents such as Dell and Sun have grown phenomenally in the past two decades, the disintegrated linkage strategy has not yet evolved in the same way as the previous industry recipe.

The focus for evaluating the backward linkage strategy in the European microcomputer industry must ultimately be on the profitability of the business. Microcomputer component firms such as Mitsubishi that entered the European market in the mid-1980s and then escalated its investment with the acquisition of an indigenous microcomputer manufacturer in 1990 on the grounds that it was involved in adjacent component areas eventually withdrew, after failing to establish a strong presence in major European markets such as the UK as well as achieving its objective to become a top ten personal computer firm worldwide.

The consistent pursuit of integrated linkage strategy among established US and Asia Pacific microcomputer firms is worth considerable attention, as most of them are not profitable in some or all segments of their microcomputer businesses. The preceding chapters have shown that the patterns of backward linkage strategy interweave with the business values of microcomputer firms. Laurent (1983 p. 76) commented that 'every manager has his own management theory, his own set of representations and preferences that in some way guide his potential behaviour in organisations...'. Numerous theorists have discussed the implications of cultural values in firms in the recent past. Considering the cultural values in achievement, universalism and specificity, Burrage (1969) suggested that there are differences between US and British firms in areas of organisation such as authority and definition of roles.

Indeed, a distinctive characteristic of the business values is the clustering pattern in accordance with firms' national origins, which can be explained by the fact that business values are articulated by founders who have established headquarters within different national culture. The founders of US and Asia Pacific microcomputer firms have not only shaped the values of their firms, but have also perpetuated them by recruiting managers that subordinate these values. Top management of microcomputer firms' shared cultural values therefore inevitably impose constraints upon their perceptions. US management who originate from a nation and culture which embodies the core value of individualism will endorse individualistic business values compatible with their personal values. Similarly, Asia Pacific managers who are from nations characterised with the core values of continuous improvement or flexibility will endorse business values that correspond to these cultural values. Among the microcomputer firms in Europe, it has been pointed out that individualistic values are embedded in US firms such as IBM and Hewlett-Packard, continuous improvement in Japanese firms such as

Acer.

Since national cultural values underlie managers' perceptions of strategic variables, a consistency between core values and backward linkage strategy can be observed. The divergent pattern of backward linkage strategy among youthful US and Asia Pacific firms substantiates the impact of the core cultural value of individualism on managerial conceptual maps which in turn influences the conformity towards the industry recipe used by established US firms. The cultural selectivity theory presented in chapter six expanded the process of isomorphism on the evolution of backward linkage strategy with a cultural dimension. It has been demonstrated that Asia Pacific firms with collective values are inclined to conform to the integrated linkage strategy whereas individualistic youthful US firms pioneered the disintegrated linkage strategy. On the general issue of business strategy, some Japanese politicians have recently expressed their views concerning its national firms' conformity to strategies initiated in the US and have asserted that conformity is the cause of Japan's recent weakness in international competition.

The implication of individualism for youthful US firms and Asia Pacific firms' approval or disapproval of the industry recipe concerning backward linkage strategy is insightful for business strategists. In retrospect, Japanese computer firms' extensive efforts to enter the mainframe computer segment also represented the replication of the industry recipe in relation to the definition of markets. Similarly, youthful US firms' innovative creation of personal computer and workstation markets was due to their non-conformity to the preconceived industry recipe. It is, therefore, suggested that microcomputer firms should evaluate their strategic inclinations critically, in the sense that individualistic US firms that are able to comprehend the broad picture of industry dynamism, think differently and challenge pre-conceived industry logic, should persist in their innovation, even when that leads to implementing a strategy disapproved of by established elements of the industry. On the contrary, collective Asia Pacific firms should evaluate the industry recipe against the logic in relation to the market and technological dynamics and resist the prevailing tendency to replicate the strategy in their attempts to reduce uncertainty. Hence, microcomputer firms' awareness of their conceptual maps would allow them to monitor their course of actions driven by their culturally oriented strategic inclinations. The important point is not to take an over-indulgent or under-indulgent view of the impact of core cultural values during the strategy process as either view may distort an objective evaluation of what is more or less critical. Managerial conceptual maps are cultural phenomena; hence backward linkage strategy should acknowledge the impact of core values as well as address the presence of economic rationalism; in other words, business strategy should be economically and culturally valid.

Taking the view that disintegrated linkage strategy is the optimum strategy, microcomputer firms that pursue integrated linkage strategy should evaluate existing strategy by clearly defining their business segments. This can be seen in the building of core businesses such as software, personal computers, workstations, storage products, services, component technology... within IBM or re-structuring business segments into areas including own-brand product, component, contract manufacturing and IT services within the Acer group during the 1990s. Then US and Asia Pacific firms should allow the microcomputer businesses to operate independently and procure on the basis of economic rationalism, which may lead to a switch from internal procurement to external sourcing in certain components. Only by doing so, will there be transparency of performance of various businesses and microcomputer firms will be able to eliminate inefficient businesses in the long run.

The pattern of microcomputer firms' integration into component areas further reiterates the importance of national culture in relation to backward linkage strategy. It has been shown that US and Asia Pacific firms draw their respective capabilities from their core cultural values, namely US firms' product design capabilities correspond with their individualistic values, Japanese and Korean firms' process manufacturing capabilities coincide with their values of continuous improvement while Korean and Taiwanese firms' people management capabilities are compatible with their value of flexibility. Core cultural values shape different nations' perceptions of firm capabilities, and support the variation of firm capabilities across nations. As core cultural values enable microcomputer firms to accumulate capabilities that are pertinent to component competitiveness, the strategic notion of leveraging internal firm resources could be expanded to that of leveraging intangible national resources. This highlights the point that the best practice within a single industry might have a national cultural limitation; in other words, firms should incorporate the strategic orientations as used by successful firms in the industry as well as those with the same nationality.

One of Wilhelm's interpretation of the text in the *Book of Changes* illustrates the importance of compatibility between core cultural values and areas of component integration. 'If a man should seek to impose galling limitations upon his own nature, it would be injurious'. Indeed, a large number of US firms, including Intel, that integrated into capital-intensive DRAMs had eventually withdrawn from this segment of the semiconductor industry prior to the mid-1980s whereas Japanese firms' substantial investment in concept-intensive software during the 1980s yielded far lower returns than the shoestring US start-ups. The predicament of US DRAM firms indicates that Japanese firms are likely to retreat from concept-intensive areas over time. In addition, it casts a pessimistic view on Taiwanese microcomputer firms such as Mitac's recent venture in enterprise resource planning software. Mitac defined the role of its new firm Sinfotek as software consultation and development as well as applications service provider; the rationale for its foundation is to expand into the software area where the Mitac Group was under-represented. The weakness of this market-oriented strategic posture is that it does not correspond with Taiwan's core value, and therefore may not be able to compete with US firms.

Moreover, the notion of culturally-constructed capabilities suggests that firms' learning curves or economies of scale in microcomputer components do not necessarily contribute to competitiveness as the ultimate competitive advantages lie within the core values of nations where they originated. As a consequence, microcomputer firms should pursue a strategy that balances internal and external consistency. To a great extent, the core value of individualism is essential for those entering concept-intensive component areas, continuous improvement for those competing in capital-intensive components and flexibility for labour-intensive components under the prevailing technological trajectory. Parallel to this, the cultural theory warns against firms' over-exposure in component areas that are not supported by appropriate core values, which reinforce criticisms such as Toshiba's failure to specialise in capital-intensive component areas where it has culturally derived competitive advantages. As a senior official in Japan's Ministry of Economy, Trade and Industry commented recently, the problem with general electronics manufacturers such as Toshiba were that they were engaged in very diverse business areas, and failed to compete in narrowly defined areas.

Nevertheless, the national cultural impact regarding the pattern of component integration is far from rigid as firm capabilities embedded in different microcomputer components may alter in the long run. It has been shown that some microcomputer component firms have demonstrated proactive strategy to exploit their culturally derived capabilities in their desire to attain competitiveness. In the context of DRAM, the individualistic US firm Micron competed with superior product design whereas the flexible Taiwanese firm TSMC developed the foundry model; both firms have created niches in terms of products and services for DRAM that contribute to changes in the competitive dynamics in the industry. The activities of Micron and TSMC emphasise the importance of the aggregated visions of individual firms towards evolution in the industry. Even though microcomputer firms cannot redefine their core values, they can utilise existing capabilities to redefine the domain of competitiveness and technological trajectory in their chosen component areas.

The above discussion points to the fact that Asia Pacific firms are well positioned in aspects of component integration; in other words, Japanese and Korean firms in capital-intensive component areas and Korean and Taiwanese firms in labour-intensive component areas. Similarly, US firms' integration in concept-intensive components optimised their national cultural advantages. However, established US firms' integration in capital-intensive component areas are not supported by the cultural selectivity theory. Interestingly enough, they successfully established themselves in microcomputer storage such as hard disk drives by employing the electronic contracting services of firms from cultures with the core value of continuous improvement. Leading US firms such as Quantum have relied on the process manufacturing capabilities of Japanese firms for component inputs into hard disk drives. Once it had perfected its disk drives for large scale production, it subcontracted some of the assembly work to Japanese firms such as Matsushita-Kotobuki Electronics during the 1980s and 1990s.

As backward linkage strategy is driven by core cultural values, institutional changes or social changes that erode existing core values over time would alter managerial conceptual maps and capabilities among firms, and would subsequently trigger off changes in the strategic pattern. For example, it is proposed that the process of westernisation in Asia Pacific that erodes the traditional collective values would paradoxically enrich the product design capabilities of their national firms. As a consequence, their competitive advantages in concept-intensive components such as software will be enhanced. On the other hand, institutional changes such as the downgrading of lifetime employment serves to de-emphasis continuous improvement and may be detrimental to Japanese firms' manufacturing process capabilities.

The relationship between national culture and business strategy is subtle but powerful. This book has shown the influences of core cultural values on US and Asia Pacific firms' backward linkage strategies within the setting of the European microcomputer industry. It illustrates that core cultural values affect managers' perceptions of the industry recipe as well as social perception of the desirability of capabilities, which are pertinent to the process of backward linkage strategy. The final question is one of balance. On the one hand, US and Asia Pacific firms strike to pursue a strategy that maximises profits; on the other hand, they are constrained by their national culture in terms of managerial perception and firm capabilities. Striking a balance between economics and national culture is therefore the ultimate challenge for business strategists.

References

Abegglen, James C. (1958), *The Japanese Factory - Aspects of its Social Organisation*, Illinois, US: The Free Press.

Abegglen, James C. and George Stalk (1985), *Kaisha: the Japanese Corporation*, New York, US: Basic Books.

Abramson, N.R., H.W. Lane, H. Nagai and H. Takagi (1993), 'A comparison of Canadian and Japanese cognitive styles: implications of management interaction', *Journal of International Business Studies, 24* (3), 575–587.

Afuah, A. (1999), 'Strategies to turn adversity into profits', *Sloan Management Review, 40* (2), 99–109.

Allport, Gordon, Philip Vernon and G. Lindzey (1913) reprinted in (1960) *Study of Values*, New York, US: Houghton Mifflin.

Anchordoguy, M. (2000), 'Japan's software industry: a failure of institutions?', *Research Policy, 29*, 391–408.

Ansoff, H. Igor [1965] (1988), *Corporate Strategy*, London, UK, New York, US, Victoria, Australia and Toronto, Canada: Penguin.

Aoyama, M. (1996), 'Beyond software factories: concurrent-development process and an evolution of software process technology in Japan', *Information and Software Technology, 38*, 131–143.

Argyres, N. (1996), 'Evidence on the role of firm capabilities in vertical integration decisions', *Strategic Management Journal, 17*, 129–150.

Bailey, J.R. and C.C. Chen (1997), 'Conceptions of self and performance-related feedback in the US, Japan and China', *Journal of International Business Studies, 28* (3), 605–626.

Barney, J. (1991), 'Firm resources and sustained competitive advantage', *Journal of Management, 17* (1), 99–120.

Barney, Jay B. [1996] (1997), *Gaining and Sustaining Competitive Advantage*, Reading, Massachusetts, US: Addison-Wesley.

Beck, J.C. and M.N. Beck (1990), 'The cultural buffer: managing human resources in a Chinese factory' in Ben B. Shaw, John E. Beck, Gerald R. Ferris and Kendrith M. Rowland (eds), *Research in Personnel and Human Resources Management*, Greenwich, US and London, UK: JAI Press Inc.

Benoit, B. and M. Dickie (2002), 'Infineon in alliance with Taiwanese chipmaker', *FT.com site*, 12 March 2002.

Berry, J.W. (1971), 'Ecological and cultural factors in spatial perceptual development', *Canadian Journal of Behavioural Science,* **3**, 324–336.

Berry, John W., Ype H. Poortinga, Marshall H. Segall and Pierre R. Dasen [1992] (1995), *Cross-cultural Psychology: Research and Applications,* Cambridge, UK and New York, US: Cambridge University Press.

Bigoness, W.J. and G.L. Blakely (1996), 'A cross-national study of managerial values', **27**, 4, 739–752.

Blackburn, J.D., G.D. Scudder and L.N. Van Wassenhove (1996) 'Improving speed and productivity of software development: a global survey of software developers', *IEEE Transactions on Software Engineering,* **22** (12), 875–885.

Bloom, R. and M.A. Naciri (1989), 'Accounting standard setting and culture: a comparative analysis of the United States, Canada, England, West Germany, Australia, New Zealand, Sweden, Japan and Switzerland', *The International Journal of Accounting,* **24** (1), 70–97.

Bohn, R.E. (1995), 'Noise and Learning in Semiconductor Manufacturing', *Management Science,* **41** (1), 31–42.

Bond, R. and P.B. Smith (1995), 'Culture and Conformity: A meta-analysis of studies using Asch's line judgement task', *Psychological Bulletin,* **119** (1), 111–137.

Bourgeois, L. (1980) 'Organisational theories: some criteria for evaluation', *Academy of Management Review,* **5**, 25–39.

Brooks, F.P. (1987), 'No silver bullet: essence and accidents of software engineering', *Computer,* April, 10–19.

Buckley, Peter J. and Ghauri, Pervez (eds) (1993), *The Internationalization of the Firm, A Reader,* London: Academic Press.

Budgen, David (1993), *Software Design,* Wokingham, UK and Reading, Massachusetts: Addison-Wesley.

Burck, G. (1940), 'International Business Machines', *Fortune,* January 1940 pp. 36–40.

Burrage, M. (1969), 'Culture and British economic growth', *The British Journal of Sociology,* **20** (2), 117–133.

Calori, R., G. Johnson and P. Sarnin (1992), 'French and British top managers' understanding of the structure and the dynamics of their industries: a cognitive analysis and comparison', *British Journal of Management,* **3**, 61–78.

Campbell-Kelly, M. (1995), 'Development and structure of the international software industry, 1950-90', *Business and Economic History,* **24**, 2, 73–110.

Carmel, E. (1997), 'American hegemony in packaged software trade and the culture of software', *The Information Society,* **13**, 125–142.

Carmel, E. and S. Becker (1995), 'A process model for packaged software development', *IEEE Transactions on Engineering Management,* **42** (1), 50–61.

Casson, Mark (1987), *The Firm and the Market,* Oxford, UK: Basil Blackwell.

Casson, Mark (1995), *Entrepreneurship and Business Culture,* Aldershot, UK: Edward Elgar.

Casson, Mark (1996), 'Culture as an economic asset' in Andrew Godley and Oliver Westall (eds), *Business History and Business Culture,* pp. 49–76.

Castells, M. and P. Hall (1994), *Technopoles of the World: The Making of 21st Century Industrial Complexes*, New York, US: Routledge.

Chandra, S. (1973), 'The effects of group pressure in perception: a cross-cultural conformity study', *International Journal of Psychology,* **8,** 37–39.

Chang, C. and A. Burgess (1991), 'Global issues, trends in software practice', *IEEE Software,* **8** (5), 4–8.

Chang, Sup Chang and Nahn Joo Chang (1994), *The Korean Management System*, Westport, Connecticut, US and London, UK: Quorum Books.

Chapman, T.L., J.J. Dempsey, G. Ramsdell and M.R. Reopel (1997), 'Purchasing: no time for lone rangers', *The McKinsey Quarterly,* **2,** 30–40.

Child, J. (1972), 'Organisational structure, environment and performance: the role of strategic choice', *Sociology,* **6,** 1–22.

Chinese Culture Connection (1987), 'Chinese values and the search for culture-free dimensions of culture', *Journal of Cross-Cultural Psychology,* **18,** 143–164.

Chung, Kae H. and Hak Chong Lee (eds) (1989), *Korean Managerial Dynamics*, New York and Westport, CO, US and London, UK: Praeger.

Chung, S. (2001), 'The learning curve and the yield factor: the case of Korea's semiconductor industry', *Applied Economics,* **33,** 473–483.

Claeys, W. (1967), 'Conformity behaviour and personality variables in Congolese students, *International Journal of Psychology,* **2,** 13–23.

Clark, Kim B., Robert H. Hayes and Christopher Lorenz (1985), *The Uneasy Alliance,* Boston, US: Harvard Business School Press.

Cole, M., J. Gay, J. Glick and D. Sharp (1971), *The Cultural Context of Learning and Thinking*, New York, US: Basic Books.

Cole, R.E. (1998), 'Learning from the quality movement: what did and didn't happen and why?', *California Management Review*, **41,** 43–74.

Coleman, J. (1988), 'Social capital and the creation of human capital', *American Journal of Sociology*, **94,** S95–S120.

Cringely, Robert X. [1992] (1996), *The Accidental Empire*, London, UK, New York, US and Toronto, Canada: Penguin.

Curry, J. and M. Kenney (1999), 'Beating the Clock', *California Management Review,* **42** (1), 8–36.

Curtis, B., H. Krasner and N. Iscoe (1988) 'A field study of the software design process for large systems', *Comm. ACM,* **11**, 1268–1287.

Cusumano, Michael A. (1991), *Japan's Software Factories: A Challenge to US Management,* New York, US: Oxford University Press.

Cusumano, Michael A. and David B. Yoffie (1998), *Competing on Internet Time,* London, UK and New York, US: Simon & Schuster.

Daft, R. and K. Weick (1984), 'Toward a model of organisations as interpretation systems', *Academy of Management Review,* **9**, 284–295.

Deal, Terrence and Allan Kennedy (1982), *Corporate Cultures,* London, UK: Penguin Books.

Deming, W. Edward (1950), *Some Theory of Sampling,* New York, US: John Wiley and Sons.

Deming, W. Edward [1982] (1991), *Out of the Crisis,* Cambridge, Mass, US: Cambridge University Press.

Deirickx, I. and K. Cool (1989), 'Asset stock accumulation and sustainability of competitive advantage', *Management Science,* **35** (12), 1514.

Deutsch, M. and H. Gerard (1955), 'A study of normative and informational social influences upon individual judgement', *Journal of Abnormal and Social Psychology,* **51**, 629–36.

DiMaggio, P.J. and W.W. Powell (1983), 'The iron cage revisited: institutional isomorphism and collective rationality in organisational fields', *American Sociological Review,* **48**, 147–160.

Donaldson, G. and J.W. Lorsch (1983) *Decision Making at the Top: The Shaping of Strategic Direction,* New York: Basic Books.

Drucker, Peter (1954) *The Practice of Management,* New York, US: Harper and Row.

Drucker, Peter (1974), *Management: Tasks, Responsibilities, Practices,* Oxford, UK: Butterworth-Heinemann Ltd.

Drucker, P.F. (1997), 'The future that has already happened', *Harvard Business Review,* **75,** September–October, pp. 20–4.

Dunning, John D. (1958), *American Investment in British Manufacturing Industry,* London, UK: George Allen & Unwin Ltd.

Dunning, John D. (1993), *Multinational Enterprises and the Global Economy,* New York, US: Addison-Wesley Publishing Ltd.

Dutton, J.E. and S.E. Jackson (1987), 'Categorising strategic issues: Links to organisational action', *Academy of Management Review,* **12** (1), 76–90.

Earley, P.C. (1994), 'Self or group? Cultural effects of training on self-efficacy and performance', *Administrative Science Quarterly,* **39** (1), 89–118.

Egelhoff, W.G. (1993), 'Great strategy or great strategy implementation - two ways of competing in global markets', *Sloan Management Review*, **34** (2), 37–50.

England, G.W. (1967), 'Personal Value Systems of American Managers', *Academy of Management Journal*, **10**, 53–68.

England, George W. (1975), *The Manager and his Values, An International Perspective*, Cambridge, MA, US: Ballinger Publishing Company.

England, G.W. (1983), 'Japanese and American Management: Theory Z and beyond', *Journal of International Business Studies*, **Fall**, 131–142.

Feather, N.T. (1995), 'Values, valences, and choice: The influence of values on the perceived attractiveness and choice of alternatives', *Journal of Personality and Social Psychology*, **68** (6), 1135–1151.

Ferguson, G. (1956), 'On transfer and the abilities of man', *Canadian Journal of Psychology*, **10**, 121–131.

Ferguson, C. (1990), 'Computers and the coming of the US keiretsu', *Harvard Business Review*, **68**, July–August, 55–72.

Ferguson, C. and C. Morris (1993), *Computer Wars: The Fall of IBM and the Future of Global Technology*, New York: Random House.

Finan, W.F. and A.M. LaMond (1985), 'Sustaining U.S. competitiveness in microelectronics: the challenge to U.S. policy', in Bruce R. Scott and George C. Lodge (eds), *U.S. Competitiveness in the World Economy*, Boston, US: Harvard Business School Press, pp. 144–175.

Fine, Charles H. (1998), *Clockspeed*, Reading, MA, US: Perseus Books.

Ford, J.D. and D.A. Baucus (1987), 'Organisational adaptation to performance downturns: an interpretation-based perspective', *Academy of Management Review*, **12** (2), 366–380.

Frederick, William C. (1995), *Values, Nature, and Culture in the American Corporation*, New York, US and Oxford, UK: Oxford University Press.

Freiberger, Paul and Michael Swaine [1984] (2000), *Fire in the Valley*, London, UK and New York, San Francisco and Washington D.C., US: McGraw-Hill.

Friedman, Milton (1953), *Essays in Positive Economics*, Chicago, US: University of Chicago Press.

Fruin, W. Mark (1997), *Knowledge Works*, Oxford, UK and New York, US: Oxford University Press.

Fukuyama, Francis (1995), *Trust: The Social Virtues and the Creation of Prosperity*, London: Hamish Hamilton Ltd.

Garrahan, Philip and Paul Stewart (1992), *The Nissan Enigma: Flexibility at work in a local economy*, London, UK: Mansell.

Gates, Bill (1996), *The Road Ahead*, London, UK: Penguin Books.

Geertz, Clifford (1983), *Local Knowledge*, NY, US: Basic Books.

Geletkanycz, M.A. (1997), 'The salience of culture's consequences: the effects of cultural values on top executive commitment to the status quo', *Strategic Management Journal,* **18** (8), 615–634.

Grant, Robert M. [1991] (1998), *Contemporary Strategy Analysis*, Oxford, UK and Malden, Massachusetts, US: Blackwell.

Gray, S.J. (1988), 'Towards a theory of cultural influence on the development of accounting systems internationally', *Abacus* **March**, 1–15.

Guth, W.D. and R. Tagiuri (1965), 'Personal values and corporate strategy', *Harvard Business Review*, **43**, September–October, 123–132.

Haire, M., E.E. Ghiselli and L.W. Porter (1966) *Managerial Thinking: An international study,* New York: Wiley.

Hambrick, D.C. and P.A. Mason (1984), 'Upper echelons: the organisation as a reflection of its top managers', *Academy of Management Review,* **9** (2), 193–206.

Hamel, Gary and C.K. Prahalad (1989), 'Collaborate with your competitors — and win', *Harvard Business Review,* **67** (1), 133–39.

Hamel, Gary and C.K. Prahalad [1994] (1996), *Competing for the Future,* Boston, US: Harvard Business School Press.

Hampden-Turner, C. (1991), 'The boundaries of business: the cross-cultural quagmire', *Harvard Business Review*, **69**, September–October, 94–96.

Hampden-Turner, Charles and Fons Trompenaars [1993] (1995), *The Seven Cultures of Capitalism,* London, UK: Piatkus.

Hannan, M. and J. Freeman (1977), 'The population ecology of organisations', *American Journal of Sociology,* **82**, 929–64.

Hatch, N.W. and D.C. Mowery (1998), 'Process innovation and learning by doing in semiconductor manufacturing', *Management Science,* **44** (11), 1461–1477.

Hayes, R.H. (1981), 'Why Japanese factories work', *Harvard Business Review,* **59,** July–August, 57–66.

Hennart, J-F. and J. Larimo (1998), 'The impact of culture on the strategy of multinational enterprises: Does national origin affect ownership decisions?', *Journal of International Business Studies,* **29** (3), 515–538.

Hofstede, Geert (1980), *Culture's Consequences: International Differences in Work-Related Values,* Beverly Hills, US: Sage Publications.

Hofstede, Geert [1991] (1994), *Cultures and Organisations*, London, UK: Harper Collins Business.

Hofstede, G. and M.H. Bond (1988), 'The Confucius connection: From cultural roots to economic growth', *Organisational Dynamics,* **16**, 4–21.

Howard, A., K. Shudo and M. Umeshima (1983), 'Motivation and values among Japanese and American mangers', *Personnel Psychology*, **36**, 883–898.

Hsu, Francis (1953), *Americans and Chinese: Two Ways of Life,* New York, US: Akerland-Schuman.

Huang, L.C. and M.B. Harris (1973), 'Conformity in Chinese and Americans: a field experiment', *Journal of Cross Cultural Psychology,* **4** (4), 427–434.

Hudson, Liam (1966), *Contrary Imaginations,* Harmondsworth, UK: Penguin.

Humes, Samuel (1993), *Managing the Multinational,* New York, US and London, UK: Prentice Hall.

Iansiti, M. and J. West (1997), 'Turning great research into great products', *Harvard Business Review*, **75**, May–June, 69–79.

Imai, Masaaki (1986), *Kaizen: The Key to Japan's Competitive Success,* New York, US: Random House Business Division.

Inglehart, R. (1981), 'Post-materialism in an environment of insecurity', *American Political Science Review*, **75**, 880–900.

Inkeles, A. and D.J. Levinson (1954), 'National character: the study of modal personality and sociocultural systems' (1969) in Gardner Lindzey and Elliot Aronson (eds), *The Handbook of Social Psychology,* Reading, Massachusetts and Menlo Park, California, US, London, UK and Don Mills, Ontario, Canada: Addison-Wesley Publishing Company.

International Data Corporation (2001), 'IDC forecasts worldwide DRAM market will shrink to \$24 billion in 2001', *IDC Press Release*, 2 March 2001.

Isoda, S. (1996), 'Software reuse in Japan', *Information and Software Technology,* **38,** 165–171.

Jackson, Tim (1997), *Inside Intel,* paper edition (1998), London, UK: Harper Collins Publisher.

Jager, Rama D. and Rafael Oritz (1997), *In the Company of Giants,* London, UK: McGraw-Hill.

Jahoda, G. (1971), 'Retinal pigmentation, illusion susceptibility and space perception', *International Journal of Psychology*, **6**, 199–208.

Japanese Human Relations Association (1988), *The Idea Book: Improvement through Total Employee Improvement,* Cambridge, MA: Productivity Press.

Jin, Sung Hwang (1994), *Economic Development and Internationalisation as Viewed through the Investment Development Path,* PhD Dissertation: University of Reading.

Jones, Geoffrey (1996), *The Evolution of International Business,* London, UK: Routledge.

Jones, J. Christopher (1970), *Design Methods: Seeds of Human Futures,* London, UK: Wiley-International.

Kay, John A. (1993), *Foundations of Corporate Success,* Oxford, UK: Oxford University Press.

Kelly, Tim (1987), *The British Computer Industry,* London, UK: Croom Helm.

Kelly, Tim and Keeble, David (1990), 'IBM: The Corporate Chameleon' in M. de Smidt and E. Wever (eds) *The Corporate Firm in a Changing World Economy,* London: Routledge.

Khera, D., M.W. Cresswell, L.W. Linholm, G.Ramanathan, J. Buzzeo and A. Nagarajan (1994), 'Increasing profitability and improving semiconductor manufacturing throughput using expert systems', *IEEE Transactions on Engineering Management,* **41** (2), 143–150.

Kim, L. (1997), 'The dynamics of Samsung's technological learning in semiconductors', *California Management Review,* **39** (3), 86–100.

Kim, J.S. and J. Choi (1997), 'Barriers to the software industry development in Japan: the structure of the industry and software manpower', *International Journal of Technology Management,* **13** (4), 395–412.

Kim, Son-Ung (1999), 'Determinants and characteristics of the corporate culture of Korean enterprises' in Henry S.R. Kao, Sinha Durganand and Bernhard Wilpert (eds), *Management and Cultural Values,* London, UK: Sage.

Kimura, Y. (1988), *The Japanese Semiconductor Industry: Structure, Competitive Strategies and Performance,* Greenwich, CN, US: JAI Press.

Kluckhohn, Clyde (1951) [1962], 'Values and value-orientations in the theory of action: an exploration in definition and classification', in Talcott Parsons and Edward A. Shils (eds), *Toward a General Theory of Action,* New York, US: Harper and Row, pp. 388–433.

Kluckhohn, Florence and Frederick Strodtbeck (1961), *Variations in Value Orientation.* Westport, CT, US: Greenwood Press.

Knight, Frank (1941), 'Anthropology and Economics', *Journal of Political Economy,* **49,** 507–23 reprinted in M.J. Herskovitz (1952) Economic Anthropology, New York, US: Alfred A. Khopf.

Knights, D. and G. Morgan (1991), 'Corporate strategy, organisations, and subjectivity: a critique', *Organisation Studies,* **12,** 2, 250–273,

Kogut, B. and H. Singh (1988), 'The effect of national culture on the choice of entry mode', *Journal of International Business Studies,* Fall, 411–432.

Kraljic, P. (1984), 'Purchasing must become supply management', *Harvard Business Review,* **62,** September–October, 109–117.

Kroeber, Alfred and Clyde Kluckhohn (1952), *Culture: A Critical Review of Concepts and Definitions,* Cambridge, MA, US: Peabody Museum.

Lachman, R. (1983), 'Modernity change of core and periphery values of factory workers', *Human Relations,* **36** (6), 563–580.

Lachman, R. (1988), 'Factors influencing workers' orientations: A secondary analysis of Israeli data', *Organisation Studies,* **99**, 487–510.

Langlois, Richard N., Thomas A. Pugel, Carmela S. Haklisch, Richard R. Nelson and William G. Egelhoff (1988), *Microelectronics Industry: An Industry in Transition,* London, UK, Boston, US and Sydney, Australia: Unwin Hyman.

Langlois, R.N. (1990), 'Creating external capabilities: innovation and vertical disintegration in the microcomputer industry', *Business and Economic History,* **19** (2), 93–102.

Langlois, R.N. (1992), 'Transaction cost economics in real time', *Industrial and corporate change,* **1** (1), 99–127.

Langlois, Richard Normand and Paul L. Robertson (1995), *'Firms, Markets and Economic Change',* London, UK and New York, US: Routledge.

Larimo, J. (1993), 'Ownership arrangements in foreign direct investments: Behaviour of Finnish firms in OECD countries', paper presented at the Annual Meetings of the European International Business Association, Lisbon, Portugal.

Laurent, A. (1983), 'The cultural diversity of western conceptions of management', *International Studies of Management and Organisation,* **13** (1), 75–96.

Lawrence, Paul R. and Nitin Nohria (2002), *Driven: How Human Nature Shapes Our Choices,* San Francisco, CA, US: Jossey-Bass.

Lee, H.C. (1989), 'Managerial characteristics of Korean firms' in Kae H. Chung and Hak Chong Lee (eds), *Korean Managerial Dynamics,* New York and Westport, CO, US and London, UK: Praeger.

Lee, S.M. and S. Yoo (1987), 'The K-Type management: A driving force of Korean prosperity', *Management International Research,* **27** (4), 68–77.

Leham Brothers (1999), *Global Semiconductor Equipment: Industry Update,* 1 October.

Levy, D.L. (1997), 'Lean production in an international supply chain', *Sloan Management Review,* Winter, 94–102.

Levy, D.L. (1995), 'International sourcing and supply chain stability', *Journal of International Business Studies,* **16** (5), 343–360.

Lewis, G. (1989), 'Computers: Japan comes on strong', *Business Week,* 23 October, 104–112.

Linvill, J.G., A.M. LaMond and R.W. Wilson (1984), *The Competition Status of the US Electronics Industry*, Washington DC, US: National Academy Press.

Lipset, Seymour Martin (1963), *The First New Nation*, London, UK: Heinemann.

Lynn, B.E. (1999), 'Culture and intellectual capital management: a key factor in successful ICM implementation', *International Journal of Technology Management*, **18**, 590–603.

Macher, J. and D.C. Mowery (1998), 'Reversal of fortune? The recovery of the U.S. semiconductor industry', *California Management Review*, **41** (1), 107–137.

Maital, S. (1990), 'Why not software factories?', *Across the Board*, October, 5-7.

Makino, S. And K.E. Neupert (2000), 'National culture, transaction costs, and the choice between joint venture and wholly owned subsidiary', *Journal of International Business Studies*, **31** (4), 705–713.

Marshall, A. [1890] (1961), *Principles of Economics*, London: Macmillan and Company.

Mashima, R. (1996), 'The turning point for Japanese software companies: can they compete in the prepackaged software market?', *Berkeley Technology Law Journal*, **11** (2), 429–459.

Matheson, L.R. and R.E. Tarjan (1998), 'Culturally induced information impactedness: a prescription for failure in software ventures', *Journal of Management Information Systems*, **15** (2), 23–39.

Mayo, Elton (1945), *The Social Problems of an Industrial Civilisation*, Cambridge, Massachusetts, US: Harvard University Press.

McCaskey, Michael B. (1982), *The Executive Challenge: Managing Change and Ambiguity*, London, UK and Boston, US: Pitman.

McClelland, David C. (1961), *The Achieving Society*, Princeton, New Jersey, USA, London, UK and Toronto, Canada: D. Van Nostrand Co. Inc.

McGuire, W.J. (1969), 'The nature of attitudes and attitude change', in G. Lindzey and E. Aronson (eds), *The Handbook of Social Psychology (Vol. 3)*, Reading, MA, USA: Addison-Wesley.

Meade, R. and W. Barnard (1973), 'Conformity and anitconformity among Americans and Chinese', *Journal of Social Psychology*, **89**, 15–25.

Meglino, B.M. and E.C. Ravlin (1998), 'Individual values in organisations: concepts, controversies and research', *Journal of Management*, **24** (3), 351–89.

Melan, E.H., R.T. Curtis, J.K. Ho, J.G. Koens and G.A. Snyder (1982), 'Quality and Reliability Assurance Systems in IBM Semiconductor Manufacturing', *IBM Journal of Research Development*, **26** (5), 613–624.

Methé, D.T., R. Toyama and J. Miyabe (1997), 'Product development strategy and organisational learning: A tale of two PC makers', *Journal of Product Innovation Management,* **14**, 323–336.

Milgram, S. (1961), 'Nationality and conformity', *Scientific American,* **205**, 45-51.

Mintzberg, H. (1976), 'Planning on the left side and managing on the right', *Harvard Business Review,* **54**, July–August, 49–58.

Mintzberg, Henry (1994), *The Rise and Fall of Strategic Planning,* Englewood Cliffs, US: Prentice-Hall.

Morgan, Gareth (1988), *Riding the Waves of Change,* San Francisco, US and London, UK: Jossey-Bass Publishers.

Moritz, Michael (1984), *The Little Kingdom: The Private Story of Apple Computer*, New York, US: Morrow.

Morris, B., N. Watson and M. Boyle (2000), 'Can Michael Dell escape the box?', *Fortune*, 16 October 2000, 92–93.

Moustakas, Clark (1967), *Creativity and Conformity,* London, UK, New York, US and Toronto, Canada: D. Van Nostrand Co.

Munday, Max (1990), *Japanese Manufacturing Investment in Wales,* Cardiff, UK: University of Wales Press.

Nahapiet, J. and S. Ghoshal (1998), 'Social capital, intellectual capital, and the organisational advantage', *Academy of Management Review*, 242–266.

Nam, S.K. and J. Slater, 'Korean Investment in Europe: Motives and Choices' in J. Slater and R. Strange (eds), *Business Relationships in East Asia,* London, UK: Routledge.

OECD (1991), *Software Engineering: The Policy Challenge*, OECD Publications: Information Computer Communications Policy.

Oliver, E.G. and K.S. Cravens (1999), 'Cultural influences on managerial choice: an empirical study of employee benefit plans in the United States', *Journal of International Business Studies*, **30** (4), 745–762.

Ouchi, William G. (1981), *Theory Z: how American business can meet the Japanese challenge,* Reading, Mass, US: Addison-Wesley.

Parnell, J.A. and T. Hatem (1999), 'Cultural antecedents of behavioural differences between American and Egyptian managers', *Journal of Management Studies,* 36 (3), 399–418.

Parsons, Talcott (1960), *Structure and Process in Modern Societies,* New York, US: The Free Press.

Parsons, Talcott and Edward A. Shils (1951), 'Categories of the orientation and organisation of action', reprinted in Talcott Parsons and Edward A. Shils (eds) (1962), *Toward a General Theory of Action,* New York, US: Harper and Row, pp. 53–110.

Pascale, Richard Tanner and Anthony G. Athos [1981] (1986), *The Art of Japanese Management,* London, UK: Penguin Books.

Penrose, Edith (1959), *The Theory of the Growth of the Firm,* Oxford, UK: Basil Blackwell.

Perrera, M.H.B. (1989), 'Towards a framework to analyse the impact of culture on accounting', *International Journal of Accounting,* **24**, 42–56.

Perrin, S. and C.P. Spencer (1981), 'Independence or conformity in the Asch experiment as a reflection of cultural and situational factors, *British Journal of Social Psychology,* **20,** 205–210.

Peters, Thomas J. and Robert H. Waterman (1982), *In Search of Excellence,* New York, US: Warner Books.

Polanyi, Michael [1958] (1962), *Personal Knowledge,* London, UK: Routledge and Kegan Paul.

Polanyi, Michael (1966), *The Tacit Dimension,* London, UK: Routledge and Kegan Paul.

Porter, Michael E. (1980), *Competitive Strategy,* New York, US: Free Press.

Porter, Michael E. (1990), *The Competitive Advantage of Nations,* London, UK: Macmillan.

Postman, L., J.S. Brüner and E. McGinnies (1948), 'Personal values as selective factors in perception', *Journal of Abnormal and Social Psychology,* **43**, 142–154.

Putnam, R. (1995), 'Bowling alone: America's declining social capital', *Journal of Democracy,* **6** (1), 65–78.

Prahalad, C.K. and G. Hamel (1990), 'The core competence of the corporation', *Harvard Business Review,* **68** (3) 79–91.

Press, Barry (1996), *PC Upgrade and Repair Bible,* Foster City, CA, Chicago, IL, Indianapolis, IN and Southlake, TX, US: IDG Books.

Rappaport, A.S. and S. Halevi (1991), 'The computerless computer company', *Harvard Business Review,* **69**, July–August, 69–80.

Redding, S. Gordon (1990), *The Spirit of Chinese Capitalism,* Berlin, Germany: De Gruyter.

Richards, E. and T.R. Reid (1990), 'Mass production comes to software', *The Washington Post,* 12 December 1990, A16.

Richardson, G.B. (1972) 'The Organisation of Industry', *Economic Journal,* **82**, 883–96

Rifkin, G. and J.A. Savage (1989), 'Is US ready for Japan software push', *Computerworld,* 8 May.

Robinson, A.A. and D.M. Schroeder (1991), 'America's most successful export to Japan: continuous improvement programs', *Sloan Management Review,* **32** (3), 67–82.

Robinson, A.G. and D.M. Schroeder (1993), 'Training, Continuous Improvement, and Human Relations: The U.S. TWI Programs and the Japanese Management Style', *California Management Review,* Winter, 35–57.

Rodgers, Buck (1986), *The IBM Way*, Glasgow, UK: William Collins.

Rohner, R. (1984), 'Toward a conception of culture for cross-cultural psychology', *Journal of Cross-Cultural Psychology,* **15**, 111–38.

Rokeach, Milton (1968), *Beliefs, Attitudes and Values*, San Francisco & Washington, US and London, UK: Jossey-Bass.

Rokeach, Milton (1973), *The Nature of Human Values*, New York, US: Free Press.

Rosenberg, N. (1963), 'Technological Change in the Machine Tool Industry, 1840–1910', *Journal of Economic History,* **23** (2), 414-443.

Rosenberg, N. and W.E. Steinmueller (1988), 'Why are Americans such poor imitators?', *American Economic Review Papers and Proceedings,* **78** (2), 229–234.

Rosenzweig, P.M. (1994), 'The New "American Challenge": Foreign Multinationals in the United States', *California Management Review,* **36** (3), 107–124.

Said, Edward W. (1993), *Culture and Imperialism,* London, UK: Vintage.

Sakai, T. (1984), 'Software: the new driving force', *Business Week,* 27 February, 96–7.

Salter, S.B. and F. Niswander (1995), 'Cultural influence on the development of accounting systems internationally', *Journal of International Business Studies,* **26** (2), 379–397.

Sandoz, Philip (1997), *Canon: Global Responsibilities and Local Decisions,* London: Penguin.

Saunders, Malcolm (1994), *Strategic Purchasing and Supply Chain Management*, London, UK: Pitman.

Saxenian, AnnaLee (1994), *Regional Advantage: Culture and Competition in Silicon Valley and Route 128,* Cambridge, MA, US: Harvard University Press.

Schein, E.H. (1981), 'Does Japanese management style have a message for American managers?', *Sloan Management Review,* **21** (1), 55–68.

Schein, Edgar H. (1985), *Organisation Culture and Leadership,* San Francisco, US: Jossey-Bass Publishers.

Schneider, S.C. (1989), 'Strategy formulation: the impact of national culture', *Organization Studies,* **10**, 149–168.

Schneider, S.C. and A. De Meyer (1991), 'Interpreting and responding to strategic issues: the impact of national culture', *Strategic Management Journal,* **12**, 307–320.

Schneider, S.C. (1989), 'Strategy formulation: the impact of national culture', *Organization Studies,* **10**, 149–168.

Schuler, R.S. and N. Rogovsky (1998), 'Understanding compensation practice variations across firms: the impact of national culture', *Journal of International Business Studies,* **29** (1), 159–177.

Schwartz, S.H. (1992), 'The universal content and structure of values: theoretical advances and empirical tests in 20 countries' in M. Zanna (ed.), *Advances in Experimental Social Psychology,* New York, US: Academic Press, pp. 1–65.

Schwartz, S.H. and W. Bilsky (1987), 'Toward a psychological structure of human values', *Journal of Personality and Social Psychology,* **53**, 550–562.

Schwartz, S.H. and W. Bilsky (1990), 'Toward a theory of the universal content and structure of values: extensions and cross-cultural replications', *Journal of Personality and Social Psychology,* **58**, 878–91.

Segall, M.H. (1986), 'Culture and Behaviour: Psychology in Global Perspective', Annual Review of Psychology, **37**, 523–64.

Segall, Marshall H., Donald T. Campbell and Melville J. Herskovits (1966), *The Influence of Culture on Visual Perception*, Indianapolis, US: Bobbs-Merrill.

Servan-Schreiber, J.J. (1968), *The American Challenge,* translated by R. Steel, New York, US: Atheneum Press Inc.

Shane, S. (1993), 'Cultural influences on national rates of innovation', Journal of Business Venturing, **8**, 59–73.

Shapero, A. and Sokol, L. (1982), 'The social dimensions of entrepreneurship', in C. Kent, D. Sexton, K. Vesper (eds), *Encyclopedia of Entrepreneurship*, Englewood Cliffs, NJ, US: Prentice Hall.

Shewhart, Walter A. (1931), *Economic Control of Manufactured Product,* Princeton, New Jersey, US: Van Nostrand.

Sieling, M.S. (1988), 'Semiconductor productivity gains linked to multiple innovations', *Monthly Labour Review,* **111**, 27–33.

Simon, Herbert A. (1957), *Administrative Behaviour*, New York: Free Press.

Song, Byong-Nak (1990), *Rise of the Korean Economy,* Hong Kong, China: Oxford University Press.

Spence, Janet T. (1985), 'Achievement American style', *American Psychologist,* December 1985, **40** (12), 1285–1295.

Spender, J-C. (1989), *Industry Recipes,* Oxford, UK: Basil Blackwell.

Spranger, Eduard (1928), *Types of Men,* translated by P. Pigors, Halle, Germany: Niemeyer.

Starbuck, W.H. and F.J. Milliken (1988), 'Executives' perceptual filters: what they notice and how they make sense' in Donald C. Hambrick (ed.),

The Executive Effect: Concepts and Methods for Studying Top Managers, Greenwich, US and London, UK: JAI Press Inc, pp. 35-66.

Steers, Richard M, Yoo Keun Shin and Gerardo R. Ungson (1989), *The Chaebol: Korea's New Industrial Might,* New York, US: Harper and Row.

Stross, Randall E. [1996] (1998), *The Microsoft Way,* London, UK: Warner Books.

Sullivan, J.J. and I. Nonaka (1986), 'The application of organisational learning theory to Japanese and American management', *Journal of International Business Studies,* **Fall**, 127–147.

Sullivan, J. and I. Nonaka (1988), 'Culture and strategic issue categorisation theory', *Management International Review,* **28**, 6–10.

Sullivan, J.J. and R.B. Peterson (1991), 'A test of theories underlying the Japanese life time employment system', **22**, 1, 79–98.

Tajima, D. and T. Matsubara (1981), 'The Computer Software Industry in Japan', *IEEE Computer,* May, 89–96.

Teece, D. and G. Pisano (1994), 'The dynamic capabilities of firms: an introduction', *Industrial and Corporate Change,* **3** (3), 497–556.

Trinadis, H.C. (1990), 'Cross-cultural studies of individualism and collectivism' in J. Berman (ed) *Nebraska Symposium on Motivation 1989,* pp.41–133, Lincoln, US: University of Nebraska Press.

Triandis, H.C. (1995), *Individualism and Collectivism,* Boulder, CO, US: Westview.

Triandis, H.C. (1999), 'Cross-cultural psychology', *Asian Journal of Social Psychology,* **2**, 127–143.

Triandis, H.C., R. Bontempro and M.J. Villareal (1988), 'Individualism and collectivism: cross-cultural perspectives on self-ingroup relationships', *Journal of Personality and Social Psychology.* **54**, 2, 323–338.

Trompenaars, Fons (1993), *Riding the Waves of Culture,* London, UK: The Economist Books.

Tylor, Edward B. (1871), *Primitive Culture,* London, UK: John Murray.

Van Hoesel, Roger (1998), *Beyond Export-led Growth: The Emergence of New Multinational Enterprises from Korea and Taiwan,* Rotterdam, the Netherlands: Tinbergen Institute Research Series.

UNCTC (1996), *Sharing Asia's Dynamism: Asian Direct Investment in the European Union,* New York, US and Geneva, Switzerland: United Nations.

United Nations (1997), *World Investment Report: Transnational Corporations, Market Structure and Competition Policy,* New York, US: UN.

Wallace, Anthony (1970), *Culture and Personality,* New York, US: Scribners.

Walters, E. Garrison (2001), *The Essential Guide to Computing,* New Jersey, US: Prentice Hall.

Wang, K.T. (1976), *A Commentary on the Art of Welfare,* Taipei, Taiwan: Chung Man.

Warburg Dillion Read, Asia (1999), *Company Report: Hyundai Electronics,* 31 August 1999.

Warner, M. (1999), 'Human resources and management in China's high-tech revolution: a study of selected computer hardware, software and related firms in the PRC', *The International Journal of Human Resources Management,* **10** (1), 1–20.

Weber, Max (1958), *The Protestant Ethic and Spirit of Capitalism,* New York, US: Scribners.

Weick, Karl E. (1979), *The Social Psychology of Organising*, Reading, MA, US: Addison-Wesley.

Weinstein, F.B., M. Uenohara and J.G. Linvill (1984), 'Technological Resources', in Daniel. I. Okimoto, Takuoano and Franklin B. Weinstein (eds), *Competitive Edge: The Semiconductor Industry in the U.S. and Japan*, Stanford, California: Stanford University Press, pp. 35–77.

Wernerfelt, B. (1984) 'A resource-based view of the firm', *Strategic Management Journal,* **5**, 171–80.

Whiting, J.W.M., E.H. Chasdi, H.F. Antonovsky and B.C. Ayres (1973), 'The learning of values' in Robert A. LeVine (ed), *Culture and Personality,* Chicago, US: University of Chicago Press, pp. 155–187.

Whitley, R. (1990), 'Eastern Asian enterprises structures and the comparative analysis of forms of business organisation', *Organisation Studies,* **11** (1), 47–74.

Williams, T.P. and S. Sogon (1984), 'Group composition and conformity behaviour in Japanese students', *Japanese Psychological Research,* **26**, 231–234.

Williamson, Oliver E. (1985), *The Economics Institution of Capitalism,* New York, US: Free Press.

Wincker, Edwin A. (1987), 'Statism and Familism on Taiwan' in George C. Lodge and Ezra F. Vogel (eds), *Ideology and Country Competitiveness,* Boston, US: Harvard Business School Press, pp. 173–206.

Winter, W. (1963), 'The perception of safety posters by Bantu industrial workers', *Psychologia Africana,* **10**, 127–135.

Winterbottom, M.R. (1958), 'The relation of need for achievement to learning experiences in independence and mastery', in J.W. Atkinson (ed), *Motives in Fantasy, Action and Society*, Princeton, NJ, USA: N.J. Nostrand, pp. 453–478.

Wollack, S., J.G. Goodale, J.P.Wijting and P.C.Smith (1971), 'Development of the survey of work values', *Journal of Applied Psychology,* **55** (4), 331–338.

Yamamoto, Takuma (1992), *Fujitsu: What Mankind can Dream Technology can Achieve,* translated by D. Belcher, Tokyo, Japan: Toyo Keizai Inc.

Yasumuro, K. (1984), 'The Contribution of the Sogo Shosha to the Multinationalisation of Japanese Industrial Enterprise' in A. Okochi and T. Inoue (eds) *Overseas Business Activities,* Tokyo, Japan: University of Tokyo Press.

Young, S.M. and Franke, G.R. (2000), 'Cultural influences on agency practitioners' ethical perceptions: a comparison of Korea and the US', *Journal of Advertising,* **29**, 1, 51–67.

Yu, F.T. (2000), 'Hong Kong's entrepreneurship: behaviours and determinants', *Entrepreneurship and Regional Development,* July-September, **12** (3), 179–195.

Zarzeski, M.T. (1996), 'Spontaneous harmonisation effect of culture and market forces on accounting disclosure practices', *Accounting Horizons,* **10** (1), 18–37.

Appendix A

Dell's Management Team (predominantly US) in 2000

US Executives	Position	Education/Previous Experience
Michael Dell	Chairman	1st year, University of Texas
Kevin Rollins	Vice Chairman	MBA Brigham Young University US management consultancy experience
James Vanderslice	Vice Chairman	Degrees from Boston College and Catholic University; IBM experience
David Allen	Vice President Worldwide Operations	Harvard MBA Previous experiences in various US multinationals
Paul Bell	Senior VP Europe/Middle East and Africa	MBA Yale School of Organisation and Management; US management consultancy experience
Carl Everett	Senior VP Personal Systems Group	Business degree from New Mexico State University; US technology firms experience
Michael Lambert	Senior VP Enterprise Systems Group	Business degree from University of Kentucky; US technology firms experience
Frank Muehleman	VP, Worldwide Home and Small Business Group	Harvard MBA; US management consultancy experience
Charles Saunders	VP Asia Pacific/Japan	Business degree from East Tennessee State University; US technology firm experience
Göran Malm	Senior VP Asia Pacific/Japan	Business degree from Gothenburg School of Economics; US and Swedish multinational experience

Source: Dell 2000 Annual Report.

Appendix B

IBM's Management Team 2000, as comprised of US managers

Chief Executive Officer
Louis Gerstner

Chief Operating Officer
Samuel Palmisano

Chief Financial Officer
John Joyce

Chief Information Officer
Philip Thompson

Senior Vice President, Marketing
Abby Kohnstamm

Senior Vice President, Strategy
Bruce Harreld

Senior Vice President, Communications
David Kalis

Senior Vice President, Human Resources
J Randall MacDonald

Server Group William Zeilter	Personal and Printing Systems Group Robert Moffat
Technology Group John Kelly	Storage Systems Group Linda Sanford

Technology and Manufacturing Nicholas Donofrio	Software Steven Mills	IBM Global Services Douglas Elix

Source: IBM 2000 Annual Report.

Appendix C

Acer's (Chinese) Management Team in 2000

Chairman	Stan Shi
General Controller	George Huang
Vice President, Technology	Fred Lin
President	Simon Lin
President	J.T. Wang
Vice President	Philip Peng
Vice President	T.Y. Lay
Vice President	Dixon Cheng
Chief Staff	Haydn Hsieh
Vice President	M.Y. Lin
Vice President	Teddy Lu
Vice President	Jerry Wang
Vice President	Howard Chan
Vice President	Jim Wong
Vice President	Robert Hwang
Vice President	Donald Hwang
Vice President	Robert Cheng
Vice President	Emily Hong
Vice President	Harvey Chang
General Auditor	Carolyn Yeh

Source: Acer 2000 Annual Report.

Appendix D

Toshiba's Top Management Team in 2000, comprised of Japanese managers

President and Chief Executive Officer	Tadashi Okamura
Senior Executive Vice Presidents	Kiyoaki Shimagami
	Akinobu Kasami
Executive Vice Presidents	Tomohiko Sasaki
	Tetsuya Mizoguchi
	Yasuo Morimoto
	Takeshi Iida
Senior Vice Presidents	Yuji Kiyokawa
	Makoto Nakagawa
	Toshiyuki Oshima
	Hiroo Okuhara
	Susumu Kohyama
	Atsutoshi Nishida
	Tadashi Matsumoto
	Takeshi Nakagawa
	Kaoru Kubo
	Masaki Matsuhashi
	Tsuyoshi Kimura
Vice Presidents	Toshitake Takagi
	Yasuo Ozaki
	Sadazumi Ryu
	Shinsuke Kawamurr
	Toshio Yonezawa
	Masro Niwano
	Ginzo Yamazaki
	Tsutomu Miyamoto
	Makoto Azuma
	Eisaburo Hamano

Source: Toshiba 2000 Annual Report.

Appendix E

Sampled Questions used in an Interview:

1. How do your firm's Scottish operations fit into the global operations of the headquarters?
2. Is the sourcing of components in this plant different from other subsidiaries, from joint ventures, from independent subcontractors or spot purchases of standardised products?
3. Can you explain the logistics of sourcing, i.e. transport and warehousing of imported components?
4. How is your production planning integrated into the launch of new products?
5. Can you identify any cross cultural communication problems with the headquarters, with other subsidiaries or with independent suppliers?
6. Are there any distinctive features about your European operations in comparision with those of your major rivals, and if so, what are they?

Index